"Kiersten's story teaches us that narcissistic abuse and coercive and controlling relationships scramble even the deepest metaphysical intuition. *Little Voices* teaches us how insidious these dynamics are, the trauma and generational issues that are activated, and how easy it is to get stuck in the cycle of confusion and self-blame. By telling her first-person story in a vulnerable and raw way, Kiersten reminds us that narcissistic and abusive relationships have a unique architecture, and represent a gradual process of grooming, gaslighting, and indoctrination. Even when the voices around her and in her are trying to guide her out, her story shines a light on how shame can be weaponized to keep anyone stuck and isolated in a toxic relationship. This book is, in essence, a compendium of red flags and can serve as a valuable teaching tool on how to listen to our inner voices and our guides; and to clearly heed these warning signs and act on them swiftly. One person's story can be a powerful lesson and motivator for change for others who find themselves in these kinds of relationships, and reminds survivors that you are not alone."

—**Dr. Ramani Durvasula**, Narcissism Expert, Licensed Clinical Psychologist, Bestselling Author, Professor of Psychology, Distinguished Speaker, and Featured Expert Guest on *Red Table Talk* with Jada Pinkett Smith and Will Smith

"I couldn't put *Little Voices* down! As someone who has experienced and written about near death and the spiritual journey which comes from it, I am blown away by Kiersten's authentic, down-to-earth approach of how becoming a later-in-life medium goes beyond a leap of faith—it's a deep dive into a knowing. If you're wondering if intuition is real and if it can save your life, this book is for you."

—**Stephanie Arnold**, Author of #1 Amazon and National Bestseller, *37 Seconds*

"*Little Voices* is a life-changing book! Not only will it make even the biggest skeptic believe in intuition, but it will also connect the dots for millions of abuse survivors. Reading how Kiersten used intuition to survive and heal from childhood sexual abuse and, later on in life, narcissistic abuse, hit home personally and was incredibly inspiring. I know many people will relate and be inspired by this book!"

—**Kelli Ellis**, Celebrity Designer, Artist, and Author
| HGTV | Bravo TV | TLC | TDN

"*Little Voices* offers a refreshing, bold, and at times, chilling account of the upside-down entangled world of relationships with a charming and handsome narcissist. Add in the power of intuition and a painful past, and readers will no doubt be impressed by her determination to find answers in detective work, as an entrepreneur and in life. Most of us become familiar with narcissists before we have a name for these individuals. No doubt, her painful examples and therapeutic explanations will help hordes of individuals learn how to recognize this dangerous personality and muster the strength to walk away from it. Kiersten writes with the ease and grace of an experienced storyteller, craftily keeping readers on the edge of their seats and anxious to dive head on into the next chapter. Kiersten, thank you for putting yourself out there!"

—**Bonnie Stevens**, Emmy Award–Winning Journalist and Editor

"*Little Voices* is the rare type of book that speaks to nearly every audience, including trauma survivors, women searching for their own identities, people struggling to connect to their intuition, entrepreneurs and aspiring entrepreneurs, people trying to improve their relationships, law enforcement, and individuals interested in mediumship and psychic abilities. It's touching, funny, dark, joyful, and disturbing—in all of the best and most intriguing ways. I highly recommend *Little Voices* for your book collection. It will inspire you to learn more about your own untapped intuitive abilities and to trust and strengthen the ones you already have. It will encourage you to be your authentic self and pursue those dreams you never thought possible."

—**Katie Beecher**, Renowned Medical and Spiritual Intuitive, Licensed Professional counselor, and Author of *Heal from Within: A Guidebook to Intuitive Wellness*

"As a Marriage and Family Therapist, I have read numerous excellent self-help books and memoirs on all kinds of abuse. Rarely have I come across one in which childhood sexual abuse, marital codependent behaviors, and partner narcissistic abuse were presented in a narrative which so painfully and yet prophetically links them together. *Little Voices* accomplishes this and so much more. With her raw, authentic detailing of the abuses she endured along with her unorthodox gifts from the spirit world, Kiersten Parsons Hathcock's memoir reminds us that until we heal the wounds within us, tragically we are drawn to external sources of validation—some healthy and some dangerous. Perhaps what is most noteworthy of Hathcock's memoir is her unwavering commitment to accountability, integrity, and truth—with herself and with others. We are not left feeling sorry for *Little Voices*. We are cheering with her and rooting for her all the way."

—**Holli Kenley**, MA, LMFT, and Author of *Breaking Through Betrayal: And Recovering the Peace Within*

"No one can understand what it's like to try to love a narcissist unless they've experienced it firsthand and Kiersten's book, *Little Voices,* is further validation of that for me. Not only was I so drawn into Kiersten's story that I read it in one sitting, but the way in which she shares her experience had me on the edge of my seat, rooting for her every step of the way. Kiersten's story takes things to a level often unexplored as she teaches us how to tap into the power of our intuition and trust our gut as a way to heal from narcissistic abuse. It's not just a compelling story on how to recover from psychological and emotional abuse, but a love story on how to honor yourself in a way only you are capable of doing. Thank you for being such an inspiration, Kiersten, and showing us what we need is already inside of us. We just have to look within."

—**Lisa E. Scott**, Bestselling Author of three books on narcissism, including *The Path Forward*

"*Little Voices* was a memoir I couldn't put down. Kiersten Parsons Hathcock's story is one that every woman should read. She gives tons of examples of how she tapped into her intuition, while also showing the humanness of what can happen when we don't listen. As a psychological and emotional abuse survivor, she could have been talking about my ex and I wouldn't have known the difference. This is a book every abuse survivor would benefit from because they would see that they are not alone. Non-abuse survivors would get the insight to why victims keep going back and some of the shame the victims feel when they go back, don't leave, or isolate from the people they love. Now, if that wasn't enough to keep a person reading, she shows you a whole other side of herself along with her special gifts. We get to see all these amazing parts of her that include being a medium and a self-taught carpenter who was on *Shark Tank*. Her story is a human story. It includes childhood sexual abuse, love, marriage, children, career, challenges, mistakes, downward spirals, intuitive gifts, helping others, and vulnerability. Her bravery and honesty are awe-inspiring. Life isn't always pretty, but learning and exposing the truth in the pain is essential to live an empowered life."

—**Rachael Wolff**, Author of *Letters from a Better Me*

"Kiersten Hathcock, as a woman and as a writer, is filled with equal parts heart and grit. I know this after reading the book she wrote, because here she is embracing life with a sweet, strong family, her thriving home-grown business, and an honest, sought-after passion for intuitive healing. All of this is despite—or maybe even because of—having endured soul-crushing abuse. Twice. But not only has Kiersten risen above the odds, now she authentically shares how and why in her memoir, so that other women might learn the power of their own inner truths. It's a must read!"

—**Janna Leadbetter**, Founder, Breaking the Silence for Women

"You've got to read this book. I'm somebody who can usually sit and read for about ten minutes at a time. But this book…I couldn't put down! I read it in one sitting. It's that good. Kiersten takes you on her journey, but it'll feel like you're right there with her. It feels like you're sitting on your couch with your best friend while she's telling you her experience. It doesn't matter if you think of yourself as an intuitive or survivor of domestic violence, you'll learn from this book. It's going to change the way we think of domestic violence, and it's going to change the way you relate to yourself."

—**Holly Jaleski,** Founder and Inventor, Grubcan

"A rich, soulful, and heartfelt journey of narcissistic abuse that mirrored my own experience so closely, at times, it took my breath away. If you are looking to gain an understanding of the dynamic played out between so many people in these relationships, Kiersten's book is a must read. Honest and vulnerable, she has helped me find my own forgiveness as to why I ended up in this cycle of abuse. Her courage in taking us through her story, gives us all courage. The love of her family gives us all an incredible example of what unconditional love looks like in action, not just words. If you are even slightly questioning the behavior of someone you love, friend, partner, or work colleague, *Little Voices* will undoubtedly give you some of those answers."

—**Shelley Buchanan**, Founder and CEO, Kindarma

"I binge read *Little Voices* in just a few days. I literally couldn't put it down. I rooted for Kiersten from beginning to end as she shared her harrowing journey with us in a way that somehow—despite highlighting life's unfairness—only helped me believe in hope and healing that much more."

—**Amy B. Scher**, Bestselling Author of *This is How I Save My Life*

"Every now and then a book comes along that vividly captures the frailty, and beauty, of stepping into our gifts and the uncertainty of what that may bring. Raw and courageous, resilient and hopeful, *Little Voices* is an unflinching portrayal of the depths into which one can fall and an inspiring account of the heights to which one can rise."

—**Bridgitte Jackson-Buckley,** Interviewer, Memoirist, and Author of *The Gift of Crisis*

LITTLE VOICES

HOW KIDS IN SPIRIT HELPED A RELUCTANT MEDIUM ESCAPE AND HEAL FROM ABUSE

KIERSTEN PARSONS HATHCOCK

Post Hill
PRESS

A POST HILL PRESS BOOK

Little Voices:
How Kids in Spirit Helped a Reluctant Medium Escape and Heal from Abuse
© 2022 by Kiersten Parsons Hathcock
All Rights Reserved

ISBN: 978-1-63758-519-1
ISBN (eBook): 978-1-63758-520-7

Cover design by Cody Corcoran
Cover artwork by Erica Vhay, "Alice"
Interior design and composition by Greg Johnson, Textbook Perfect

Post Hill Press
New York • Nashville
posthillpress.com

Published in the United States of America
1 2 3 4 5 6 7 8 9 10

Contents

Author's Note

I want to assure you—the reader—that despite the subject matter, *Little Voices* does not contain graphic detail of child murder cases. I do, however, share examples of narcissistic abuse I endured while in a toxic relationship and recount my revelation of childhood sexual abuse after having repressed memories for over thirty years. If you are an abuse survivor, please know that reading my book might trigger intense feelings and memories from your own life.

At its core, *Little Voices* is a story about learning to trust your intuition and use it as a roadmap for life. And it's a story about never-ending love despite pain and loss.

Please know that I changed certain names and locations in the book. To ensure that I recounted events as honestly and accurately as possible—I poured over emails, screenshots, documents, and witness testimony while writing *Little Voices*. With that said, my memoir is written from *my* perspective. From *my* memory. From *my* truth.

Foreword

By Mark Pucci, NYPD Detective (Ret.)
Founder/Chief Investigator
New York Private Detective Services

Spending most of my adult life as a detective, private investigator, or investigation supervisor, both in public service as a detective in the NYPD and in the private sector working cases nationwide, I unconsciously developed a sixth sense—an implicit intuition—for reading people and uncovering the truth. While most of the police detectives and professional investigators I know and have worked with will not openly admit to using their intuition to solve cases, it's succinctly presumed that following our gut feelings often makes the difference in discovering hidden evidence to solve a case. In certain extreme circumstances, intuition may even prove to be the factor that inevitably saves your life or the life of your partner.

I strongly believe that developing the ability to listen, understand, trust, and then follow my intuition has definitively made me a better detective and quite possibly resulted in many of my greatest successes and accomplishments as a police detective and private investigator.

Thinking back to before Kiersten and I had the opportunity to speak on the phone, I remember asking myself, "What is this furniture company CEO from Arizona doing volunteering to assist on a high-profile missing persons case in Long Island, New York?" That being said, when I finally had the chance to speak to Kiersten on the phone for the first time, my intuition kicked into full gear. Much to my surprise, not long into our conversation, I realized that she was unlike any other intuitive medium I had spoken to throughout the years. She explained to me that she recently discovered that she possessed certain abilities that might assist investigators in finding missing persons and that she was simply looking to volunteer her time because she cared. I eventually came to understand, as time went on and as I got to know Kiersten personally, that she had truly been given a gift for helping others in this way...especially kids.

More precisely, what I love about Kiersten—as is illustrated in her book—is that she's just a regular person thrown into supernatural experiences. Unbeknownst to her at that time, those experiences had meaning far beyond what she could see. The belief in what we can't see, especially as a detective looking for quantifiable, tangible evidence, is extremely difficult. However, Kiersten makes it easy to believe. In her moving story, we see that she is just like most of us—extremely logical and fact-driven. The most amazing part of her journey is that she wasn't looking for any of what has happened to her...it simply found her.

Thankfully, in writing this book, Kiersten was brave enough to share her undercover life as a reluctant medium and her amazing journey of survival and healing from abuse. After reading her book, I hope you find the same strength and fearlessness and that you learn to trust your own intuition. What Kiersten reveals to all of us is a hands-on roadmap for life, as it's been proven in my personal experience, for truth and justice as well.

Introduction

I always wanted to fit in—to be seen as normal. Normal family. Normal life path. Writing this book—and experiencing what I have since 2009—threw any chance of being seen as *normal* out the window. And I'm finally okay with that. It just took forty-seven years for me to get here.

The irony of my plight to be normal is that I finally realize intuition *is* actually normal. We all have it, even if we're not openly talking about it. It's one of the reasons I decided to write this book. As you'll discover in the pages of this memoir, for someone who's wired to trust scientific proof rather than faith, becoming a late-in-life medium proved a difficult journey. Like most folks who aren't raised to believe in the unseen, I couldn't wrap my head around why, in the middle of my life, I could suddenly hear and see kids in spirit. My heart raced, and the hair on my arms stood up every time a child came to me with a message.

In the beginning, I saw so much and yet, very little at the same time. I couldn't see how the kids would eventually step in to help me as much as I was helping them. There was a reason they were coming to me. My inner child knew why even if I didn't. The reason would be horrifying, unbelievable, and...something I'd never imagined in a million years.

My journey to trust the small voice inside me—and the small voices outside of me—has been life-changing. Not only did I learn to honor my intuition, but because of it, I survived and eventually escaped the cycle of abuse.

Now, finally, I'm on the other side of the pain, the fear, and the uncertainty. Even so, I'm confident that, as much as I've learned over the past eleven years as a reluctant medium, I certainly don't have all the answers to why we are here and why we endure what we do. But I do believe there's a plan for our lives that's much bigger than we can see. With that said, I want to share what resonated the most when I started to recognize intuition as a gift that we all possess. At the end of the book, you'll find a few tips and techniques that helped me develop and trust my intuition as well as heal from a lifetime of hidden abuse.

My hope is that, after reading about my journey, you'll not only develop more faith in your intuition but you'll see that part of yourself as a compass—a normal, everyday compass that you can use to help you get where you're meant to go. If you're an abuse survivor, I hope you know that no matter where you are in your journey, you are a warrior. And if you use your intuition as a guide, you'll always find a lighted path...even in the darkness.

2011

"You're close...but it's the big one," she said.

Her tiny voice rang clear and sweet, as though she was standing in front of me. It had been a few months since the little blonde-haired girl whose name started with a "C" began communicating with me. In my mind's eye, she looked to be no older than eight. No one else could hear her or see her, but for some reason, I could.

Walking over to the tallest tree, I asked in my mind, "Are you sure it's this one?"

"I'm sure."

Out of nowhere, chills ran up and down my entire body. I welcomed the familiar sign of confirmation. Standing in the hot sun, I surveyed the ground beneath the hundred-year-old tree as beads of sweat ran down my back. Readying myself, I leaned the shovel against a nearby tree and pulled my blonde hair back into a ponytail while I stared at the spot. As a self-taught carpenter and furniture designer, I was used to manual labor, but this felt different. Harder. My hands were sweaty as I thought about the weight of it all and what I had to confront to get to the truth.

I'd do anything for these kids, but clearly, the universe was reveling in some kind of sick joke. I was being guided to dig up the past. But first, I'd have to face a lifelong fear. As I stepped closer to the base of the tree, I glanced up to see hundreds of spiders encased in a blanket of webbing hanging from the branches. I immediately jumped back, trying desperately to slow my breathing. Spiders had always terrified me. From the time I was a small child, even the sight of the tiniest eight-legged creature sent me running and screaming for help. And now, as luck would have it, all of the arachnids in the world were in one place waiting to pounce on me. *What kind of fresh hell was I in?* A part of me wanted to take this intuitive gift and shove it, but I didn't. Instead, I carefully wiped away scores of cobwebs with my shovel handle and carved out a place to stand beneath the outstretched arms of the elm. I was ready to dig and had convinced myself that if I didn't look up, I'd be okay.

I dug for an hour, all the while feeling nervous about what I'd find as I shoveled out hardpacked soil and tossed it into a mound. As the mound grew taller, I grew more anxious. Wiping sweat from my brow onto my dirt-stained jeans, I looked around the yard, making sure that I had indeed been guided to the correct tree. I panicked for a minute because I could no longer hear the girl. *Where did she go?*

All I could do was trust what she'd already told me. As I continued to plunge my shovel into the ground, flashes of visions I saw weeks ago played like a movie in my mind. They revealed grisly details of her abduction and murder, making me all the more determined to keep going. She needed my help, and I needed her to help me understand why she was coming to me.

A little more than an hour into shoveling, I was ready to ditch my sweat-soaked halter top for another shirt.

That's when I felt a tug on my ponytail.

I turned, searching for another soul in the yard. The entire backyard was empty, but I wasn't alone. She was making sure I knew she was still there.

Even though I was intuitively led to that spot that day, I truly didn't understand just how much was left to uncover.

CHAPTER 1

The Road to Spirit

Standing in our already-sweltering LA garage during an early June morning in 2009, I savored the scent of Baltic birch plywood that I'd just run through the table saw. My 400-square-foot workshop was built during my favorite musical era—the 1940s. Now that the roar of the saw had faded, it was time to hit *play* on a few Billie Holiday tunes. Donning a toolbelt, jeans, white tank top, ponytail, and flip flops, I walked over to the workbench where I planned to start crafting the umpteenth toy box. The sun lit up the bench like a spotlight. I was in the right spot.

In the two years since I started my furniture company, the scent of cut wood came to symbolize quiet solitude and solace. Looking back, I hadn't realized just how much I needed that time alone in my workshop, but I knew I adored my sawdust oasis.

As I reached for the hand jigsaw to carve out the leaf-shaped lids of the toy box, I thought back on my unusual journey going from corporate to carpentry. Most days, I felt content with my new role as a work-from-home mom who built kids' furniture while taking care of her own kids. Other days, I'd reminiscence on the fast-paced, exciting years I spent working in the television industry in Chicago.

I was in my mid-thirties and seemingly happy—except that I wasn't. In years past, I saw my world in vibrant technicolor—but since moving to Burbank, California in 2006, the colors of my life were more muted. Gray, almost. I couldn't put my finger on it. I was too young for a mid-life crisis, and I genuinely found pleasure in all that I did, but nothing really set me on fire anymore. I considered going to counseling, but what was I going to talk about? Sure, we'd moved around the country a few times, and my husband, Scott, had endured a couple of unexpected layoffs. But all in all, we were good. Aside from worrying about our second grader's sudden onset stuttering, I had little to fret about.

After cutting the leaf-shaped lids, I went into assembly mode. I'd gotten so used to building toy boxes that I could easily craft a box without much mental effort. It allowed me to continue searching my mind for answers to my gray state of being. Answers did not come that day, nor for several months after, until September when I stepped out of my comfort zone and into a strange new world.

* * *

Staring at the New Age tapestry on the wall of the tiny waiting room, I reminded myself that my midwestern family wouldn't approve. *How the hell did I get here?* I thought as I nervously sat down on the edge of a red velvet-covered chair and fumbled with my phone. I was in such unfamiliar territory. The weird symbols on the wall and the smell of incense did nothing to calm my nerves.

I'd passed this particular psychic shop a million times on my way to pick up the kids from school or when I dashed to the lumberyard for more plywood.

"This is crazy," I mumbled to myself as my anxiety climbed. *Maybe I should just leave.*

At that very moment, Sophia, a short, silver-haired woman in her sixties dressed in a flowy chiffon dress, came out from the room next door, sat down across from me, and asked what kind of reading I would like. Looking down at the floor, I told her I had no idea; I just felt the urge to venture in that day. She knew that was a lie—just me trying to prop up my got-it-all-together façade. I didn't have the courage to immediately tell her about my gray life. She carefully reached for my hand, held it in hers with eyes closed, and proceeded to change the course of my life.

First, she revealed specific details about my life, my habits, and my family's past, like the fact that my mom's father was emotionally abusive. No way could she have otherwise known these things. Clearly, the Universe had rightly pegged me as a skeptic. I had always been very scientific by nature. Though I wasn't traditionally religious, I did believe in some kind of higher power. In order to share the messages I truly needed to hear, Sophia first had to share things that she couldn't possibly have looked up online. And that she did.

Feeling more open and trusting, I told her I felt a weird emptiness in my life—like I was looking through gray-colored glasses—but couldn't put my finger on why. I had a wonderful husband, two awesome kids, a growing furniture company, and a fantastic group of friends. So, what was the deal?

Without addressing what I had just said about the gray, Sophia said in a matter-of-fact tone, "You will help millions of kids. In fact, you will help people all over the world, but you have much healing to do first. Your life has always revolved around children—others, your own, and finally, you even built a business around kids. You're very good at making things happen outside of yourself, but you've not yet gone inside to heal. You have gifts like I do, but you won't have a shop like this. You'll use yours in different ways."

An unstoppable ear-to-ear grin spread across my face, outing my disbelief. And yet, I wanted to believe her. Maybe it was the spot-on details she shared in the beginning. Maybe I just wanted to believe that my life had more purpose than building high-end kids' furniture. Or maybe I'd inhaled too much polyurethane in the garage.

My mind latched onto the more ominous bit of information. *Why do I need to heal? And from what?*

She sat back in her upholstered chair as if she was preparing to tell me devastating news. "A seed of negativity was planted when you were very little."

Wait, what? Was that the gray? Can I just pluck it out? Who put it there? How old was I when it was planted? I had so many questions but didn't feel brave enough to ask.

My head spun as Sophia wrapped up our session by talking about all things being revealed in their own time. She did share that she saw me writing multiple books, and even shared a vision of some sort of healing center set in the middle of a field of tall pine trees. She said I would be a big part of making that center a reality. Sophia said she hoped I would eventually move forward with the healing center she saw in her vision because it was what our world needed—for her own kids and for generations to come.

Dumbfounded, I stared at Sophia as though I was in a trance. Her voice snapped me out of my paralyzed state when she asked if I had three children.

"I have two kids," I replied.

"Hmmm…well, forgive me for asking such a personal question, but have you endured a miscarriage or an abortion? I'm only asking because I see her clear as day. She has longish brown curly hair, this third soul."

"No, it's okay. I haven't had an abortion or a miscarriage."

"Well, sometimes these things reveal themselves later on," she replied.

In true-to-form fashion, my practical mind took over. Unless we adopted, there was no way another child was possible. My husband's vasectomy assured us of that.

Wrapping up the session, Sophia started giving me guidance on what to do next. She encouraged me to meditate and really get in touch with who I was as a person. "Everything you need is inside of you," she said. This was my birthday—September 9th, 2009. I was thirty-six.

* * *

For weeks after my session with Sophia, I took daily walks around the neighborhood hoping they would give me space to solve the mystery of the negative seed that had been planted. Maybe if I thought about it enough without interruption by my kiddos, it would come to me. It never did, so I forced the whole interaction to the back of my mind. While the gray was still ever-present, I couldn't waste my time on the musings of an old psychic woman. I had things to do, toy boxes to build, and kids to shuttle to and from school. I didn't even really have time for meditation like Sophia had prescribed.

Instead of dwelling on that psychic nonsense, I spent time worrying about how we could better help our son—a second-grader—cope with his newly diagnosed anxiety disorder.

Scott and I started researching holistic ways to help quell Noah's anxiety after we did what all good parents do: made an appointment with a psychiatrist—who turned out to be a pompous ass. Noah saw through him immediately. We had no choice but to trust the doc because he was the expert, and he felt Noah needed something to help his nervous system calm down. That something was an SSRI. Soon, we learned that the medication didn't do anything but make Noah feel, in his words, "down, and I don't know why." This was enough to push us to research additional alternative treatment options. We'd heard enough stories about kids becoming suicidal on anti-anxiety and antidepressant medication that we knew we had to find another solution.

The thing is, I'm a natural-born detective who prides herself on finding stuff most people can't. But even I'll admit that figuring out how to help Noah—aside from traditional medicine—was difficult. As synchronicity would have it, two folks who were dear friends with one of my friends were coming to LA from the UK and they taught a form of Japanese energy healing called Reiki. Prior to their arrival in the States, I'd read that energy balancing might help Noah, but I didn't know anything about it.

One night after they arrived, Scott and I invited the Reiki teachers, Doug and Mike, to our little yellow house in Burbank. While we sipped on gin cocktails in our living room, we laughed at their British sense of humor and got to know their journey to *woo woo*. After about an hour of chit-chat, we started talking Reiki.

The skeptic in me knew I needed to see how this Reiki thing worked, but I was admittedly nervous. Hands-on healing seemed so foreign to me and went against my scientific wiring, but I kept an open mind. There had to be something to it if these two were teaching classes on it. After explaining that Reiki energy is intelligent and goes wherever it's needed in the body, Doug asked if he could pull the white midcentury-style kitchen chair into the living room. I felt my pulse quicken when he asked if I would sit down in front of him for a mini Reiki session. Nervously, I sat down and prepared for what was to come. He said it would last for about ten minutes.

The moment Doug simply put his hands on my shoulders, I felt woozy and hot. He hadn't done anything but place his hands on me, but the woozy feeling progressed to the point where I was feeling nauseous and dizzy. Not wanting to disappoint him but knowing I couldn't go on any longer, I spoke up.

"Doug, I'm so sorry but I'm feeling nauseous. Maybe I'm doing it wrong."

"Oh no, you're not doing anything wrong...but let's get you to a place where you can lie down."

Doug helped me to our bedroom, which was, thankfully, right off the living room.

Sitting on the edge of our bed, Doug asked if I was feeling better. I nodded my head as the heat in my body started to cool.

"Kiers, is there any chance you could be pregnant?" he asked quietly in his soothing British accent.

"Um, no. Scott took care of that after Grace was born."

"Hmmm, because that type of reaction is common if you've had issues in the reproductive area or are currently pregnant."

"Well, I have had ovarian cysts—PCOS, to be exact."

"Ah, well, that's likely the culprit," he said.

Something in his voice made me question if he truly believed my reaction was related to PCOS. All I knew at that moment was that after he took his hands off me and I rested for a bit in our bedroom, I felt new again.

This five-minute demonstration on the power of Reiki was all it took for me to understand that there was indeed truth to this strange practice. Before heading off to their hotel, Doug and Mike encouraged me to think about Reiki healing for Noah. All I had to do was learn it myself. Even though it felt foreign and weird, I thought, *If it can help Noah, I'm in.* I figured it was worth a shot because we were running out of options and I was worried about him.

A few days later, I became Reiki certified in a beige-colored hotel room in north LA. Doug and Mike taught me the first two levels of the therapy, which meant I could start working with Noah.

Much to my surprise, Noah didn't balk at me when I offered to try out my skills on him. The energy balancing seemed to reduce his anxiety, but admittedly I didn't detect as much of a difference in him as I detected in myself. I felt more in tune with myself than I had in many years, and I noticed that my hands would become extremely hot out of nowhere. I didn't understand how and why it all worked the way it did, but I was grateful to have opened my mind to Reiki healing.

* * *

Over the next three months, my garage life monopolized most of my daylight hours, but I took time to perform Reiki on Noah when he seemed super anxious. Thanks to this new technique I learned, Noah seemed a little more balanced, and he loved not having to play the game where Mr. Psychiatrist condescendingly pretended to care for a total of fifteen minutes and Noah pretended to offer honest feedback. I was a happy mama knowing I could make a difference in his small but anxious world. The peace that came with my quiet, sawdust-filled workshop and the realization that Noah felt better made me feel more balanced.

My crazy idea to start building and selling furniture out of our garage, in order to not have to go back to a corporate job, was working. My home-grown company, Mod Mom Furniture, had expanded until I was building two to three toy boxes per week and selling them to folks all over the US and Canada, as well as celebrity clients who lived on the wealthy side of Los Angeles. Sawdust covered me from head to toe, daily.

After dropping the kids at school, I'd swing open the workshop door to start my shift. But in 2010, three years into building the Mod Mom brand, life was changing for me in ways that had nothing to do with business. I was hearing and seeing things that could only be explained as a byproduct of lack of sleep, exhaustion, and paint fumes. Or so I thought.

One spring day, I opened the shop like normal. I wasn't known to be the most organized carpenter. Most times, my workshop was littered with half-empty coffee mugs and energy bar wrappers in addition to a layer of sawdust that I swore every day I'd clean up— but never did.

After locating my toolbelt, I slung it around my hips over top of my three-year-old True Religion jeans that bared the scars of a woodworker. They were my holey work jeans, and I wore them almost every day for three years.

It was time to get to work. I remembered that I'd just bought a few half-inch screws that I needed for attaching toy box legs.

"Honey, do you know where the screws I just bought went?" I yelled to Scott from the garage. He was working his sales gig for a tech company from home that day.

"Didn't you put them on your main workbench when you came in?" Scott shouted back.

"Yeah, I did. I must have moved them and not realized it."

Now, where were those screws? I thought. *Oh, there they are, in an area of the garage I never venture. That's weird. Okay, back to work.*

Knee-deep in sanding a Gracie Toy Box and getting ready to install leg brackets, I reached over for the box of screws that I'd just put next to me. They were gone again. I frantically looked around the room and found them staring at me from the chop saw bench. I was the only person in the garage. I had not put them there; I never put screws on my chop saw. At least, I didn't think I put them there. Well, whatever happened, I didn't have time to ponder the anomaly. I pushed it to the back of my mind and returned to work.

"Mom!"

As much work as I had to do, when one of my kids calls, I see what they need. I stopped installing brackets and marched into the kitchen where the noise was coming from.

Wait.

They're at school.

Immediately, my entire body chilled and the hair on my arms stood straight up. I tried to ignore my reaction and focus on who could have been outside.

I scanned the room, stopping at the window. There wasn't a soul in sight. Still, goosebumps covered my entire body. Ignoring the chills I felt, I shrugged, chalking it up to some kid that wasn't mine. I felt kind of silly for forgetting that my kids were at school, and went back to work.

Progressively over the next few months, I started experiencing an escalation of all these weird things.

I started hearing voices.

I smelled cigarette smoke that wasn't there.

Music I didn't know filled my head.

The TV turned on and off by itself.

Shadows moved across the garage.

I had chills. Lots of chills.

I felt like I was being watched all the time.

I did what any normal person would do—I ignored it until I couldn't push it away anymore. Searching my mind for answers, I suddenly remembered other odd occurrences in our previous house. Shadows that both Noah and I would see, but no one else would pay attention to, flashed across my mind in a series of montage moments. I only remember those because, while we were sitting on the couch watching TV together, I could see Noah's head move when he saw the same shadow crossing the room. Somehow, I'd managed to bury that memory in my overcrowded brain. *Maybe this had been happening for a while but was ramping up for some reason?* Whatever it was, it was freaking me out.

For months, I struggled with determining what was real and what wasn't real. I was still hearing, seeing, and smelling things that other people didn't. I didn't tell anyone except Scott. He took it in stride and kept reassuring me that I was perfectly fine, but we both knew that wasn't completely true. Nothing about my heightened senses felt normal.

One evening while getting ready for bed, the hair on my arms started standing up while I struggled to find my voice.

"Scott, do you see that over there?" I whispered, pointing to a shape I saw in the corner of the bedroom.

"I don't, hon, but I believe you're seeing it."

It made me feel a little better that he didn't think I'd lost my mind, but I sure wished he could see it too. Maybe then I'd really believe that I wasn't about to be carted off to the psych ward.

* * *

Belief in seeing and hearing things not visible to the naked eye was never part of my upbringing or adult life. Growing up in Defiance, Ohio, I was all about what I could see and touch and what my parents and others perceived about me. Being the daughter of two teachers taught me the value of hard work, community, and self-discipline. My dad coached our high school football team and my mom taught junior high kids with learning disabilities, and I did everything I could to make my parents—and everyone around me—proud. I followed the rules to a "T." Stepping out of line and bringing shame to my family wasn't an option. I was terrified of letting anyone down—a telltale sign of perfectionism.

My parents grew up Baptist but they didn't go to church as adults. The only time I went to church as a child was when I'd stay at my Grandma's house. With dad's football coaching keeping him busy on Friday and Saturday, they didn't want to spend our family day in church. I can't say I was ever angry about that choice, although every time I walked into a church, I felt chills up and down my body.

I picked a college that was four hours away to officially test the rule-breaking waters. A couple of not-so-upstanding guys, four menial jobs that helped me get through school, a badly constructed fake ID, and a few dozen beers later, I packed my diploma into the car and headed south to Charlotte, North Carolina. Being on my own for the first time in my life, knowing hardly anyone in the Queen City, gave me both a sense of freedom and fear. I alternated between thinking, *Yay, I'm doing this!* and *oh, God, I'm doing this!*

Shortly after starting a computer training job in Charlotte, I was invited by a new friend to Vinnie's Sardine Bar where, much to my surprise, I met the love of my life. Scott Hathcock, a tall, handsome, dark-haired, Southern gentleman from Alabama more than caught my eye as he walked into the greasy dive bar. A few minutes later, our friend, Leigh, introduced us to one another. In my oversized Adidas jacket, cheeky grin, and faded jeans, I offered him a fried cheese stick. He was amused by my gesture and politely accepted it before saying he'd return the favor with a drink of my choice. Not only was he strikingly handsome at 6'2", he was hilarious. And much to my delight, he thought I was funny, too, when I joked about how many wallets I stole on the way through the crowded bar to the restroom. He felt like home to me—like my college friends from Ohio, especially because he oddly didn't have a Southern accent.

Believe it or not, four months after sharing fried cheese sticks at Vinnie's, we were engaged at his parent's Alabama home, surrounded by his extended family. To quote Scott's dad, "It was about time." We'd known each other for four whole months, after all. But the thing was, we felt as if we'd known each other for lifetimes.

A year later—at the ages of twenty-three and twenty-five—we married on the steps of a Roosevelt-era manor. Our adventure started with a move to Birmingham, Alabama, where Noah was born, then on to Atlanta, Georgia, working for numerous TV networks on the un-sexy side of the business. Scott was in affiliate sales for cable networks, which meant that climbing the ladder came with a moving truck.

Eventually, Scott was relocated with Playboy TV Networks to the Windy City. In Chicago, I landed a wonderful marketing job with A&E and The History Channel. For three years, we juggled fast-paced careers and our little bundle of joy, spending a lot of time on the L train going back and forth from our downtown offices to our brownstone in the Wrigleyville area. Grace's birth in 2002 spurred a desire to ditch the hectic city life for a quieter one in a smaller town. We sold our house and moved south to a town called Hebron, Kentucky, where Scott landed a job in nearby Cincinnati, Ohio.

While I loved the idea of being home full-time with the kids, it was a tough adjustment. I was used to the fast-paced TV ad sales life, and a big part of me wanted that back in some shape or form.

Nine months later, an unexpected layoff threw us into panic mode but ultimately moved us towards our destiny. We just didn't see it that way at the time. We sold much of what we had, including our 4,000-square-foot home, and set off for LA without jobs and with the little we had in savings, and our cashed-out 401Ks.

The move to California made me seriously reconsider my TV career. With a one-year-old and a five-year-old in tow, the last thing I wanted to do was put them in a new daycare after they'd gotten used to being with me every day. Plus, we realized that if I went to work full-time, we'd spend almost my entire salary on childcare costs. Scott landed a job at E! Television Networks, so we could both stop holding our breath, but we still needed additional income to live extremely modestly in a 1,000-square-foot 1940s home in Sherman Oaks. I started taking on freelance projects but we needed something steadier.

"Obviously, we need more money," I said to Scott one afternoon while we watched our little ones play in the backyard garden. "I can't make enough working contract jobs, so I'm thinking of becoming a nanny. After all, I don't want to be forced into a hooker life. This is LA, ya know."

He laughed. "Hooking is not in your wheelhouse, honey."

He knew me well. But seriously, every movie we watched during our early time in LA involved someone who moved to the City of Angels and ended up selling themselves or drugs. I knew what was at stake.

The next day, I nervously placed an ad on Craigslist after building and publishing my own website. *Voilà*. I was instantly Mary Poppins without all the flying about. Two lovely families saw my ad and contacted me right away.

For two years, I cared for two adorable babies and helped shepherd them into toddlerhood. My days consisted of trips to and from Noah's elementary school pushing a second-hand double stroller for Grace, who was two-years-old at the time, and my charges who became part of our family. When I made the decision to nanny, I was terrified. I loved children but I questioned if I'd be any good at taking care of other people's kids.

I discovered over the two-year period from 2004 to 2006 that the kids were the easiest part of nannying. Having left a successful corporate career where I earned accolades and plaques validating my worth, my new title took some hard adjustment. Still, I knew my gut was spot on when I had the idea to dive into the world of caregiving. It was the right move for our family during those years.

I wouldn't trade that time for the world, but I will say it was my inside look at what it meant to not be climbing the ladder—something I was programmed to do as an overachiever. And no matter how many "art projects" I did with my babes, I missed being creative and strategic. I missed the thrill of dreaming up marketing campaign ideas. Luckily, there were garage sales!

"Hon, I just made our garage look like The Gap," I sheepishly proclaimed when Scott walked through the front door one day.

I really did have a knack for marketing design. As Scott lifted the heavy 1940s garage door, I heard an audible gasp. Okay, maybe not a gasp, but an impressed grunt at how much I'd gotten done and how much our dilapidated garage looked like a department store. It didn't surprise him though, because he was used to coming home to my manic projects. Once, I built a plywood highway system in our backyard for the kids to ride their bikes on. Another time I threw Scott a surprise birthday party decked out with a handmade plywood karaoke stage, tiki bar, and surfboard bar table. My instincts were saying it was time to get back to my creative roots, but I was still unsure what to do.

One night, after we settled our kiddos into bed, I sank to the sofa with a sigh. "Now that the kids are older and the babies are moving onto preschool, I've been thinking about building furniture. I think there's a market for a particular kind of plywood kids' furniture."

"You think?" Scott asked.

"You know how we've been looking for a mid-century modern toy box on Craigslist? Well, I started searching current retailers to see if anyone is making that type of storage right now, and there's only one company creating one toy box design. And get this—they're charging four hundred dollars for it. When I saw their design, I immediately saw a cool new design in my mind's eye inspired by Grandma's old split-top record player. My gut is screaming that I need to do this. I know it sounds crazy, but...." I waited to see if *he* thought it sounded crazy.

He looked me right in the eyes. "I think you can do anything you set your mind to, Kiers."

I leaned in for a hug, grateful for his support and love. Our life together hadn't been easy with all of the moves and financial worry, but we loved and respected one another. Even through the hard times. In that moment, I was reminded how my gut knew almost instantly that I should marry him, just like it knew I was supposed to give this furniture thing a try.

Mod Mom Furniture was born that day in 2007, and I thought life couldn't get any more interesting. Little did I know that in two years it was going to get a *lot* more interesting. And terrifying, at times.

CHAPTER 2

Awakening

After visiting Sophia in the psychic shop, the spooky stuff ramped up. Not only was the TV going on and off on its own, but I started to see more than shadows walking around my home.

One afternoon, while working at my kitchen table, I saw the apparition of a small boy walk into the kitchen. He had dark hair and wore a white shirt with white shorts. My entire body chilled as I sat frozen, staring him in the eyes. Just as I was getting ready to say hello, he vanished. I held my breath for what seemed like an eternity before exhaling, trying to make sense of what I'd seen. Just then, the living room TV turned on as if validating what had happened.

I frantically researched apparitions on Google. The search engine never let me down when I was figuring out how to design and build furniture, so I figured it would help make sense of my current situation. For the most part, I looked for articles about spirituality and spirits in general. What I found ran the gamut from after-life stories to near death experiences to spiritual *woo woo*. I wasn't that much of a believer despite what I was seeing. I still thought there was half a chance I was going crazy.

More incidents like the little boy in my kitchen occurred, but one night while we were drifting off to sleep, Scott whispered, "Honey, do you see that girl with long black hair standing in the doorway?"

Relief engulfed me. Finally, he saw what I did.

"Yep...I sure do," I said. "You have no idea how happy I am that you see her, too. I am pretty certain I saw her in the garage with me today. I have to figure out how to come to grips with this and find out what she, and all of the kids showing up in our house, want. They keep staring at me, but I don't know how to talk to them. I think I'm going to have to Google it. I can't believe I'm saying any of this right now."

Scott chuckled. "I love that your mind goes to Google, Kiers. I wish we knew why it was happening, but at least you know I just saw one, too. You're really not crazy...you do know that, right?"

"You mean you're not about to cart me off to the psych ward?" I replied with a smile. "I don't know what to think, I mean...I believe that it's really happening. I'm just still so confused as to why and how."

"Try to get some sleep, hon, he said leaning in to kiss me on my forehead. We'll figure this out. I love you."

While Scott found easy slumber, I spent most of the night with eyes wide open thinking about everything. I didn't have any definitive answers, but I knew deep down that something had changed in me.

The next morning, I called my Reiki masters, and they explained that I was energetically more receptive, having gone through training. But still, not everyone who learns Reiki starts seeing apparitions. Google became my best friend, but there had to be more to it. *Why me? Why now?* I was pretty sure the internet couldn't answer all my questions, but I had faith I'd be able to research how to navigate it all.

Every month brought a new unexplainable experience—some I still wish I could wipe from my memory. One night around 3:00 AM, I dreamed about being buried alive. I was a blond boy in a red plaid flannel shirt who looked to be around the age of five. Strong, calloused hands were squeezing tight around my neck before I was laid in a shallow grave. Darkness surrounded me, but I could still make out tall pine trees surrounding me in the glow of the half-moon. The sensation of dirt being tossed in my face was the last thing I saw before I was suddenly back in our bedroom.

Scott woke to the sounds of me screaming, "I'm not dead yet! I'm not dead yet!"

"Kiers, you're dreaming...it's OK. You're safe," he soothed.

Drenched in sweat and almost to the point of hyperventilating, I searched for his face to ground me. Once I realized I was safe in our home, I clung to him. He held me tight against his chest while my tears soaked his t-shirt. I couldn't speak for a few minutes.

"Can you tell me more about it, hon?" Scott asked once I was no longer in hysterics.

I relayed the scene to him, but this time from more of a bird's-eye view. Afterward, we talked about how strange it was that I was dreaming of a child I didn't know and that I wasn't watching it play out like an episode of *CSI* but living it.

Eventually, I fell back to sleep from sheer exhaustion, but once the sun came up and the coffee was brewed, I pulled out my laptop and started googling all things paranormal.

I searched the internet for scientific studies on the afterlife, spirit phenomenon, alternate realities, and spiritual awakenings. After a couple of hours of research, my mind, which was now filled with too much information about the strange phenomenon I was experiencing, began to crave normalcy. And I knew just how to make that happen—I had a toy box to build. I tried to give myself a break from the *Twilight Zone* life I'd been living by cranking up the radio in my workshop and calling a few friends in between sanding toy box parts. Hearing their voices made me feel like I wasn't losing my mind. While I didn't say anything to them about what I was going through, I wondered if they could hear and feel how off-kilter I felt.

During a break that day, I sat down at my computer and opened up Facebook. Surfing the feed helped me feel grounded in reality and connected to my friends and family who weren't living in LA. Sitting at my desk in the kitchen while I scarfed down a sandwich, I perused the feed, laughing at jokes and fawning over baby photos until I landed on a post about a memorial celebration. I was immediately drawn to the photos of a young boy named Nate Pannell, who had passed away in the town I grew up in—Defiance, Ohio. He was the son of two fellow Defiance High School alumni a bit older than me. I knew of them but didn't know them well.

Staring at the photo of Nate, I heard what I thought was his voice. It rang in my head. I was terrified at first. *Was this real?* I wasn't sure if I was really talking to *him*, or if my mind was making it all up. After all, I'd never experienced anything like this while surfing Facebook. Staring at his photo, I could see him in my mind's eye, and chills ran up and down my body. I noticed the chills were predominantly on the left side of my body and made note of that, too. I had no idea what it meant, but it stood out.

I suspended disbelief long enough to hear Nate talk about his family and share specific messages he wanted me to share with them. That part terrified me, but I continued listening while I reached for a pen and paper to write down what he was saying. In between his messages, I asked him, in my mind, if he had more to share. He would either say yes and continue or no and then plead with me to reach out to his parents.

After he spoke, I sat frozen in my chair, thinking about what just happened. The last thing I wanted to do was reach out to grieving parents, who may or may not receive my guidance well. Their family had been through so much already. *What if I was wrong and none of it was real? What if they saw me as someone trying to somehow take advantage of their situation?* I didn't know how I'd react if someone reached out to me this way. Finally, I rose from my chair, knowing I needed time to think about all of it, and beelined it for our bedroom.

Sitting on the edge of the bed with my notes in hand, I knew I had a choice to make. For now, it was to hide what had happened and go about life as normal. Normal was easier.

I opened the drawer of my bedside table and stuffed the messages inside. I knew I needed time, so I waited to be filled with courage and knowledge that what Nate asked me to do was the right thing.

The courage came two days later when I least expected it: I wasn't even thinking about Nate until, out of the blue, peace came over me. Still terrified to take the next step, I obsessed over what it would mean to try. Even if they slammed the door in my face. Even if I was going to be the laughingstock of my hometown after word got around. I gently pulled my notes out of the drawer and crafted a quick introductory message to his mom, Denise. I nervously hit the *send* button, hoping that I was doing the right thing. And it was indeed the right thing. Denise responded kindly, which started a back-and-forth exchange that led to a phone call and, later, an in-person meeting in Defiance when I was home visiting my parents.

About four years after I shared Nate's messages with his family, I asked Nate's father, John, if he wouldn't mind writing what the experience was like for them. By that time, I was running a nonprofit that helped grieving parents and thought a testimonial about his experience would be helpful for other parents.

John agreed, and about a week later, he shared his account of their experience with me via email. As I read the letter, I slowly sat back in my chair, astonished by what John wrote:

Almost four years ago, I was just surviving being a bereaved parent of a child who has passed away. It was a daily struggle getting through a day without a total meltdown and the overwhelming feeling that I didn't want to live the rest of my life in the role of a grieving parent. It was in the midst of one of my many meltdowns that I remember my wife coming upstairs, in tears, telling me she got a message from Nate, our son who had passed away at the age of 13 from an AVM. I tried to listen to what she was telling me, but it seemed Greek to me because I couldn't get past my own doubt. She tells me that she got an email from this lady in California about how strange it may seem, but she thinks she has a message for us from our son. If we were willing, we could give her a call.

Denise called her and they spoke for almost an hour. Denise was trying to relay the information from the four pages of notes she took while Kiersten talked. The only comfort this brought to me was that for the first time since Nate's death, I had seen tears of joy versus tears of sorrow. Denise and Kiersten kept in contact, but I kept my distance. One day, I remember Denise telling me that Kiersten was going to be in the area and wanted to meet with us.

Out of obligation to Denise, growing skepticism, and just a dash of curiosity, I agreed to meet with Kiersten. My anxiety level that day was extremely high. I remember when Kiersten sat down with us at our dining room table. It was my wife, our younger son, Jack, my wife's aunt Sally, Kiersten, and myself. There was a lot of small talk, and I listened intently trying to find what the catch was. Over the next three and a half hours, what I got were answers, hope, and explanations. I had questions on authenticity as to who Kiersten was and what her motives were. I found Kiersten to be one of the most genuine people I have had the pleasure of meeting. She spoke from the heart. She relayed to us information as it was interpreted by her. What I found was she spoke with a gift. Her heart was pure. Her interpretation spot-on. She offered validation that was unquestionably accurate. She gave us peace knowing that our son was fine. Kiersten taught me events that occur are not just coincidences.

Kiersten opened up a form of communication between my son and me that allowed me to go from being a grieving parent just existing to being a bereaved parent who is allowed to live. She has *helped us by being a conduit for question-and-answer sessions, she has taught us what it means to look for the hidden meaning; most importantly, she gave us our youngest son back. You see, until that time, there wasn't much communication between him, his mother, and me. I know a large amount of time that first night meeting Kiersten, she spent talking with Jack. I have never asked either one what exactly was said, but whatever it was made a difference in that young man's life.*

Meeting Kiersten and being open to her gift has not taken away the fact that we lost our oldest son. That is something we live with every day. Having Kiersten reaching out to us, opening herself up to us, putting it all out there, all for us, and never asking for anything in return, has given us peace.

Kiersten, I know that my statement doesn't even start to do justice to what you have given us.

—John Pannell

Up until then, I had no idea the impact the messages and visit made on his entire family. I knew they greatly appreciated that I reached out to them, but I didn't fully grasp how much it shaped the course of their lives.

With tears streaming down my cheeks, I read about the healing that Nate had facilitated by sharing messages with me. Of course, I knew what the whole experience did for me, and I'm eternally grateful. Nate and his beautiful family helped me understand that what I was experiencing wasn't just my imagination. It was very real and very important for all of us. I just had to have the courage to trust.

* * *

Nate wasn't the only child who decided to pay a visit in 2010. Some children just popped in without messages, while others asked me to write down what they were saying and save it for later. Most times, they were related to someone I knew, but sometimes they would pop in like Nate did while I was reading an article or watching a news program. I could count on a new child coming to me at least once a month. The validation I received from Nate's family reassured me that it was all very real, but I continued to keep it under wraps for fear of being called crazy. Scott was my only confidante at the time.

I still didn't know why they were bending my ear, but I figured maybe they liked that I was a mom and a goofy one at that. Or maybe no one else was available, and I was at the end of the *Hey, she can hear us!* line. My mind raced as I tried to figure out *why* children who had passed on were coming to me.

One teenager in spirit named Matt had committed suicide, and he told me about being scared to move on into the light. I didn't know this particular teen but I knew the other teen in spirit who brought him to me so that I could help him. The only problem was that *how* I was supposed to guide him into the light was a mystery to me.

Thankfully, I had already learned from watching my new favorite show, *Ghost Whisperer*, that he needed to step into the light. But where was the light? Was Matt the only one who would come to me for help, or did this come with the territory of being a covert psychic medium of sorts?

Once again, I found myself turning to the internet—my trusted advisor. I literally Googled "how to cross spirits into the light." Turns out, it's relatively easy to find online. I figured out how to create a bright light doorway in my mind, but he wouldn't pass through it. He was scared that he would go to hell because he committed suicide. By this time in late 2010, I'd experienced enough to assure him that he had nothing to fear. From what I'd already learned from Nate and several other kids, I knew enough to tell him that when he crossed, he wouldn't be going to hell. Rather, he would cross into the light and meet with loved ones who were already on the other side. And I knew he could come back and forth after he crossed.

Once he was convinced that there was nothing to fear, I asked if he saw the light I created in my mind, and he said yes. Then, after making me promise he could come back and forth and that he wasn't going to hell, he walked into the light door. Goosebumps covered me from head to toe when he made his exit. It was one of the most touching moments of my life.

Unlike my encounter with Nate, the chills that accompanied Matt's arrival were predominantly on my right side. As time went on, I deciphered that if a spirit had already crossed into the light, I would feel chills on my left side. If not, I would feel them on my right side. I was becoming a decoder in addition to being a medium.

Thankfully, Matt did come back to me after he crossed. I was covered in chills on my left side when he thanked me for helping him. And then, just as quickly as he came in, he was gone again.

* * *

In 2010, around the same time that I learned to open light doors for spirits, we continued to search for more alternatives to help Noah with his severe anxiety. I mentioned to a friend that Noah was still struggling, despite the Reiki healing I was providing, and she told me about her daughter and another girl who had visited a professional energy healer a few hours north of LA and how it had made all the difference for both of them. Grateful for the referral, I immediately booked an appointment.

Upon arrival, we found a welcoming, brown-haired, middle-aged, erudite woman who truly wanted to help Noah. She didn't look the least bit woo-woo, which calmed me, and helped Noah accept her as normal.

She greeted us in the waiting room and guided us to a meeting area. I had butterflies in my stomach as we all sat down at a round table.

"Noah, you are an incredibly creative person whose nervous system is on overload," she explained to him. "I can see from looking at you that the space between the left and right brain is actually much smaller than most. You are in a constant state of taking everything in on both the left and right sides of the brain, so much so that the nervous system becomes overwhelmed and a rhythmic response mechanism is created to soothe the mind and body. In a nutshell, it's why you started stuttering out of nowhere."

This was already the best visit to a doctor ever, in my opinion. Not only did she intuitively understand him from the get-go, but she also did not make him feel broken, as traditional medicine had succeeded in doing. Everything was right with him—she considered him highly gifted with the mind of a detail-oriented director. This completely resonated with my own intuition about my precious son.

And get this: she saw children for free or for a small donation to a nonprofit she'd founded. We didn't have a lot of extra cash, so we donated whatever we could afford at each visit—sometimes only twenty dollars. She went on to explain that Noah was highly sensitive. We had already figured that out in kindergarten, but it was wonderful to hear it again three years later.

During the appointment, she laid him down on the table and surveyed his energetic field by waving her hands in a circular motion a few inches above him. She picked up on vitamin deficiencies and recommended specific foods and regimens. After several appointments, we noticed a difference in his anxiety and his stuttering.

As far as I was concerned, this woman was Mother freakin' Teresa. We continued to travel north every three months. While the visits had everything to do with Noah and nothing to do with me, one day she asked to speak with me privately after her session with him.

Noah busied himself in the waiting room drawing Anime figures in his sketch pad. Meanwhile, she and I walked into her nearby office lined with bookshelves filled to the brim with texts on every kind of holistic treatment and herbal remedies. I nervously took a seat in the chair in front of her desk, wondering why she pulled me aside. She sat down at her desk and smiled warmly, making me feel more at ease.

"There are many children in spirit around you," she started. "The work you do and are meant to do is really important."

"Oh my God...how did you know?" I asked with a dumbfounded look on my face. "I haven't told anyone except for my husband."

"I can see and hear them, that's how I know."

"It's been happening for a year now," I explained. "I thought I was losing my mind at first."

"You are most certainly not losing your mind," she said.

Her instinctive understanding stunned me. She went on to explain that she's had her gift since she was a child, and it proved very useful when she worked as a police officer turned FBI agent before she started her healing practice.

Wait—what? This incredible woman who had multiple graduate degrees, worked all over the world, and saw highly sensitive children for free, had been a pistol-wearing FBI detective at one time? I was gobsmacked.

Naturally, after hearing what she said, I called Scott on the way home and told him about our conversation. Little did we know, this was just the start of many "holy shit" moments in our lives. The next one came when I stayed with my dear friend, Kelly, and learned about a little girl named Carrie.

* * *

I felt like I'd been digging for days beneath that tree. In actuality, it had only been a few hours. The weight of the clay-like dirt was heavy on my shovel, and hard on my shoulder. Still, I pressed on. It wasn't unusual for me to put my all into whatever I did—I'd been doing that my whole life. I knew I couldn't stop until I found what Carrie, in spirit, kept urging me to find—evidence that she was abducted and brought to Kelly's house decades ago. This was not going to be easy, but I was determined.

"Kelly, how much longer do we have until we're supposed to go downtown and meet your friends?" I asked.

Kelly looked at her watch. "You still have about two hours.... Any luck yet?"

"I wish I could say yes," I said, wiping sweat from my brow.

Kelly and I had been friends since we were little; we were like sisters. Visits to her home had always been filled with wine drinking, laughter, kids' birthday parties gone awry, and hilarious recaps of what we remembered from our formative years.

But in 2010—the same time I started to awaken intuitively—my stays with Kelly also included some strange, unexplainable goings-on. I started to notice that my toes would feel like they were being tugged on from beneath the blanket while I slept in her guest room. As if that wasn't creepy enough, I felt as if there were others in the room I couldn't see. You know that feeling you get when someone is staring at you, so you turn to look, and there they are? That's how I felt.

My dear friend endured the woo-woo ride with me and never once said, "You're flat-out losing your mind, Kiers." In fact, Kelly remained super supportive. When I started telling her about what was happening whenever I stayed at her house, she was open and relieved. She even confided that a few strange things were happening that she couldn't explain—toys with dead batteries had been lighting up and making noise, her razor would fly across the shower stall when she was in it, and the dogs and cats were acting out of sorts and refusing to come inside.

By this time, Nate and Noah's healer had helped me understand that I wasn't losing my mind when it pertained to what was happening at Kelly's. I knew there was truth to what I was seeing and feeling, and Kelly knew it, too.

Prior to the visit where I dug beneath the spider tree, I started to tap into what was happening at Kelly's. Sitting at the kitchen table one day after dropping the kids off at school, I was sipping my coffee, cherishing a few minutes of quiet before I had to start building toy box orders. Out of nowhere, I saw a vision of a young girl with blonde hair who looked to be around eight years old flash across my mind. Then I heard her. She said her name started with a C and that she'd been kidnapped and murdered in the 1970s. And she said there was evidence in Kelly's backyard. I noticed, again, that chills covered my body, but they were mostly showing up on my right side. I made a mental note that she hadn't crossed into the light yet.

As usual, I grabbed a piece of paper off my nearby desk and jotted down notes. It was the most disturbing message I'd received to date. Immediately, I called Scott at work to tell him about it, and when my friend Stacey called to ask about getting the kids together, I told her, too. My gut told me she was a safe person with whom to share, and my gut was right. She, too, had experienced a strange phenomenon but admitted that most of the time, she buried her head in the sand about it all.

Then it was time to call Kelly.

"I don't know any children with the initial C who passed in the 1970s, but I believe you," she said. "And I wonder if it's connected to the weird shit that's happening in my house."

"Do you know anything about who owned your house before you bought it?" I asked.

"I don't know much actually, but maybe it's time to find out."

I hadn't really done any research at that point; I was simply following the little girl's instructions. After I hung up, I started looking for reports of missing kids who fit the description. Later that night, Scott and my friend Stacey started researching as well. We jokingly called ourselves the Scooby-Doo gang; it helped to minimize the fact that this was really serious, dark stuff. We were spooked, but on a positive note, it seemed the more I trusted my own intuition, the more my husband believed in it, too. And the more Stacey felt comfortable trusting in—not ignoring—her intuition as well.

Scott thought maybe it was time that he spoke with a psychic himself. He was curious about possible job prospects after being laid off by a major TV network. I recommended that he call Vicki, a psychic medium I'd come to know and trust as I traversed my awakening. Maybe she could tell him something about his next career move.

A week later, I flew to Kelly's house, hellbent on getting to the bottom of what really happened there years prior. While I was digging beneath the tree, Scott went to his in-person reading with Vicki in LA. I knew her to be incredibly intuitive, as well as gorgeous, down-to-earth, and not the least bit carnival-side-show fortune teller. It's why I was drawn to her and why he immediately felt he could trust her.

After they discussed Scott's next career move, he asked if she could tell him anything about Kelly's house. He said I was there and that some weird stuff was going down. Before he could say anything else, she blurted out, "There's some really, really dark energy at that house."

"The house was used for horrific crimes for many years," Vicki went on to explain. "There's a little girl whose name begins with a C. Carrie? Something like that. She is desperate to get her message across, and Kiersten is the one she feels most comfortable with."

Vicki went on to give more detail, including a possible date range and the nature of the dark energy at the house—murder and sexual violence. Scott called me immediately after his session to relay Vicki's messages. Minutes before the phone even rang, chills covered me from head to toe.

Shortly after hearing what Vicki picked up intuitively, I heard the voice of a little girl urging me to dig deeper at the base of the spider tree. Messages in the form of visions filled my head. Flashes of scenes of sexual and physical abuse I knew I could never unsee played on a loop. I was in tears with the realization of what this poor child had endured, which made me all the more determined to shovel deeper and faster.

While I was knee-deep in hard-packed soil, Scott was busy digging up dirt online. He found a profile of a child who went missing in the mid-1970s. Her name was Carrie. Immediately after finding her, he sent me a text letting me know he was sending the link via email.

With adrenalin coursing through my veins, I ran inside the house to tell Kelly that Scott had found a possible match. She and I sat side-by-side at her kitchen table as I opened my laptop. Once I clicked the profile link, my heart settled in the pit of my stomach.

It was her.

Confirmation chills up and down my body quickly followed.

We sat in silence for a few minutes, staring at the missing person's page. I felt for Kelly—knowing that this would change the way she felt about her home—but the heartbreak I felt for Carrie was immeasurable. This poor child had been waiting all of these years for help. And for some reason, she chose me.

I was more determined than ever now, but after a full day of digging four feet deep into the rock-hard ground, my blistered hands and I knew that a break was needed as the sun started to set. It was time to head to a downtown bar to meet up with Kelly's friends.

Kelly relayed the story of Carrie to her friends, who were all on pins and needles as each "and then" came out of our mouths. I instinctively knew I wouldn't have enough time to complete the job before hopping on my return flight the next day, and I felt panicked because of it. I couldn't let Carrie down. Kelly promised to help get justice for this precious soul, and I knew through shared efforts, more would be revealed.

But I wasn't ready to give up on the physical uncovering just yet. I set my alarm for the crack of dawn and made it my mission to dig as much as I could before I had to be at the airport. I prepared my blistered hands for more work and quietly slid open the glass door to the backyard. I walked over to the hole and was hit with the paralyzing realization that where I'd spent hours digging just yesterday was now mostly filled in with dirt. I don't know how long I stood there, staring at the area before I snapped out of my frozen state. My scientific mind looked for the cause, thinking maybe the dogs had pushed the dirt back in, but the large mound of clumpy earth I shoveled out of the ground the day before hadn't moved.

How did this happen, and why does the dirt look like it's slanted in the hole? Because of that, and the fact that it wasn't completely filled, it seemed to be conveying a message. Being fairly new to this whole mediumship thing, I knew I needed help from a professional. I immediately called a trusted medium I knew named Megan, expecting to get her voicemail. Thankfully, she was an early bird that day, too.

Megan had a particular knack for mediumship and house clearings. I filled her in a bit about Kelly's house, the messages I was channeling, and the newly dug hole now filled with light brown dirt that was slanted.

"Carrie is trying to tell you you're in the right vicinity but need to dig closer to the fence," Megan explained.

"Wait, so the dirt…*she* did that?" I asked, dumbfounded. "How does spirit manifest dirt?"

"She did do it," Megan replied. "She wanted to let you know you're close, and she's incredibly grateful you're listening to her and trying to help."

If only I had more time.

* * *

I spent the flight home staring into the cloud-filled sky, thinking about everything that happened at Kelly's house. Lost in thought, resting my temple against the airplane window, I wondered if there was really some larger force at play and a reason I was chosen for this particular job. *Why me? Why now?*

I spent a lot of time talking to my new psychic friends—asking them about their experiences and how they handled the weight of it all. They all said they grew up knowing their senses were dialed up a notch. They went to workshops to learn how to better tune in to the world we can't see and they accepted it as something they aspired to perfect.

I wasn't one of those people. I felt like I was living a "normal" life until I wasn't. One day my life was about furniture and trips to Target, and the next, I was channeling children who had died. Through all of my head-scratching, a constant, quiet voice continued saying, "Trust it. One day at a time." That's exactly what I decided to do.

Daily life played out as usual, but in between normal activities, Scott, Stacey, and I were all doing what we could to see if we could find more information about Carrie. Kelly was part of the unofficial club now, too, only she did her part from thousands of miles away. From LA, Stacey and I both channeled important details about what happened to Carrie and kept a log of them. For some reason, when she and I were together, our candle burned brighter. We could see more.

Kelly was also doing a little digging about the history of her house. She asked neighbors who lived near her home in the 1970s if they remembered anything about the folks who lived there. They did. Along with memories of loud parties and trash bags used for window shades, they recounted men coming in and out of the house quite a bit, which led them to believe drugs were being sold there. In fact, Kelly said when they moved in and were digging a garden in the backyard, they found hypodermic needles. It looked like the neighbors' assumptions were spot-on. But darkness cloaked the house in more ways than drugs.

I doubt the thought of murder and sexual abuse ever crossed the neighbors' minds. While I can't share specific details of this cold case due to its sensitive nature—and for my own protection—I will say that Carrie told us exactly how she was kidnapped and the type of car they were in when they lured her. When Kelly questioned the neighbors, they described seeing the exact car—make and color—that Carrie told us about.

I started keeping records of everything we were discovering in a folder. I was determined to stay organized, but I was admittedly clueless about how to move forward with all of the notes. Until Kelly called.

"Kiers, you're not going to believe this, but we have a connection to Carrie," Kelly said with excitement in her voice.

"What do you mean?"

"Well, you know the family daycare that both of my kids attend? It was opened back in the 1970s. I was talking with one of the relatives, Jill, whose mother started the daycare and asked if she remembered a missing child case during that time frame. I mentioned the name Carrie. She immediately teared up and said, 'Yes, I more than remember it. Carrie was one of our kids. They never found her.'"

"Oh my God. I can't believe she remembers her."

I was floored. It was another one of the *holy shit* moments we were all coming to expect.

"Kiers, we have a connection to her mother through the daycare," Kelly went on. "Jill's entire family not only knows her, but they are still close with her. This can't be a coincidence."

With this news, I needed more stability than my own two feet. Sitting down on the garage steps, I said, "Okay, Kel, I'm shaking and have chills from head to toe. We have to do this. Oh God, how in the world are we gonna do this?"

Eventually, I felt guided to write a letter to Carrie's mom, Mary. But first, we needed to find out if she was even open to hearing from me. Kelly asked Jill if she would ask Carrie's mom if she was open to receiving a letter. A day later, Kelly got the okay.

I spent most of the night pouring everything into a four-page letter for Mary. I included photos of our family and reassurances that I was not looking for anything, nor was I a professional medium by trade—I simply wanted to get the messages to her. While I can't share the letter in its entirety due to a multitude of reasons that include privacy and protection, here's the first part:

Dear Mary,

Thank you for agreeing to read what I've come to learn over the past two months. I'm sure over the years you've heard from a lot of psychics, so I completely understand if you're skeptical. Please know that I am not a medium by profession but I've known of my gift for some time. And in regards to what I'm about to share about your wonderful daughter, I did reach out to two trusted professional mediums who validated the messages coming to me without any prior knowledge or tips.

Let me first say how sorry I am that you've had to endure such pain. I'm a 37-year-old mom of two and my heart breaks for you and your family. But let me also begin with letting you know that the constant thread in my communications with Carrie revolves around her telling me what an amazing mom you are and how much she loves you. She is worried about you because she knows you struggle every day with her loss...

At the end of the letter, I gave her my contact information and a link to my furniture company website, and I asked her to please keep my identity secret.

It took a little time to hear back, as expected. Meanwhile, I started channeling other children who'd suffered similar fates. I kept file folders of information on them as well. They were still considered missing. It was as if a line of children had begun forming behind Carrie.

About two weeks later, I heard back from Mary. She wanted to talk. My heart pounded out of my chest as I dialed her number. Our conversation lasted about thirty minutes, and in that time, she told me she believed what I shared with her to be true. The details in the letter seemed to match what happened, even if they didn't match public reports.

Mary also said she believed that her daughter was helping all the other children in spirit find a way to get their messages to me. In fact, it was reminiscent of who her daughter was during her life. I was overcome with emotion that Carrie was able to get her message to her mom, but I was sad that I hadn't been able to get to the evidence beneath the tree.

"In due time, you will find it. And more," Carrie said, out of nowhere after I hung up the phone with Mary. I heard her as clearly as if she were standing beside me. Since I was used to that sort of thing now, it didn't shock me. I simply nodded, thankful for her reassurance.

As a practical thinker, of course, I thought about Kelly finishing the digging, but I also knew her husband was skeptical of it all and frankly, didn't want a giant hole or a damaged tree in his yard. I didn't want to put her in a difficult position. Kelly and Mike had already dug up evidence that helped prove that what I was hearing was true. When they first bought the place, while working on the yard, they'd found friendship bracelets from the eighties, needles, and more.

I believed Mary, and I also knew that if I could connect with law enforcement, they might be able to dig a little deeper.

Again, the Universe made a connection I never thought possible. Turns out, one of Kelly's friends is a police detective. Kelly agreed to ask if he would be open to information about a missing person cold case. Lucky for me, he was. I sat down at my computer and penned another four-page letter with details, dates, and web links. He called me immediately after reading the email. It was the first of multiple detective connections I would make over the years.

CHAPTER 3

Sharks

Flipping back and forth between the unseen world and my "real world" wasn't as hard as I thought it would be. In fact, my furniture business became something of a respite from the heaviness of the messages I received from children in spirit. I was happy to focus on the future of my wooden world. Then my dad threw something at me to elevate my business.

"Kiddo, did you see that new show on ABC called *Shark Tank*?"

"No, but I'll check it out. Is it about SeaWorld or something like that?"

"No, it's for businesses like yours," he said with a chuckle. "You can potentially get an investment deal by pitching your company to a team of big-time investors." He went on to explain the show a bit more.

"Dad, that sounds scary as hell," I replied. "I'll check it out, but, honestly, it makes me nervous to think that I could get skewered on national TV." Which was ironic, I know, considering I spoke with dead people.

After checking out a snippet of the show on the internet, I was overwhelmed with fear. It lasted for about ten minutes before I threw up my hands in resignation; I already knew deep down that I had to give it a shot. I sent a text to my dad telling him I was about to apply for the show. Then, I filled out the online application and figured I'd let the Universe decide the next steps.

A few weeks later, I kept hitting the replay button on my voicemail message to hear the producer say I made it to the next round. It finally sunk in—this was real. I just needed to send in a video, so they knew if I was "TV material," and I had to fill out a lengthy questionnaire. Like most of the leaps of faith in my life, this one was scary, too. I had to fight through more fear just to make the video that would potentially get me to the next round of casting. I filmed the video in our messy, sawdusty garage with the help of Scott, who manned the camera.

My rational brain wondered how bad this *Shark Tank* thing could actually be. After all, my new life was filled with spirit and murders—some of the scariest stuff I've ever encountered. How bad could a tank full of wealthy business people really be? I sent off the video via email and played the waiting game.

* * *

Life continued as usual—Target trips, school, toy boxes, spirit communication, and neighborhood parties filled the hours of our lives. I still felt grateful to be able to stay home with the kids while making money at the same time. In fact, when Grace wasn't at school or with our neighbors' kids, she hunkered down with me in the garage, covered in sawdust. She has always been a very independent, social, risk-taker who loves being in the middle of the action. It makes what I'm about to share all the more bizarre.

Normally, Grace would ask if she could run down the street to play with Chloe and Emily—but things were changing. At first, I couldn't figure out why. Out of the blue, she started becoming clingy. She didn't want to leave my side and she was asking if I could walk her everywhere. We were watching our independent eight-year-old morph into a fearful child, and I couldn't see the reason.

During the same time, Carrie was around me a lot. I knew she hadn't crossed into the light yet, so I told her she could stay as long as she wanted until she felt it was her time to go. I was happy that she felt safe with me. It wasn't until I spoke with Megan, the incredibly gifted medium who helped me on the day I was digging for evidence, that I finally started to see why Grace's personality had changed.

"Kiers, I think Carrie is attaching herself to Grace," Megan explained.

"Wait...Grace is taking on Carrie's fear of not going anywhere without me?"

"Yes, she doesn't understand that it's affecting Grace the way it is. We need to tell her she can't attach to her."

I pondered that for a minute and knew in my soul she was right. Carrie was eight when she was abducted and murdered—Grace's current age. With tears in my eyes, I explained to Carrie (in my head) that I understood her fear, but it was transferring to Grace and changing who she was born to be. I reassured her that Grace would be just fine. She understood—she loved our Little G and didn't want her to be fearful, even if Grace didn't understand why she was feeling that way.

One day later, we decided to take the kids to a pizza joint complete with a mini arcade. Grace's favorite game was the Claw—the game where you insert copious amounts of money into the machine that narrowly misses giving you a cute stuffed animal.

We were used to feeding what felt like the total of Grace's college fund into the game without reward, but this time was different. We gave her ten dollars, and I kid you not, our pint-sized claw master won every time she put her dollar in the slot. We couldn't believe our eyes. Other diners and staff started noticing her windfall, clapping and proclaiming, "You need to take that girl to Vegas!" By about the eighth win in a row, I realized this was much more than luck—Carrie was helping Grace. She felt sad for inadvertently attaching fear to Grace and made up for it with the arcade game.

To say that Grace was excited would be an understatement. She was the queen of the world, or at the very least, the queen of the claw game. Little did she know, a sweet soul named Carrie was by her side—not only helping her beat the claw machine but getting her back to her fearless self.

"Mom, can I go play with Chloe and Emily?" Grace asked one afternoon.

"Sure, sweetheart. Do you want me to walk…?"

I couldn't even finish my question before I heard the front door slam.

All was right with the world again.

* * *

I'd been happily gluing up another Owyn Toy Box when the call came in. I could barely hear the phone ringing over the sound of classic country music filling the garage.

It was them. The *Shark Tank* people. I don't remember hearing everything they said because I was already starting to freak out that I had successfully set myself up for embarrassment in more than a million homes.

I quickly wrote down all of the details: where, when, and what to do next. From what I could tell, for about a month, I would be working on my "pitch" with a producer. Thank God I had a month to prepare.

One of the first things I did was go on LinkedIn and ask for help. I didn't know enough about calculating valuation and other MBA business concepts. It was virtual crickets until a woman named Katie reached out. She was not only amazingly kind, but she was also very accomplished. Back then, when Katie wasn't designing furniture for major brands, she was leading the American Society of Furniture Designers as vice president.

Unlike most LinkedIn connections, we became fast friends in no time. Katie and I are both driven, sensitive, fun-loving people, and she happened to think that what I'd built had the potential to blow up in a good way. Not only did she help me calculate projections, but she also introduced me to the Amish manufacturers I would partner with for five years. The more we talked, the more confidence I gained. I began thinking that the crazy garage business I started might just be worth something bigger than I ever imagined.

Over the next month, I immersed myself in my crash course, Katie-led MBA, while I finished up regular toy box orders and worked with *Shark Tank* producers on my two-minute pitch. Night after night, I practiced my elevator speech. I knew I had to nail it if I wanted to get a deal. Four years and about a million splinters led me to this moment—I couldn't blow it.

The producers coached me on what they felt I should say and then talked about wardrobe. It quickly became apparent that they wanted "Tool Time" Kiersten akin to the show *Home Improvement*—otherwise known as a white tank top and jeans-wearing carpenter—more than they wanted Entrepreneur Kiersten. I'd always been good at taking direction, but this production note did not sit right with me. After all, the reason I had a successful company to begin with had everything to do with my experience as a marketer.

I knew I couldn't just flat-out say no, so I compromised. I told the production head that I would wear a dress and heels as I would wear to any investor meeting, but I would sling my tool belt around my waist to show that I did indeed build the designs.

After a few weeks of prep, the day of the "pre-pitch" was upon us. The producers explained that those of us chosen to be on the show were expected to practice our pitch in front of the production and legal teams the Friday before our live Sunday filming. I was nervous like anyone would be, but I was also confident because I trusted my preparation. Plus, not only had I given presentations for a living as a computer trainer and salesperson, but I had also taught presentation skills classes. I revised my pitch multiple times, per my producers, but practiced enough to believe I had it down pat.

Like cattle, we were corralled onto a sound stage at the Sony Pictures lot. I was standing off to the side—on deck—as the panic feeling set in. I'd rehearsed my pitch a million times, but I was drawing a blank. What was I supposed to say? How did I kick it off? Sweat started pouring off me.

"Kiersten, you're up," said one of the line producers.

In front of what now seemed like hundreds of people, I pitched my first line. And then I blanked. I could not remember what I was supposed to say next. This wasn't like me. I apologized and tried again and bombed again. I could feel the tears welling up in my eyes. How could I be blowing my shot? What if they decided right then and there to nix me from the live filming list?

The executive producer of the show pulled me aside and encouraged me to keep practicing. They were sure it was just nerves. I assured them that it wasn't nerves. I'd given hundreds of presentations, sometimes in front of thousands of people. The only thing I could figure out was I had allowed the producers to tweak my pitch to the point where I didn't recognize it anymore. My intuition was screaming that I should scrap the pitch.

After a few minutes, I walked up to the executive producer and my line producer while the next participant was prepping to pitch and mustered the courage to tell them I was planning to rewrite my pitch. Unsurprisingly, this declaration was not met with enthusiasm. I was told that I just needed to practice the one I'd already written a few more times.

"Trust us, we've seen this before," they said. "You do not want to revise the pitch you've worked on for weeks with only a day and a half until filming."

"If I want to get a deal, I have to change it," I countered.

On the way home over the hill into the Valley, I called Scott to tell him I bombed the rehearsal. I told him I was going to rewrite the pitch, and he was more than supportive. My Blackberry reminded me that a whole camp of *Shark Tank* folks felt differently. I opened my email to read several messages discouraging me from rewriting the pitch. By the time I made it home, I was still determined to change my fate. I no longer felt fear, but rather a steady calm about my new direction.

I just knew I had to trust my gut on this one. On the way to watch Grace cheer with her Little League cheer team at Burbank High, I started scratching out notes on an old receipt I found in my purse. Scott drove while I crafted my new pitch. It was practically writing itself as if I were channeling it.

I wrote, "If someone had told me ten years ago I would be running my own internationally known furniture company out of my garage, I would have said they were crazy. Ten years ago, I didn't even know what a jigsaw was."

I was in the zone. I had this…maybe.

* * *

I felt pretty good driving over to the hotel to meet up with the other *Shark Tank* participants on that October morning in 2010, where we were to be shuttled to the Sony Pictures production lot. I was the only local contestant which meant I was able to sleep in my own bed the night before filming. When I arrived at the hotel lobby, I chatted with a few folks who seemed to be experiencing my emotions—a numb calm.

The sun hadn't come up yet as we were piling into rented vans for our trek to the production lot. I was tired but excited and in great need of coffee. What I did not need was someone practicing their pitch on me as we bounced along LA streets for what seemed like hours. "Accommodating Kiersten" listened and smiled, but inside I was willing the man to stop pitching at me. He was the only one speaking in a van full of *Shark Tank* hopefuls who could have used less ego and more silence that morning.

We arrived as the sun was starting to light up the studio lot. I was happy to be freed from the van and led to my own personal green room the size of a small office. We were given approximate filming times but were also told delays were likely. I was pretty damn excited to have my own space to practice my pitch and to talk with Katie and Scott on the phone. The funny thing about me is that, while I love people, I consider myself completely overwhelmed by them most of the time. I was starting to understand just how much my sensitivity to people's energy—living and dead—affected my everyday life. Having this time and space was just what I needed.

In between getting called into hair and makeup, where they created the "mom" makeup look for me, I paced my small room reciting my pitch over and over. I knew we couldn't take any notes or documents into the Tank. Not only did we have to memorize our pitch, but we also had to memorize projections, sales numbers, and everything in between.

Suddenly, there was a knock on the door. My producer came to check on me and asked how I was feeling. I said I felt good and calm. He remarked that I looked skinnier than the last time he saw me on Friday, which I chalked up to be a typical Hollywood remark. Maybe I was, or maybe the brown wrap dress with the tool belt and camo-colored heels made me look ten pounds lighter.

As luck would have it, the Universe would throw one more thing on my plate that day: a sudden onset period. Oh yes, I was going into the Tank worried that at some point, I would be showing more than I wanted to on national TV. I was too embarrassed and shy to ask one of the production staff to help me find the super-plus-oh-God-please-don't-let-me-down tampons, so I used what I had (read: everything I could find that didn't make me look like I was wearing a diaper), which wasn't enough and I knew it. Nothing like a little curveball on filming day, but I was getting pretty used to those by now. I half expected another child in spirit to walk up to me while I was in the Tank to add to the list of surprises and hurdles. I prayed our production schedule would stay on course. I only had about five hours until I was up to bat.

Shortly before I was called onto the sound stage, a production assistant came to get me for a quick on-air interview. I felt like I was floating at this point. I hadn't expected this—it threw me for a second. I managed to pull myself together and give an interview. Looking back, I am stunned by my calm, put-together demeanor. The interviewer even commented on camera that I didn't look nervous. It just felt out-of-body in many ways. If I didn't have the footage to look back on, it would all be a blur.

Right after the interview, I was told to follow a production assistant onto the set. I wasn't going right into the Tank, but I was on deck. This meant I was sequestered in a dark, curtained-off area but could hear what was happening on the other side. I heard the Sharks telling the current contestant they'd never dream of doing business with him. I recognized him as the guy on the bus earlier that day. Just then, my producer popped into my holding cell. "Are you ready?"

I must have answered the question with less than the normal amount of enthusiasm he expected, because he asked, "Um…do you need a Coke or something…you know, to get pumped up?"

"Oh, thanks, but no, I'm fine," I replied. "I feel ready and calm."

He still looked worried and tried his hand at giving his best quiet pep talk, hoping to see more life in me. I smiled with a reassuring look that hopefully conveyed I wouldn't let him down.

Little did I know, I was going into the mode I do when I'm in the zone.

We began the walk to the *Shark Tank* doors. My hammer was banging against my leg as we snaked our way through the dark soundstage. A makeup artist was there to powder me up again. Afterward, I was told to stand on a particular mark and that when the doors swung open, a camera crew would be in front of me with a dolly moving backward. I was also told that once I walked through the door and hit my mark in front of the Sharks, I would have to spend about two minutes just looking at each one of them so the cameras could capture it for editing. I couldn't even start my pitch right away! It was at that moment that I began to pray. In my mind, I asked for two things: 1) I needed my grandmother Juanita to be with me in spirit, and 2) I prayed to not become the poster woman for Tampax on national TV.

The makeup artist stepped back from me, as did the rest of the production team who were saying they were rooting for me, and the doors swung wide open. It was time.

I made my way through the fake hallway set lined with floor-to-ceiling images of shark-infested waters and finally stepped onto the mark. After two minutes of looking up and down the line of the Sharks, I took a deep breath, opened my mouth, and out flew my two-day-old pitch:

"Hello, my name is Kiersten Hathcock and my company is Mod Mom Furniture. I'm seeking ninety-thousand dollars in exchange for twenty-five percent of the company.

"If someone had told me ten years ago that I'd be running an internationally known furniture company out of my garage, I would've told them they're crazy. I didn't even know what a jigsaw was then.

"Just three and a half years ago, we were like most families I know. The toys were starting to overtake the house but we wanted a toy box that was going to fit in with our modern furniture and, frankly, there was virtually nothing on the market, or what was, we couldn't afford, so I taught myself how to design and build a toy box. I knew I wanted it to be eco-friendly, have lids that lift on and off like puzzle pieces, so it makes toy clean-up a little more fun, and fit in nicely in any room of the house. It occurred to me that we're not the only family with this same need. At the time, I

had just left my corporate job to spend more time with my kids, so I was doing whatever I could to bring in money—I nannied and did freelance marketing work. I honestly figured maybe I'd sell a couple toy boxes a month to local stores. But I underestimated the power of social media and viral marketing.

"Which brings me to where I am now. Seven days a week, I'm in my garage covered in sawdust with a backlog of orders, having to turn down retailers from seventeen different countries because I can't handle the volume on my own. My products have been featured in magazines like Elle Décor, Better Homes and Gardens, Dwell Magazine, as well as TV shows and international design books—all without me approaching any of them. I'm even receiving orders from Hollywood celebrities and famous interior designers now. The other day, I read something online that said Mod Mom Furniture was a 'globally coveted brand,' alongside a few of my competitors who are making two million per year, and I have a sneaking suspicion they're not in their garages at 11:00 p.m. finishing toy boxes.

"With your help, I'll be able to increase manufacturing by getting it out of my garage—where I physically can only build three per week—and into an Amish furniture manufacturer in my home state of Ohio who can build one hundred per week. And that's just the start. I'll be able to grow the brand internationally as well as design products and case goods for existing customers and for larger companies like Crate and Barrel's kids' division, Land of Nod, who reached out to me about exclusive designs. This blows my mind because I don't have a design degree but my work is being recognized by the design world.

"What started with a table saw and a mom has grown into a globally recognized brand which, with the right resources, has unlimited potential. The brand is respected. The demand is there. Please join me in making Mod Mom the next million-dollar furniture company."

I was in the Tank for about an hour, even though the TV segment is edited down to about thirteen minutes. By the grace of God, I pitched my heart out, remembering pretty much every word of my speech. When the Sharks started asking questions, I was prepared. I even countered their request to reveal all my pricing, including wholesale rates. I told them I was happy to share it with them but I would need to write it down on a piece of paper and pass it down the line. They were surprised that I said I wouldn't vocalize my rates but completely understood and respected why I wouldn't "out" all that on national TV.

I received an offer early on from Mr. Wonderful. It went a little differently than what was edited together on the show. I felt relief right away because I had at least one offer about ten minutes after stepping onto the stage.

The Sharks were amazingly kind, unlike what I heard happening with the contestant before me. I could feel the respect and interest in my story and my products. After I received the second offer, I was allowed to call Scott. I took the opportunity. I stepped back into the *Shark Tank* hallway—between the fake tanks—and the production team got Scott on the phone. They wanted this part on film, too. A camera was literally about three feet from my face as the phone rang on Scott's end.

"Honey! Oh my God...I got two offers!" I practically shouted into the phone.

"That is incredible, hon. I knew you would. Way to go! Who's offering?"

"Okay, so the first is Robert Herjavec and the second is, um...oh God, I can't remember his name...um...the bald guy."

Scott started laughing, as did the production team around me. My husband agreed that I should take whatever deal felt best and told me he loved me before we hung up.

The choice was an obvious one just based on the terms of the deal alone. I knew who I was going to go with before I called Scott. And it's not shocking to me that my phone call to him was not included in the final cut that aired on April 1, 2011. I'm guessing "the bald guy" wasn't how they wanted Kevin O'Leary described, but it sure made a lot of folks laugh.

I was on cloud nine after I left the Tank. My producer came up and gave me a giant hug and told me what a great job I'd done. I'd managed to get a deal and not embarrass myself in more ways than one. They interviewed me on camera where I talked about just how long and hard it was to get to this place. I built over three hundred pieces by myself over a four-year period. I was so emotional during the pitch and the interview afterward that I teared up a couple of times. The Sharks had heard during the question-and-answer portion that Scott was laid off, and that this opportunity now was everything to us.

Everyone from the carpenters on set to young production assistants hugged me and told me how much they rooted for me during filming. It felt good to know that, by trusting my own intuition, I knocked it out of the park. What happened during the live taping was a far cry from what they all saw just two days earlier, when I was listening to everyone but myself.

With a grateful heart, I drove home to Scott and the kids, who had a beautiful dinner prepared for me. I technically was not allowed to tell anyone what happened in the Tank because it would be months before the actual show aired. I was bound by legal contracts, but I knew I had to tell Katie and my family. The kids were bouncing around the house yelling, "Mom, you did it!" which brought tears to my eyes. They knew the gravity of our situation and how much we had been struggling financially, even though we tried to shield them from that.

I got into my usual jeans and t-shirt and ate dinner laughing and carrying on about what happened to our little family that day. More than anything, I was happy to know my kids saw me fight for something that seemed like a crazy idea four years prior, but ultimately ended up being one of the best ideas of my life. I was finally starting to see how trusting my own intuition and believing in what my soul knew to be real was the way to go, no matter how crazy it seemed to others. If I trusted it, it was like having a roadmap for life.

CHAPTER 4

Reality

I wasn't just using my intuition in business; I was taking it very seriously in other areas of my life, too. My friend and fellow medium, Karen Andersen, told me, "Kiersten, you have a whole line of children in spirit waiting to talk with you." It echoed what Noah's therapist had said that day in her office. And the file folders stacked on my desk full of notes from children in spirit were proof of this, too. But still, the one child who stuck by my side day and night was Carrie. She even made it clear she'd been with me much longer than I knew. I had no idea at the time, but when she said it, it resonated deeply.

The Owyn Toy Box—one of my biggest sellers—was one of those toy boxes I designed and thought to myself at the time, "How the heck did I come up with that?" I am in love with modern organic design, but this design felt epic because it came to me easily and clearly. I had a feeling when I crafted it in 2008 that it would become a huge success. And it has, for well over a decade.

What I didn't know was how and why the design came to me. I can remember exactly where I was sitting on the driveway blacktop when I sketched it out on wood pieces, but I didn't know how it got to my cluttered, forgetful brain until Carrie told me. While sitting at the kitchen table looking over invoices, I heard her voice in my head.

She explained that the tree design—a branch with two leaf lids—came to me in such sharp color in 2008 because she was communicating with me. Of course, I didn't realize it at the time because I hadn't started to understand that I even had afterlife communication abilities. Little did I know when I designed the Owyn Toy Box, she was sharing the message about the tree at Kelly's house where I would end up digging for evidence. The tree held proof of the fate of multiple children.

The realization that I had been channeling her before I realized it floored me. As a friend once said, "Creative inspiration is spiritual." I hadn't thought of any of my work that way. I just assumed—like many artists do—that the design ideas were intrinsic. Yet again, I was blown away by how little I truly knew about life on earth. The only thing I grasped was that all of it was much bigger than what we can see with the naked eye. Aside from helping me with furniture designs, the spirit world was doing everything it could to get me to wake up to one of my life purposes: to help children on the other side.

* * *

Meanwhile, in the "land of the living," I was waiting for Robert Herjavec to call. I held out hope week after week, but the phone did not ring. Finally, after the second month of not hearing from him, I called the executive producer of *Shark Tank*.

"Kiersten, I'm so sorry you haven't heard from him yet," he said. "I'll see if I can get ahold of him myself and let him know you're still waiting to hear back."

"Okay, thank you. I really appreciate your help."

I hung up the phone with the renewed hope that I was about to start the due diligence part of the deal. After all, my new friends from the show—who got deals—were already in due diligence or beyond with their investors. My investor was MIA until the phone rang while on a walk in the equestrian area of Burbank. Robert was cordial but his initial words were, "Kiersten, forgive me, but what is the name of your company and what was our deal?"

I immediately stopped walking. I had a kick-in-the-gut feeling, but refused to allow myself to think that, ultimately, Robert truly didn't want to do a deal with me. I blocked those thoughts, as I was good at doing with much of life, and pressed on. Whatever he asked for, I would give him. Projections. Sales numbers. My Mod Mom world was an open book, and he was asking to take a second look.

We arranged to talk after I sent him the information I shared on the Tank. After we hung up, I continued my walk home, passing galloping horses and friendly neighbors. At that moment, I felt excited again. I was finally on my way to a deal.

Despite crossing all my fingers and toes for two weeks, the phone didn't ring after I shared the info with him. I decided to call his secretary. We played a lot of phone tag but I eventually got a phone meeting on the books for two weeks down the road. My intuition was telling me it wasn't going to happen, but I pushed it away and thought positively, like that book *The Secret* tells you to do.

The secret that wasn't obvious to me was that Robert simply lost interest after the taping. He looked at my numbers and said, "You're still a little bit too small. Why don't you come back in six months to a year?"

You can probably guess what happened next. I blinked back tears while I struggled to come to grips with the reality of that one moment. Then I went out and bought a six-pack of Corona and sobbed while drinking beer on our kitchen floor. *How was I going to do this?* To think—due to all the layoffs—we were on the verge of personal bankruptcy with absolutely no investment in Mod Mom. I'd gone from over the moon to splayed out ready, for a Mack truck to run over me.

Many questions turned repeatedly in my mind. *How did Scott and I—two hard-working people—get here? Why didn't Robert want to invest in my company? Why didn't I choose Kevin? How could this be happening?*

I took full advantage of the quiet house with the kids at school and grieved this massive loss. I dreaded telling Scott but I called anyway.

"But didn't you get a deal in the Tank?" he asked, incredulous.

"I did, but both of us have the right to back out during due diligence," I replied with a Corona bottle in hand. "And he chose to back out, even though I gave him nothing different than I did the day of filming."

The rest of the day was a blur. I knew I had to move forward, but now everyone was going to think I got a deal when the show aired. I had four months to figure out what to do before the big primetime airing on ABC.

We were working against the clock, and I needed to do something behind the scenes. I resigned myself to the inevitable bankruptcy we would face, but not without a mountain of resentment. It was hard on our marriage because no matter how much I knew that Scott was not at fault for the multiple layoffs, I still questioned why I gave up my career for his if this is where we ended up—me covered in sawdust daily and a date with bankruptcy court.

Then I got a reprieve: my family and friends-like-family invested roughly thirty thousand dollars in Mod Mom Furniture. This second wind inspired me to keep pursuing what I knew I was meant to do. I felt like I was on better ground and ready to grow my business internationally.

April 1, 2011 finally arrived. It was the day my *Shark Tank* adventure would air on ABC. Scott sweetly rented a massive TV for our viewing party, and we invited our closest friends to watch the episode I was slotted in. I was nervous to see how they edited my pitch, but feeling like the underdog story of the bunch was comforting.

Four months prior to the airing, an entire TV crew came to the house to film what they call the "home package." They wanted to film me in the garage using my power tools, and they wanted footage of our family playing in the backyard. Clearly, they had an idea as to how they wanted to craft my story. Scott and I chuckled that they had us looking in the newspaper for jobs, which neither one of us had done since high school. The visual was what they wanted to capture, but we lived in Burbank (aka, the Valley), and everyone knows the only jobs you get in the paper require fake boobs and a tanned birthday suit. Still, we obliged and laughed on the inside.

Crowded in our tiny living room, everyone started cheering when my segment came on. It was surreal, to say the least. I sat with bated breath, wondering how they'd cut the footage together, and breathed a sigh of relief that it was indeed the underdog story I'd hoped they'd tell. At some point during my *Shark Tank* segment, my website crashed, and my phone sounded like I had hit the lottery. Notifications were going off left and right from all the emails coming in, but I knew that if I tried to field them immediately, I'd be swamped for hours. I'll never forget just how grateful I felt for the opportunity and how happy I was that I looked fear in the face and did it anyway. This is a life lesson that would repeat over and over again.

The show brought a slew of attention from consumers, retailers, and the press. The day after the premiere, responding to the emails alone became a full-time job. The airing itself didn't do a lot to boost sales, but it did elevate the brand from a marketing perspective.

Three days after *Shark Tank* aired, I flew to North Carolina to something called High Point Market. Katie told me about it and booked me as a keynote speaker for the annual American Society of Furniture Designers dinner. Katie and I—both introverts with extrovert moments—did well together. We walked the massive furniture and interior design world trade show and met folks like Ty Pennington and other bigwigs in the industry, and then we went back to our hotel to hide out and eat takeout on our beds.

In addition to owning my mediumship sensitivity, I was starting to finally understand why, throughout my whole life, I felt drained when I was in the middle of a big crowd. I recognized again how hard it was to keep my energy level high. It felt as if I needed a cape; I was absorbing everyone's vibes. The bed picnic became a welcome respite from the chaos that is High Point, North Carolina in April.

I returned from Market with a better understanding of the home furnishings world and a longing for two days of nothing but sleep. That wouldn't be possible, of course, but it was a nice thought. I had a company to build, despite everyone thinking I'd partnered with Robert Herjavec. I also had to figure out how to handle all of the spirit messages that were starting to bombard me.

CHAPTER 5

True Angels

About a month after the airing, I was on a plane to NYC to tape *The Nate Berkus Show*. The PR department at ABC booked me as a guest to talk to Nate about my time in the *Tank*, which just so happened to be another ABC-owned TV show.

On the flight to the Big Apple, I thought about how to handle the inevitable question: "How is it being partners with Robert?" I had to find a way to sugarcoat it—a difficult task because I was still hurt that what I thought was real wasn't real after all. I focused on how my family and friends came together, and how it was the best possible outcome for me when Robert didn't ink a deal off-camera.

The show went well, and Nate even introduced me to an icon in the children's furniture design business out of the kindness of his heart. Before I knew it, my quick trip to the East Coast was over and I boarded a plane to Burbank, happy to get back to my family.

Life felt unchanged in many ways. The gray had subsided a bit with all of the excitement of *Shark Tank*, but I knew it was still there. I couldn't escape it no matter what. I started to recognize it as more of a pit in my stomach that I couldn't explain.

On the business front, I was still running Mod Mom, but now I had an Amish manufacturer and didn't have to build everything on my own. We were dealing with the emotions that come with declaring personal bankruptcy, and I continued to come to grips with my new life as an undercover intuitive medium.

I still struggled with getting my arms around the *why* of it all. Unlike Nate Pannell and the other children who came to me with messages of love and hope, most of the children coming now were flashing images of sexual abuse they endured that could have been the plot of last week's crime drama. Many times in 2011, I felt that all too familiar burning in my throat before my eyes welled up. It was not easy stuff to stomach.

Thankfully, the few mediums I knew and trusted were incredibly helpful—they explained that this was my calling to help children who suffered in this way. I still didn't know why but at least I knew it was real.

The funny thing about "gifts" is that they morph and change—mine would change depending on the spirit who was communicating.

One of the "gifts" I started to recognize during this time was the gift of feeling. Not only would I feel what others feel in real-time—both the living and those in spirit—but I would also feel how they died. Sometimes the pain would come out of nowhere, and I would have to ask, "Is this my pain or someone else's?" And then I would have to let the spirit know that I got the message and to please let up. Ever since I can remember, I have been a very feeling person, but this took empathy to a whole new level.

When I think back to the beginning of my awakening in 2009, before I started channeling children, the first sense that was heightened for me was hearing. It's ironic because I've always had trouble with my ears. As a child, I had multiple sets of tubes implanted to help with chronic ear infections. I suffered hearing loss at high-frequency ranges, but this didn't affect my ability to hear spirit at all. And it certainly didn't stop me from hearing what I was meant to hear in Palm Springs, California with a friend from LA just several months before I sat with Sophia the psychic. It was my first memory of hearing spirit full-on.

During that trip, Ann and I booked a cheap room at a hotel spa outside of the mod, retro desert town known as a playground for the Hollywood elite to get a little R&R. The sprawling resort sits on sacred land. We ended up being put in a separate house that sat alone on a hill—it was considered the best accommodation on the property. Our ticket to the golden palace was sheer luck. Our standard hotel room had suffered some pretty bad water damage and smelled horrendous. We asked if we could change rooms, and they went above and beyond.

That night, after lots of laughs and a few drinks, we went to sleep in our separate rooms thanks to the swanky upgrade we received. The next morning, I woke to the sound of Native American chanting, horses running, and gunshots cutting through the air. *What the heck was my friend watching over there in her room?* The noise got louder and louder until I realized it was definitely not coming from a TV in another room. Holding my breath, I scanned the room until my eyes stopped at the drape-covered bedroom window. I knew instantly I'd found the source. After I forced myself to walk to the window, I gingerly pulled the curtains apart and cautiously peeked outside. *What the hell?*

I was staring into the empty desert, yet still hearing chanting, horses galloping, and gunfire. While I stood frozen at the window, the noise faded into the sound of cars on the highway at the bottom of the hill.

Once the chanting completely disappeared, I snapped out of my paralyzed state. I dove back into bed and pulled the covers up to my neck as if I were protecting myself from what I'd heard.

Carefully, I slid my hands outside of the covers to grab my phone from the side table and sent Scott a text telling him what had happened. He was shocked but not concerned in a "Let's get you to the nearest psychiatrist" way. In fact—when I think back—he's never said that. Ever.

Thank goodness, since this was a preview of what was to come: a life filled with things others don't freely hear or see.

* * *

Post–*Shark Tank* life in LA was peppered with exciting projects, family life, and many souls in spirit trying to get my attention. As if that weren't enough, going through the bankruptcy process made it abundantly clear that another layoff might mean complete financial devastation and homelessness. This fear hung like a dark cloud over us despite Scott landing a new job in the tech side of the entertainment industry. We felt at home in California and didn't think we'd ever move, but we couldn't ignore the high cost of living in LA.

On the flip side, we'd done that whole song and dance of moving away from the media mecca of Chicago to Cincinnati, only to experience an unexpected job loss. This was on our minds as well. As one can imagine—or maybe has experienced firsthand—moving outside of the industry is a recipe for disaster in the face of sudden layoffs.

Much to my surprise, my grandmother in spirit came through with a doozy of a message while I was driving to pick up the kids from school.

"Kierstie, you're going to be moving soon," she said.

"Really?" I asked. "I just don't know how that's possible."

"It's possible…just trust."

It was rare for me to channel personal guidance, but when it came through, I paid attention. I filed this little nugget away with no clue how it would happen and kept on living life as usual.

Shortly after receiving the moving nudge, Scott and I had a rare chance to get away together for a night of our own in Palm Springs. While unpacking before heading to the pool, my phone told me I had a new email message. Much to my surprise, an angel investor out of San Francisco was inquiring about Mod Mom and asked if my deal went through with Robert. These types of messages came in quite a bit via email, but this one felt different.

My intuition told me this one was important. I knew I had to write him back right away. I explained the situation and, much to my surprise, he replied quickly. We made plans to talk on the phone after I returned home.

That night, Scott and I sipped wine on the patio attached to our lovely mid-century modern hotel room and talked about the surprise email. The sun was setting, creating a beautiful glow in the sky, highlighting the palms in our sightline. I'll never forget looking over at Scott sitting to my right and then noticing something out of the corner of my eye just feet from us in the lush grass in front of our patio. When I focused straight on, I saw a Native American woman in full garb sitting atop a majestic horse. I blinked—and she was still there. Time stood still as we stared at one another. She didn't speak, but the moment was filled with an energy of hope and transformation. And then the moment was gone—she disappeared into the dry, desert air.

"Honey, are you okay?" Scott asked, noticing I'd been staring at nothing for a minute or two.

"Yeah, I think so. I just saw a Native American woman on a horse staring at me. Right there."

"Well, it is Palm Springs," he said. "Remember that time you were here on a girls' weekend and you heard the chanting? Maybe it's a sign?"

I knew deep down it was some kind of prophetic sign. She seemed to be staring at me, asking me to stand tall and proud. It was only a matter of time before I would know exactly what her presence meant.

* * *

A day later, I stood at my workbench sanding a small panel of plywood. I was thinking about the woman on the horse as the sound of Patsy Cline's "Crazy" filled every inch of the garage. Because I'd always been analytical and scientific in nature, the woo-woo stuff still felt half-crazy and half-calming, even though it was real. I knew in the quiet of my soul that there was a much bigger picture I had yet to grasp.

All I could do was try not to control it—just let it happen—and continue to glue up the sides of a Grace Toy Box before I reached back out to the investor who expressed interest in Mod Mom.

He asked me to put together a proposal, and I quickly created a pitch deck outlining three different investment levels. A few days later, he called to give me his offer: he wanted to invest at the highest level—$100,000. "What you've done is not an everyday occurrence. Not all moms go into the garage without carpentry experience or design know-how and build a company like you have. I believe in you. This investment won't make me or break me—I simply want to help."

Help? He was a freakin' savior! I tried to sound calm and professional when I accepted, but as soon as I hung up, I jumped up and down screaming with tears of gratitude and joy running down my cheeks. The high I felt was beyond explanation. I started calling everyone I loved to tell them the news. Mod Mom was back on track, and so were we.

The only piece of this deal that terrified me was that I knew one day I'd become more vocal about my life as an undercover medium, and I'd have to share it with him. It's much easier to be the woman who won a deal on *Shark Tank* than the one who talks to the dead. Still, I knew to push away this fear and just live in the joy of the moment. I had an investor who not only believed in me and the power to grow the brand but also believed in being a good, caring, compassionate person who would help a stranger. He is a true angel on earth.

* * *

Like the investor, many different types of angels were coming into my life. Jane was one of those people. She became one of my dearest friends who happened to need a little help herself during the summer of 2012.

Helping her open the bank account that sweltering summer day wasn't the hard part. Helping her navigate the inevitable after moving out of a house she shared with her husband would prove one of the hardest things my brave friend would go through in her thirty-eight years. I was happy to help her because 1) I didn't want to see my friend continue to be trapped in an abusive relationship, and 2) we could help each other. The only way out for her was *out*.

Now that Mod Mom received funding, I could afford to pay someone else to manage some of the operational duties that were preventing me from having time to grow the business.

Jane is an amazingly organized, smart, beautiful woman whom I trust immensely. I knew she would be the perfect person to run operations, billing, order intake, shipping, and day-to-day account management duties. The ten-thousand-dollar retainer I offered meant that she could rent a place for herself and her three kids and help me manage the administrative side of Mod Mom for one year, in addition to her full-time job.

I met her at the bank, and we deposited the check into her new bank account. Then we hatched a plan to make sure she had furniture for the new apartment we knew she would secure. Scott and I purchased a few Craigslist pieces for her and gave her what we could from our home. At that time—even with the gift of intuition—I had no idea just how full-circle this would all come down the road. All I knew was that my friend was enduring psychological and verbal abuse and I wanted peace for her and her children.

We eventually helped her move—which was a secret operation until the very last minute—and we lent an ear and a shoulder when she needed to talk about all of the retaliation tactics her husband used against her for having the nerve to leave. This was my first inside look at what it meant to be in a relationship with a narcissist. Except, even then, I didn't know what that truly meant. I wasn't living it like she was, so I didn't understand the depths of hidden pain. I knew he was probably similar to other LA men but with the "added bonus" of a hateful temper. I had no idea just how hard it is to leave someone like this—near impossible for most, especially when kids are involved. I thanked God that I wasn't in a relationship like that and that Jane was finally out on her own.

* * *

My life was starting to resemble a reality TV show. The cast of characters included old friends who were freaking out that I continued to accept and acknowledge my intuitive gifts, people in spirit who needed help or just wanted to get messages across, my more than understanding family, and my new spiritual friends who knew not to go too far with anything that smelled like woo-woo psychic ramblings or I'd freak out. It was my own personal *Twilight Zone*.

The messages that were coming in about a move for us were getting louder. I couldn't tune them out. One day, I came in from the sweltering garage to grab a glass of soda and clear as day, I heard "Arizona." My head whipped around looking for the spirit with a geographic agenda. I saw no one. I went back to sanding but couldn't get "Arizona" out of my mind.

Later that night, I sat down with something called a pendulum. It looks like a necklace with a crystal on the end of it. I'd been taught to use it to visualize what my intuition was telling me. I could hold it over my hand and ask questions, and it would spin one way for yes, and another for no. It was freaky but it worked most of the time, specifically when I didn't have a vested interest in the outcome. And it would prove helpful later in pinpointing the location of evidence for law enforcement.

My gut told me to get out my iPad so I could hold the pendulum over a map of the Southwest. I became determined to figure this Arizona thing out if it killed me. We'd visited a few times, but to say we'd be moving there sounded crazy. After all, Scott had a good job in the industry, and we weren't moving to a town where we couldn't get work.

I sat down at the kitchen table and placed my iPad on the tabletop. Carefully, I held the pendulum over the map of Arizona. It started spinning above Arizona in a *Yes* position, indicating we were indeed being guided to relocate to the desert state. I sat back in wonder. The only part of Arizona I knew was Phoenix—we'd been there a few times with friends. It was definitely not where either of us felt we wanted to live, and—much to my delight—as I hovered the pendulum over that particular city, it spun in the *No* direction. I followed suit in the southern part of Arizona. Again, it spun *No*. Then I moved the pendulum to a town called Flagstaff in Northern Arizona. I'd never heard of it. Being from Ohio, I didn't know much of the West except for LA and San Francisco.

"Hmmmm, that's interesting," I mumbled as I watched the divining tool spin in a massive *Yes* circle over Flagstaff. I had to know more, so I started Googling.

Turns out Flagstaff—a prominent stop at seven thousand feet elevation on Route 66—is pretty famous. Its cowboys-and-Native Americans heritage is legendary, and the location makes it one of the best American cities to live in year-round. I had no idea there were mountains in Arizona, let alone cities with four seasons and average yearly snowfalls over eight feet. What was this little gem of a town, and why was I being told we'd move there?

I told Scott about it, and we both sighed. We were getting tired of the LA lifestyle (massive traffic and even larger egos) but how could we even think about moving? Scott's job was located in Burbank, and there was no changing that. Or so we thought...

A week after the pendulum incident, Scott walked through the door with the news: His office in Burbank was being shut down. My stomach flipped, and I immediately thought the worst. Thankfully, I was wrong.

"Kiers, it's not a bad thing, I promise," he assured me in his calm voice. "The office is shutting down, but the parent company overseas wants to keep me on. I'm the only one."

"Wait, what does this mean?" I asked, halfway knowing that it meant something bigger than just working from home.

He grinned. "It means we can move. And if it's somewhere in the West, I'll be able to travel to clients."

The realization that we were being guided to Flagstaff smacked me right in the face. After everything we'd been through, how could I not trust this? At the same time, we were trying to figure out how to help Scott's parents make the move West from North Carolina to be closer to us, but we knew neither of us could afford for them to live in the LA area. We could barely afford it ourselves.

Scott told his parents to check out Flagstaff. They loved the idea of moving to Flag, as the locals call it, to be closer to us. They just didn't know how much closer to us they'd really be. We didn't let that cat out of the bag right away because we had to figure out feasibility first.

We kept pinching ourselves when we realized that this was indeed real. Scott's parents came out to visit us in LA, and we all took a road trip to the historic mountain town to check it out and look for housing. When the Universe conspires with you, it makes it easy to find what you want and need. We headed back down the mountain to LA with a lease in hand—it wasn't ours, but it was the first step. Larry and Judy had found a little mountain cabin to rent and would be relocating from the South in a month or so.

We helped them move into their home in July 2012, and it was during that same weekend that we decided to look for a place of our own. We found one easily that was half the rent we were paying in Burbank. The only thing we had left to do was tell the kids. We knew Noah would be relieved to get out of the smog-filled, overcrowded metropolis that is LA.

Conversely, we knew Grace would not be happy to leave her friends and the Hollywood lifestyle. They both reacted as expected: Noah was happy and Grace screamed bloody murder with tears running down her face. We cried with her but reassured her it would be a good move and that she would quickly make friends. It was heartbreaking, but Scott and I knew we were doing what was ultimately best for both of them.

The move itself is a bit of a blur. I remember heading back with Scott, renting a U-Haul truck, and loading everything we owned into it for the trek across California to the land of the lumberjacks. Somehow, we managed to neatly nestle ourselves into a beautiful four-bedroom home within the city limits of Flagstaff. The neighborhood was pristine—almost like a movie set compared to where we lived in LA. I remember that the quiet of the mountain town took a little getting used to those first few weeks. After all, we were accustomed to hearing sirens and city noise after living in the heart of Burbank.

It was wonderful to be close to Scott's parents, and we were eternally grateful for the calm the move brought to Noah. Grace was still reeling from the uproot, and who could blame her? She loved that city and her gaggle of friends. Thankfully, school was about to start. We kept our fingers crossed that the change wouldn't be too overwhelming for either of them.

They both adjusted pretty quickly to their new lives as ex-Hollywood kids, and that tidbit definitely helped their street cred. Grace shared with her new besties that she went to school with some of the kids you see on Disney Channel. She was quickly deemed a cool kid with connections, and when you're in third grade, that's exactly what you want to be.

Scott continued to work for the overseas company. I pushed forward with plans to grow Mod Mom. One of the perks of leaving Burbank was that the world felt less crowded for me...the seen *and* unseen world.

Towards the end of our stint in LA, I had been feeling increasingly bombarded by spirit. The children who were meant to talk to me always made their way to the front, but there were others vying for my attention as well. Many recognized that I had figured out how to help some of them cross into the light. In Flagstaff, it was much quieter. It was less congested on all fronts, and I felt the tension melt away. I didn't feel the pressure to cross scores of spirits into the light. However, I did notice an upswing in the messages I was receiving from children. It was becoming clear that maybe Sophia the psychic knew what she was talking about three years prior.

CHAPTER 6

This Little Light of Mine

Our new mountain home gave me space to think and feel more than I did in LA. We didn't have much to worry about because things were going well with Scott's job and Mod Mom. It left me with time to contemplate the afterlife as I knew it, and figure out a plan to move forward and help more than just my small circle.

As a "fixer/doer" personality, I knew I needed to finally own that channeling was part of my life. I wanted to put myself out there as a volunteer medium who passes messages from children in spirit to their parents, as I'd done with Nate Pannell and his family.

Before the end of 2012, I created a website called the Little Light Project, named after the little lights in spirit. I took a deep breath and penned a blog post on modmomfurniture.com outing myself as a medium. My hands trembled as I clicked *publish*:

I've gone over how I would say this a million times in my head. And as I sit here at the computer drinking coffee out of a mug that says, "I'm a carpenter," I am reminded that I really am so many different things all wrapped up in this 39-yr-old body of mine. We all are, aren't we?!? So many times, we get labeled and pigeon-holed into narrow categories because it's easier for all of us to process who that person is within a rigid framework. I'm guilty of doing it, too. And boy is it easy to do that during election season.

But it's not that simple, is it?

I have been keeping a secret about a "side" of me out of fear. Fear that I would be judged. Fear that it would hurt my business. Fear that I would let people down. I've come to the realization over the past year that we are not meant to live in fear. It holds us back. We're given gifts and talents not for us to hide away, but to really own, respect, and share. Basically, stand in our truth.

So, here's mine. In addition to being a daughter, a wife, mom, carpenter, designer, CEO, amateur hair cutter, and a whole slew of other things, I am a medium. I was born with the gift of being able to communicate with loved ones who have passed on.

This gift of mine is something I've always had but turned off at a very early age. Probably due to fear. It started to awaken in me about three years ago but really came on full force over the past year and a half. Out of nowhere, I started to hear and see things other people were not. And for the most part, the messages I was receiving were from children who have passed. There is so very much to this complicated story of mine, but in a nutshell, I have been helping families reconnect with children who have crossed in an effort to help everyone begin to heal. This isn't something I do for income (I do not charge for my help) and I do not seek out the children; they come to me. Some I know through friends or family and some are complete strangers.

In an effort to stand in my truth and move forward with what I know will ultimately be one of the most important things I do in my lifetime, I started a website called The Little Light Project (LLP). You can read more about how it works and how a handful of families feel about the work I'm doing and more importantly, how it is helping them cope with their loss.

I know this is a very controversial subject and I completely respect if you do not believe in such things. All I know is that for me, this is very real and is my truth. It might not be yours, but it is mine and I want to do the best I can in my lifetime to live authentically.

So, there you have it. No more hiding for me. I wouldn't be able to stand in my truth without the support of my amazing family, colleagues and friends who love me for me. It's hard to put into words how thankful I am for their support. And I especially want to thank my husband, Scott. It takes a strong man with a lot of faith in God and his wife to endure what he has had to go through over the past few years. His love and support have given me the strength and confidence to do what I'm doing now. Scott, I love you and thank you immensely for not putting me in an institution. And mostly for believing in me, even when I didn't believe in myself.

As always, thank you immensely for your support of Mod Mom Furniture! I am working on incorporating more giving through MMF by donating a percentage of sales to organizations that help abused and ill children. Check out a sneak peek of a beautiful wooden Nativity set we will be replicating, retailing and donating a portion of sales to charity on the Mod Mom Facebook page. It's a design by Scott's late grandfather, Sam Brown, who was a Baptist minister and carpenter.

I sincerely hope every one of you reading this has the opportunity to live your authentic life, and ditch the fear. Coincidentally, my dear friend told me that today is National Coming Out Day. I couldn't have picked a better day. :)[*]

I breathed a sigh of relief reading the comments. They weren't damning and no one called me crazy, which I considered a victory. All I had to do was wait to see if parents of children who had passed on would find my website.

---

[*] http://modmomfurniture.blogspot.com/2012/10/this-little-light-of-mine.html

Much to my delight, they did. I didn't advertise, yet families all over the world found me. If their child came through, I let them know via email. I also made it clear that I couldn't force anything; I wasn't like a traditionally paid psychic medium who booked appointments. If I read the email from the parent and the child in spirit showed up in front of me, I'd get to work. Otherwise, I'd keep them on a list in case they came in at a later time.

I figured if this was part of my life purpose, then I needed to make it known that I was here. If it was meant to be, it would be. I didn't charge money—I simply volunteered my time and set aside a few hours a week to read messages and channel. Eventually, I brought on other mediums who volunteered their time as well.

While running the Little Light Project, I met a wonderful mother named Camilla. We became friends after meeting in a Facebook group for grieving parents where I volunteered my time as a medium. After tragically losing her newborn daughter, she turned to the grieving parents' group for support and love. I am beyond grateful to know her and her beautiful family and daughter in spirit. In addition to passing spirit messages, I was able to help Camilla understand the incredible intuitive gifts she possesses. In turn, she helped me gain confidence in my own abilities and would go on to help me in more ways than I could have imagined at the time.

* * *

We were all adjusting to the move pretty well, but I still felt a bit anxious about where my life was heading and why we were guided to this particular place. Karen Anderson, my psychic medium friend from LA who also volunteered her time with grieving parents and the Little Light Project, talked to me on the phone about six months after we moved to Arizona. I don't remember much of the talk, but I do remember her saying, "Kiers, you moved to Flagstaff to heal." This was the second time in my life I was told I had healing to do; first, by Sophia, and then, by Karen.

I tried desperately to make heads or tails of it. On a spiritual level, it made sense because Flagstaff is extremely close to Sedona—a spiritual mecca for many. I didn't understand why this was the case, but I knew psychic shops lined the streets of Sedona, and people came from all over the world to experience something called a vortex.

Flagstaff is a liberal mountain town with a rich Native American culture and history, making it a very healing place for many. I was good at connecting the dots in my life, and this was as close as I could get to checking the box on why I moved here. Time would tell just what Karen and Sophia meant.

During the same period, I was mentally blocking the fact that I was becoming increasingly frustrated with Scott. For many years, I felt like I was being suffocated by his love, but I went along with it. For an independent introvert who needed quiet time, always being around people took its toll on me. It's one of the reasons I did well working by myself in my garage.

He wanted to do everything with me and even said at one point that I was all he ever needed in life. While that's a beautiful idea, when it plays out in real life, it feels claustrophobic. I felt a lot of guilt about my feelings, knowing that many women would kill for that kind of attention.

I didn't truly know how to say no. Almost every time Scott asked to go with me on a solo walk or trip, I would reply, "Sure, honey." I didn't know how to stop pleasing everyone, including Scott, even if it was a detriment to my own sanity.

As we made new friends and hosted neighborhood parties, I felt like I was having fake fun. Talking about homeowner's association fines and the weather just didn't cut it anymore. I was forever changed by the children in spirit, knowing there was much more to life than surface shit.

Scott was bonding with our new friends who were similarly musical, but I was noticing he seemed to crave attention more and more—at least when he took to the karaoke stage. I snapped one night at a singing party. He was asking folks to come back upstairs to listen to more music while I was chatting downstairs with some of the ladies. Upon hearing him calling to everyone, I uncharacteristically yelled loudly, "No, Scott!" The room froze. I couldn't contain my irritation, which was such a total departure from my accommodating nature that it shocked everyone, including Scott.

I was, again, in the familiar position of being hostess and supporter similar to the role I played in LA. This time around, it felt exhausting. I liked preparing for the parties more than mingling with everyone.

In my non-hostess life, I was running the Little Light Project, recording details of kidnappings and murders, helping grieving parents receive messages from their kids in spirit, and running Mod Mom. No one in our new circle could relate to what I did, so I relied on my friendships with other spiritually open people who were spread all over the US.

Because Scott believed wholeheartedly in my intuitive gifts, he started asking me to tap into the energy of everything in his life. Instead of going within, he asked for a lot of advice. And who could blame him? He realized that I was privy to information that many people weren't (or didn't know they were), but it left me feeling like I had three kids. Carrying the weight of him, in addition to the heaviness of what I was channeling, became overwhelming. I was unknowingly running out of steam on all fronts.

No wonder Scott sought attention elsewhere through new friends; I wasn't feeling fully connected to him as I had in the past, and I was just plain worn out from all of my jobs. I even started having panic attacks during sex with Scott. I wasn't sure what that was, but I knew all too well how to push it down and not deal with it. My solace became my meditative walks through the pine forest trails. I needed those walks alone.

* * *

One of the perks of outing myself as someone who connects to the afterlife was how many good-hearted, spiritual people came out of the woodwork and into the center of my life. Of course, one of the downfalls of outing myself as a medium was the exact opposite of that: folks with their own agendas came out in full force, too. Discernment is a tough lesson to learn when you innately want to give everyone the benefit of the doubt. It's something that's taken decades to learn.

Yvette and Jason required zero discernment on my part. I knew instantly, when Yvette reached out to me, that she was as genuine as they come. Some call that a soul connection. Whatever it was, it was real, true, and powerful.

"Kiersten, my name is Yvette Fournier and I found your Little Light Project website, and would love to talk," she wrote.

Yvette, a beautiful, silver-haired grieving mother, shared how she was holding healing sessions for grieving parents in Old Saybrook, Connecticut. What she didn't say in that first exchange was that her son, Jason, who had passed away in 1998 from a heroin overdose at the age of twenty-three, had been urging her, in spirit, to contact me.

When she shared this, I instantly felt Jason in the room. At that point, I'd been channeling the spirit and working with grieving parents and law enforcement for roughly two years, and I'd never encountered a mother who could channel her child the way Yvette could with Jason. Typically, grief is a block. Therefore, it's much harder for parents to channel their own kids.

I would learn, in the coming years, that Yvette and I had a lot in common. However, right off the bat, I knew she was the real deal. She, too, wasn't looking to channel spirit when it happened. She was simply going through the most horrendous time in her life when Jason started sharing messages of support and guidance. I was blown away by her ability to connect with him. I remember passing a few messages to Yvette in the early days, but what I found was that primarily, she was passing messages from Jason to me. Little did I know, I'd met two of my guardian angels—one in body and one in spirit.

During the same time period that we were getting to know one another, I was in the process of making the Little Light Project a full-fledged 501c3 nonprofit, in addition to running Mod Mom full time. Yvette and I talked about everything under the sun and Jason always threw in his two cents. He cracks me up because he does not hold back.

From the first time I connected with them, I knew their place in my life would be forever, even though I'd never laid eyes on either of them. I later came to learn that both Jason and Yvette endured childhood sexual abuse. In fact, the abuse Jason endured contributed greatly to his descent into the world of heroin. I didn't realize how instrumental they would be in saving my life, as well as my soul. I just knew that the three of us would go on to work together, helping others in some way.

* * *

Shortly after I wrote the hefty check for the incorporation of the Little Light Project, we found ourselves in a familiar position of job loss, yet again. Much to our surprise, Scott's contract had not been renewed, making it the third layoff in eight years. I knew deep down that it wasn't Scott's fault, and we both agreed that despite it all, moving from LA was still the best decision, but I couldn't help but feel the familiar sting of resentment. Like the times before, I processed most of that internally and tried to put on a happy face as we plotted the next steps. We had done what we said we wouldn't do again—move to a town that didn't even have a TV station, let alone a TV industry.

Scott went to work looking for options in town, only to find jobs paying about a quarter of what he was previously making. He dove into a job at the local radio station, continuing to interview for other positions with better pay. On the Mod Mom front, I focused on listening to my intuition and asking about possible licensing opportunities for the Mod Mom line of designs. An industry friend and fellow designer suggested I talk to Stanley Furniture. He even offered to make the connection happen. The furniture dinosaur who once made $333 million in revenue in one year was interested in talking with me. It couldn't have come at a better time.

I put myself on a plane to Charlotte, North Carolina, armed with determination and a kickass PowerPoint presentation meant for a room full of Stanley leadership execs—all men, I must add. I must have done something right because the president of the company wanted to talk more about how we could partner. We began eight months of talks, ultimately leading to a salaried spokesperson offer for their youth division called Young America. In addition, we crafted a licensing deal for existing and new designs under the Mod Mom brand. Stanley projected roughly five million in sales for Mod Mom designs for the first year alone.

I'd finally made it happen! Just two years after *Shark Tank*, I'd landed a dream deal with a respected giant in the industry. Scott and I were practically jumping up and down because my salaried position alone ensured we had more than enough to live comfortably in Flagstaff.

In February of 2014, I started working remotely as a spokesperson for Young America while we ironed out the last details of the licensing agreement. Everything felt kismet and guided. I finally felt like our financial rollercoaster was coming to a stop after years of ups and downs.

* * *

On the personal front, coming out as a medium and legitimizing the Little Light Project didn't necessarily bring more inquiries than what I was already receiving—but it did mean that more and more children in spirit were coming in to share their stories and messages. Even if their families hadn't made their way to me yet, they were communicating with me. It dawned on me that, when I fully committed to this part of my life, the floodgates opened.

In addition to the pattern I was seeing involving children who had been sexually abused and murdered, I noticed that some of the kids coming to me had been miscarried or aborted. And some had committed suicide, like the boy I helped cross into the light.

For the most part, I channeled children who had endured heaviness in life and death. My work with law enforcement was picking up as well. I was now in contact with multiple detectives around the country as the visions intensified and expanded.

While milling around the house in late 2013, a new vision came in.

Belt buckle.

Forest that looks like it's in the Midwest.

Fear.

First-person perspective.

The flash of visions startled me because I understood that what I was seeing involved a child who was being sexually abused or had been abused at some point. It was an all-too-familiar scene—one I'd come to expect when a new message would come in.

What I didn't expect to see was my five-year-old face looking back at me.

Wait! What was happening? Why am I in this vision? And who's with me?

I walked over to the bed and sat, stunned and waiting to feel fully present again. I knew that the heaviness in my stomach wasn't going away anytime soon. What I'd just seen was life-changing, despite not having enough info to put all the puzzle pieces together just yet.

I reached out to my intuitive friends to share what happened that day, and they helped validate that I was indeed the one in the visions. More scenes of abuse flooded my mind over the course of the next month. I'd be walking down the street with my daughter when, out of nowhere, I saw myself as a five-year-old in a bathroom I didn't recognize. Apparently, my subconscious was showing me tiny bits, knowing I was finally ready to connect the dots.

Had I not been channeling children in spirit, and working with cops for two years, I doubt I would have trusted that the visions were real. The validation I received was the foundation I needed to understand that I, too, was a childhood sexual abuse survivor. I just had no recollection of it until age forty, when my subconscious was ready to let me see the truth.

My abuser had always been known as a playboy of sorts, and it spread widely that he had his way with scores of women during his decade-long marriage to his wife. *But child abuse?* I still had a hard time wrapping my head around it. After all, I had very few memories of my childhood in general.

One day, while cleaning up the kitchen, I heard a voice followed by the smell of cigarette smoke.

"Kierstie, age doesn't matter to him," said the voice of my deceased grandmother, Juanita, who had smoked when she was alive. "It stems from a cycle of abuse that goes generations back."

I stopped loading the dishwasher and put my hands on the counter, bracing myself because my legs were about to buckle. I couldn't catch my breath. My grandmother had just confirmed that I was indeed abused and raped by him. She went on to say that I wasn't the only child, and then showed me the number five.

Five? Had there been five victims total? How was this possible?

I think I was in shock for a week. No matter how much proof piled up, I continued to shake my head in disbelief, wondering how I could have forgotten it.

My detective mind went into overdrive, which helped to quell the emotional avalanche that was to come. I knew that what was ahead was not going to be easy but, as usual, I thought more about how it would affect others—like my parents, and my abuser's ex-wife.

I didn't even make the connection between my labored breathing and increased need to use an inhaler, and the childhood abuse I had just discovered. I figured I couldn't breathe because we moved from sea level to 7,000 feet elevation. And to be fair, I'm sure it had a little something to do with the elevation, but it wasn't until I sought help from a local hypnotherapist that I connected more dots.

The palms of my hands started sweating as I drove across town to Dr. Proiette's office. My anxiety calmed when I stepped through her front door to find a warm, light-filled home adorned with many plants. She led me into her peaceful but professional office. I took a seat in what appeared to be a massage-type chair that reclined.

My appointment with Dr. Proiette started with some casual conversation about life in general. I was comforted by her because she, too, is highly intuitive. I felt sure that she would be able to help me uncover more memories, but I didn't realize she would help me breathe a little easier after just an hour in her office.

The skeptic in me was blown away during my hypnotherapy session, where we brought subconscious memories to the conscious mind. I'd been using an asthma inhaler for what I thought were allergies and altitude-related issues that sent me to the floor, gasping for air after a very easy bike ride. None of what was happening made much sense because, when we lived in LA, I ran four days a week.

While I saw improvement with the inhaler, my lung capacity didn't improve as I had hoped. During our session, Dr. Proiette asked if I had lung issues. I was shocked because I hadn't said a word to her about it. After confirming that I did, she said, "After this session

with me, I believe you will see a big difference in your lung capacity."
I was hopeful but still doubtful.

It was time to go back in time. Dr. Proiette pushed the lever that reclined my chair and explained what we were going to do. Suddenly, my anxiety was back in full force but I took a deep breath and told myself to calm down. She was here to help me—there was nothing to fear.

I closed my eyes and listened to her calming voice ask me to, in my mind, visualize stepping down a large white staircase, one step at a time. I did what she instructed and felt every part of my body relax. Once I got to the bottom stair, I was ready to learn more about what I endured.

While in a very meditative, relaxed state of hypnotherapy, where my subconscious could be accessed, I brought forward more detail about the memories I'd experienced on a conscious level. This allowed me to bring them into the conscious mind, as I was fully awake during the session.

After facing the memories while still under hypnosis, Dr. Proiette led me through an exercise to help release the energy of what happened many years ago. She guided me to envision myself small but growing taller. I envisioned my abuser as tall but growing smaller until he was so tiny that I could throw him, and then step on him. At one point, I literally felt myself getting lighter as the energy released, and I fully embraced that none of what I endured was my fault.

Almost immediately after, breathing felt easier. Dr. Proiette explained that Chinese medicine posits that sadness and grief are stored in your lungs, and it seemed true for me. It stood to reason that the closer I got to the truth of what my body and subconscious memory knew, the more I felt it physically. As a Reiki-certified practitioner, I believed in the power of energy healing and understood how the body is deeply affected by emotion. But up until now, I hadn't realized I'd been carrying all of it since I was three years old—the age when the abuse started.

I left Dr. Proiette's office feeling such a sense of accomplishment and hope. I even stopped using my inhaler on my daily walks. It was clear I was starting to heal from a lifetime of hidden abuse. I finally had my answer to what Sophia and Karen were talking about. And I finally knew why those kids in spirit were coming to me.

CHAPTER 7

Midlife Unraveling

The time had come to tell my parents what I'd discovered. I knew it would be a shock to them, but I also knew I couldn't keep it from them. They'd always been loving parents who protected their daughters as much as humanly possible. I knew I couldn't speak the words without having them written down on paper. I ended up putting it in letter form, and read it to them when they were visiting in December of 2013:

Mom and Dad,

I need to share some stuff with you that has come up over the past few months. I've finally figured out why I have such an intense connection to these child abuse cases.

Please know what I'm about to tell you, which has nothing to do with either of you, is still in NO way your fault, it's not my fault, it just is, and frankly I'm so happy to finally have some answers. I'm truly in a good place. In fact, I'm more than fine. And I'm not looking for answers or information, but more so needing to share this with you for my own healing and clearing of the energy. I know I'm here in this life to stop the cycle of abuse, and being silent about it will not do that. If I don't clear it now, energetically, it could still affect my kids as that energy is very real and very dark and is like a magnet.

I've been seeing Dr. Proiette, one of our LLP board members who does hypnotherapy, as well as seeking advice from mediums I know and a few I don't, after flashes of memories started to come back. Dr. Proiette calls them repressed memories. They involve my uncle. I asked you about him months ago, and if we'd camping, because my subconscious was slowly revealing what happened to me when I was a child.

I've come to learn that my uncle sexually abused me sporadically between ages 3-6, which is one of the reasons I don't have memories from that period of time. To protect my psyche, my subconscious completely repressed it all, but signs of it have shown up in various ways throughout my life. It wasn't until recently that my subconscious started to release the memories. Through therapy and readings/visions, I've been able to piece it together but I don't want to go into too much detail because it's not something I want in your head. And I've only been privy to a bit of detail for the same reason. I can tell you from what we've been able to discern, he made things into a game at first. Hide and seek, etc. I was very trusting, as 3-year-olds are, but then it turned and terrified me so much that I completely disassociated from it to protect myself. This is very common with child sexual abuse survivors, and the repression typically lasts until between the ages 40-50.

As I now have the luxury of trusting what I'm getting intuitively and trust my colleagues who also receive intuitive messages so for me, this was very easy to piece together. And then throw on top of that that 99% of the kids in spirit coming to me were sexually abused makes all of that make more sense. I just figured they were coming to me because I'm a mom.

When I started looking for the tangible signs in my life, I thought back to potty training. Mom, you've always said I was such a sweet, compliant kid but when it came to potty training, you wanted to throw me out the window. It was during this period (right around age 3) that the abuse started, and I wanted no attention directed at them due to what he did. It had nothing to do with your potty-training techniques or anything like that. It had everything to do with him.

I've been given several flashes over the last six months and through hypnosis, realized that he, at times, would use Benadryl (antihistamine) on me in larger doses to drug me. I've seen flashes of a bedroom with full size bed, outdoor camping site, and a bathroom. Grandma has come in several times to myself and several mediums saying, "He liked girls . . . didn't matter the age." I reached out to Karen, a medium out of San Francisco whom I did not know, for clarification and validation. I was referred to her, not knowing at the time that she also suffered abuse as a child by a family member. She said that my uncle has done a very good job of hiding this very dark side of him—the pedophilia side—and that I am not the only child he abused. There are roughly 5 other children, but my sister is not one of them. It finally stopped for me before age 6 because I was getting stronger and more defiant, and there was also something going on with his marriage at the time.

When I look back over my life, after unearthing this knowledge, so much makes sense, and I'm truly so glad to have this information now. I've had intimacy issues and major issues with feeling claustrophobic, even in loving embraces, my whole life. It started getting more pronounced the closer I got to recovering these memories. I couldn't even let Scott hold me for a long time because at some point panic would set in and I'd want to bolt. I'd say, "Okay, okay," and then I'd push him away. Even cuddling with one of my kids with their weight on me felt panicky, and I never understood it. There are particular sexual acts that I have had violent reactions to and didn't know why. And truthfully, I've never been comfortable with my reproductive parts and have been unusually modest my whole life, which are tell-tale signs of abuse.

This also brings me to the vaginal surgery I had when I was in college. Through Dr. Proiette, my own guidance, and help from mediums, it has been determined that my hymen was damaged as a young child and healed but with scar tissue. Research of child abuse victims shows this is not uncommon but, at the time and without knowledge of abuse, the doctors wouldn't have put two and two together. Even small things like truly dreading gynecological appointments and requesting the doctor use the smallest speculum because of the pain all make sense now.

Please know I am not telling you this to hurt you but rather to heal and move forward. It is absolutely not your fault, so please do not take that on. You do not need to do anything with this information. I will, in time, talk to my aunt about it and may confront him, but I'll know better as I move through this.

I am truly better than ever now that I understand how it all fits together. It's a relief in many ways. Three years ago, a medium said to me, "These kids are here to help you as much as you are helping them," but that it wasn't the right time for me to understand how/why. Now, I get it.

I hit the jackpot with parents – you are truly the best on the planet – so please know that is truly what I feel in my heart and soul and nothing he did could change the great feelings I have about my loving childhood. It was your love and support that helped me become who I am today despite suffering abuse at the hands of him.

I love you both very much and am proud to be your daughter. I hope so much you understand why I needed to tell you. It's not just for me, but for my kids and all the kids who have experienced *what I did. Without the gift of mediumship, therapy, and other intuitive mediums helping me, I would not have been able to stop the cycle and release the energy, which was wreaking havoc on my body. And now I'm free to move forward with greater understanding and purpose. I want that for others who struggle to move forward and I know we can help provide those services at The Little Light Project.*

I love you both very much,

Kiersten

As I read the letter aloud to my parents, with Scott holding my hand, tears streamed down their faces. I, however, was almost emotionless. I'd come to operate this way since understanding the full picture. Maybe it was just my way of protecting myself, but I truly thought that since I'd figured it out, I could just go on living life normally once I shared it with my family. If I checked the boxes, I could move on.

My parents were stunned, as anyone would be, and they knew me well enough to know that I was not inventing things that weren't there. After all, they also witnessed firsthand the truth of messages I had passed from spirit. On the other hand, it's terribly difficult to accept that someone they trusted did horrible things to their daughter when they weren't looking. And they didn't know to look. I sensed doubt in them that I first read as shock, but I would come to learn that what I was seeing was the tangled spiderweb of emotions and coping mechanisms something like this brings out. As parents, they were devastated that they couldn't protect their little girl, and as my father said, he wanted to wring my uncle's neck—or worse.

The next step was to let my aunt know what had happened, and how I put it all together. Most importantly, I had to share with her why I trusted these visions and why others do, too. Despite my attempt to cushion the blow as much as possible, my aunt did not take it well and believed I was mistaken. She said the memories and visions weren't real. He could fool around on her for their entire marriage with roughly one hundred women, so the story goes, but it was not possible for her to think he targeted young girls. Denial is a very powerful state of mind, especially when deep down one thinks it actually might be true.

She wasn't the only one questioning what I'd come to learn about my past. My mom also started to wonder about the validity of my claims after I told her what I knew. Much of this waffling had to do with the fact that I was being open about what I knew I endured, and people were asking questions.

One family member stopped talking to me altogether and vowed to never have anything to do with me again. I remember being told, in a letter from my mom, that it was very hard on everyone. She said she understood their hurt feelings because it was "never something that could be proved and no one had an inkling it happened." She did mention that she was still having a hard time believing it, but that my dad said he wouldn't put anything past my uncle. It was a tough letter to read.

I was asked to keep my truth off of Facebook to protect my uncle's family. If there's one thing I've learned since my revelation years ago, it's that survivors are almost always asked to protect their abusers and their families.

They expected me to keep quiet, even after proclaiming that I was going to be vocal about what I endured. I did not keep quiet because it is not my job to keep his secrets.

I remember feeling as though I wanted to move on to help others as quickly as possible. I made that my focus. We even incorporated a few free programs for childhood sexual abuse survivors at the Little Light Project, now a full-fledged 501c3. Life was moving forward as planned, in spite of all I'd uncovered. I began checking boxes left and right—but as it turned out, not the right ones.

* * *

Four months after I uncovered the childhood sexual abuse I endured, I was on cloud nine getting ready for the High Point Market furniture trade show in April of 2014. Equal parts nervous and excited, I hoped my public declaration about the "woo-woo" side of me wasn't going to hurt my partnership with Stanley Furniture. No one said a word, nor did they recognize that I did anything other than try to help highly sensitive kids and their families.

"Are you going to tell Stanley about what you're doing?" Scott asked.

"I've told them I founded a nonprofit that helps sensitive kids by pulling together professionals from Western and Eastern medicine."

"You do," he replied. "But you also talk to dead kids who've been killed by predators, so it's going to be interesting to see how it goes down in North Carolina."

"Yep, it will be interesting for sure," I replied. "You might want to pop some popcorn for this."

Three days before heading to High Point Market to film videos for Stanley, meet with HGTV, and meet my cardboard cut-out that Stanley printed for the showroom, I received an email from my boss, the VP of Marketing. They were moving the meeting where I would be speaking to over one hundred furniture reps—who were mostly male—about my new role, and they wanted me to move my flight to accommodate the change.

I'd faced my share of chauvinism in my time as a carpenter, so I felt confident I could handle the meeting, no matter when it was scheduled, but I didn't want to change my flight schedule last minute. I told my boss I would keep my original schedule and just work from the hotel. He gave me the okay, and I started packing. Tool-belt—check. Spokesperson-like clothing—check. It was all becoming very real. And admittedly, I enjoyed shifting my focus from abuse or death for a bit. Touting the selling points of American-made kids' furniture was a welcome respite.

Industry friends of mine were sharing my new spokesperson role on Facebook, and we were plotting to meet up while in town for Market. My friend, Amy, tagged a male friend of hers—a designer named Tony—and mentioned that if he hadn't met me yet, he was in for a treat. Tony immediately looked into my work, my life, and my new job, and sent me a Facebook friend request. We connected, and he wrote me privately. He was very complimentary of what I'd built and even suggested working on a kids' line together. Always feeling like the underdog, I felt flattered that this twenty-year veteran designer thought my brand was up to snuff. After all, he'd designed for some big names around the world.

Amy, another friend named Trisha, Tony, and I chatted away online telling jokes and preparing to meet up at Market. My nerves were calming, knowing I had people to cling to when I needed a break from all the spokesperson stuff. And to boot, I was being accepted and respected by a real furniture designer. The only thing left to do was get on the plane bound for Charlotte, North Carolina.

CHAPTER 8

The Rabbit Hole

In addition to making plans to get together as a group, Tony reached out to me on Facebook Messenger to ask if we could have dinner while I was in town. I'd had work dinners with other men throughout my marriage, but for some reason, his request felt slightly inappropriate. Other than getting to know me better, there was no clear purpose like most work dinners I attend. Instead of agreeing to a one-on-one dinner, I suggested I pop by his showroom on Friday. Plus, we were already scheduled to dine together with our friends the next night so we already had a dinner planned.

I completely understand, Tony replied when I wrote to tell him I'd stop by the showroom.

Then he told me he wanted to talk about his Dad and the abuse he suffered as a child. He knew I was a survivor because he'd been reading what I was posting on the Little Light Project Facebook page.

Oh Tony, I'm so sorry you went through that, and with your father, I replied, thinking he meant he endured sexual abuse at the hands of his father. *My distant uncle was the one who abused me, I can't imagine it being my father.*

Little dots started moving on my screen—he was typing.

My dad didn't sexually abuse me, but he did abuse me. I also wonder sometimes about memories I have of my mom's boyfriends.

I didn't quite know what to write other than how sorry I was that he endured any and all of it. I wasn't sure what else to say to someone who was in the kind of pain I knew all too well. And I wasn't picking up on anything intuitively to share with him regarding his memories of his mom's boyfriends, which sometimes happened when survivors shared information with me. On more than one occasion, I saw flashes of what they endured. In Tony's case, I didn't see anything, but I felt a lot of empathy for him.

We signed off saying we were looking forward to meeting up at the showroom, and I continued preparing for my trip to North Carolina.

I boarded the plane on Tuesday, ready to celebrate the fact that I'd finally done it—I'd succeeded at growing Mod Mom Furniture, and I still had all fingers intact. After many years of hardship and struggle—and countless hours of building everything by hand—I was finally going to scale up my furniture company.

My plane touched down in North Carolina, and I quickly powered up my phone to see what I'd missed. Text messages flooded in.

"Did you see the press release?" was in several messages. Scott asked this question, too. I had no idea what they were talking about. I reached out to my husband immediately after getting off the plane, and he said, "Kiers, Stanley Furniture just put out a release saying they are shutting down production of their youth furniture division." That very sentence spun my head around and simultaneously punched me in the gut.

Did I just lose my job and licensing deal? I could feel tears welling up in my eyes as I gathered my things and walked off the plane. Then it hit me: this was the real reason they were trying to get me to push my flight back.

Standing outside one of the airport terminal shops, I dialed the VP of Marketing at Stanley. He confirmed that it wasn't an April fools' joke, and said they couldn't have told me what was happening because they were a publicly-traded company. The team hoped I would move my flight back, meaning I would have stayed in Flagstaff when the release hit the press. He also confirmed that I lost my job and licensing deal.

Stanley offered to fly me back to Arizona immediately, but I said no. I knew what I had to do and it wasn't head back to Flagstaff. I was, at the time, the main breadwinner. As much as I wanted to curl up in a ball, I needed to make something happen, and fast.

They agreed to pay all of my expenses at Market—thankfully, they understood they owed me at least that much. We also planned to meet at the Stanley headquarters on Thursday to discuss my year-long contract and payout.

Walking through the airport to the rental car lot, I was in such shock that I could barely see straight. The deal that had taken seven months to solidify was now in ruins, and I had to figure out how to fix it. *How could they string me along like this?* They had to have known they were in big trouble back when they started negotiating with me. I couldn't help but think that maybe they considered me their Hail Mary pass, but it came too late.

As I stood at the rental car counter, tears stained the paperwork I signed for my economy car. The poor woman handing me the keys felt bad for me—even she thought I'd gotten the shaft after I told her why I was such an emotional mess. She comforted me with her soothing Southern accent and gave me a giant hug before I pulled out of the lot. I was grateful for Southern hospitality.

The drive from Charlotte to Greensboro felt especially long; I couldn't stop wiping tears from my eyes. The blow of the loss set in, causing fear to fill every molecule of my being. The only thing I could do was hold out hope that they'd keep me on as a spokesperson for the other lines of furniture they owned.

I spent Wednesday waiting to hear from the CEO and senior executives at Stanley. Mostly, I cried in my hotel room, bought a six-pack of Corona, and reached out to everyone I knew who might be able to help me meet with other big brands. Many wonderful people made connections for me that day. My industry friends' hearts were huge—they did whatever they could to help me.

While sitting at my hotel room desk, I got a Facebook message from Tony. He had read the release that seemed to spell the end of my stint with Stanley. Much to my delight, he told me he knew I would make something else happen, and said that Stanley would be crazy to let me go completely. This lifted my spirits a bit. After all, he was a somebody in the industry. He knew what he was talking about, or at least I hoped he did.

I tried to sleep, hoping that my Stanley meeting the next day would help clear up the questions I had about my fate with the company. After tossing and turning all night, I woke with a huge pit in my stomach. One that wouldn't go away even as I sat down for lunch with the CEO and VP of Marketing in Stanley's elegant dining room.

"Thanks so much for understanding, Kiersten," said the CEO.

"I understand that you were in a horrible spot having to make this decision," I replied. "My heart goes out to the families who are being affected by the factory closing."

We chatted more about the position they were in, and how they got to the point of knowing there was no turning back. It was why they kept pushing back the signing of the licensing deal we'd worked on for so long. It went from talk of mailing it to me, to, "Why don't we have you sign this when you come down to Market in April."

I could tell they weren't eager to talk about the elephant in the room, so I spoke up. At this point, I had nothing to lose. "Again, I know this is super hard, but I would like to know if you have plans to keep me on as spokesperson for the other Stanley brands and, if not, I'd like to discuss how my current spokesperson contract will be paid out."

Maybe they thought I'd simply be happy having lunch in their posh cafeteria, and would gleefully skip out of the building because I understood the position they were in, but that wasn't going to happen.

Looking me dead in the eyes, he said, "We don't have plans to keep you on, but we're going to see that you get two months' severance, which I'm sure you know is very fair."

"With all due respect, that's only two months of my twelve-month contract," I replied, my face turning red as fire. "I still have ten months left, and as you know, my husband cut back his hours so I could accept this spokesperson position."

"Yes, but two months is all we can and will be providing," he reiterated, offering that I was welcome to come back to the cafeteria daily for lunch if I'd like. As if lunch made up for a year-long contract that he wasn't going to payout.

I couldn't wait to leave. Trying desperately to keep the waterworks at bay, I thanked them for lunch, told them I'd be in touch regarding severance, and excused myself from the table. The minute I exited, the burning in my throat started my descent into full-on sobbing as I snaked my way around the building to the parking lot around back. I entered my safe haven of a rental car.

During the twenty-minute drive back to my hotel, I pulled myself together and thought about why they seemed so sure of themselves despite the fact that we had a signed contract. Ultimately, the Stanley execs knew we didn't have money to pay a big-time lawyer, so they pretty much had me where they needed me: desperate and powerless. I knew what I had to do, and there was no better place than High Point Market to land another deal.

By Friday, I was back in fierce determination mode. I scheduled meetings with CEOs who were very compassionate after hearing the news.

I headed to Market ready to make things happen, but first I had to meet Tony in his manufacturer's showroom. He looked just like his Facebook photos—tall and dark-haired with beautiful blue eyes. Tony even wore the signature black biker jacket that I'd seen in his profile photo. His voice was what struck me the most, though. Later, I would learn that many people told him that he had a perfect voice for radio, and they were right.

I was slightly nervous, but he quickly made me feel comfortable. With smiling eyes, he leaned in for a hug that felt oddly familiar. His cologne covered the faint scent of cigarette smoke, a vice he didn't hide from the world. He was charming, supportive, compassionate, and respectful. Even though we'd just met, I felt like he was someone I'd known for a very long time. I thought it was odd that I was covered in head-to-toe chills when I met him, but I chalked it up to lots of energy in the room.

Tony seemed very excited to meet, which was a bit surprising considering he was the design star and I was newly unemployed. After we talked for a bit while sitting on one of his sofa designs, and he took a selfie of us, he asked me to go with him for a smoke break. I didn't smoke but I obliged, feeling happy to go with him. He had a secret spot in the building that was perfect for his sneaky smoke breaks. I made a mental note of his rebel ways, and afterward, went back into the showroom with him to talk a bit more.

About the time I was planning to leave, my phone needed charging and, much to my delight, Tony offered to walk me over to what he felt was the best spot for such a thing. The lounge he spoke of was in a different building, which gave us time to chat more on the way over.

Tony sat down with me, and we talked about what I'd been doing with the Little Light Project, which he professed he loved so much that he'd shared it with friends on Facebook. After about ten minutes, he abruptly said he needed to get back to the showroom. His energy felt anxious to me, though I understood that he needed to get back to work. Before parting ways, we both said we were looking forward to our group dinner the next night.

Later that day, I made my way back to the hotel to rest before more evening festivities. I pulled myself off the couch when it was time to get ready for a women-only industry event. Trisha and Amy, the two friends I was seeing the next night with Tony, were going with me to a mixer for roughly sixty women leaders in the industry. Despite knowing that I was in for a night of small talk with many people I didn't know, I was still excited to chat with Trisha and Amy. As soon as I arrived at the event, I determined the time was right for a gin and tonic. I needed something to take the edge of all that energy in the room.

Standing in line at the makeshift bar, I looked down at my phone to see a Facebook message from Tony:

Dear Kiersten,

So, I need to bare my soul. Something very profound happened to me the very first second I saw you online. And, I mean the very first second. It was a feeling so strong and so beyond words, I literally sat in my chair and felt completely paralyzed. And later, on 3/31, I wrote the first piece of poetry I've ever written in my life. You can read it on my FB profile page. It's actually the caption to my Profile Banner Photo. What nobody knows, nor will ever know, is that I wrote this about my feelings for you. Please don't worry!! I will never bring this up again. In fact, I will take an aspirin or something and get over it as quickly as possible. But I want you to know, it's truly shaken me to my core. I have literally been sick to my stomach ever since then.

Please know that I have no delusions, and I know very well the reality. I also feel certain you suspected, or even completely knew this already. It's why I'm writing to you now. I know I would not be able to keep from saying something to you, so I figured writing it will spare you that uncomfortable moment in person.

What's most important to me is that I don't lose you as a friend because I have these feelings. I'm sure the aspirin, or maybe some magic kale smoothie drink, will eventually cure this. I'll find the way. Seriously though, if this makes you uncomfortable for me *to be at dinner tomorrow, please tell me! I will find a good excuse to miss it.*

I didn't have to meet you today to confirm it either. This came from your spirit through universe that transcends your physical presence. But I still felt so nervous today. I needed to run away basically.

I pray to the universe that this doesn't put me in the same pile of guys who most certainly and constantly throw themselves at your feet. Especially after writing this to you at Market, where you've already experienced the wolves!

No matter what you think of me now, I know I will be adoring you, watching proudly, respecting, and loving you from afar. You are such a precious, precious person. And I know deep in my soul, you will achieve your goals.

With my warmest heartfelt feelings,

Tony

Everything around me disappeared when I read that letter. There was no noise. No sound. No one clamored to talk with one another. It took a minute before I realized where I was standing. Feeling taken aback by reading his message, I had to immediately read it again. I was flattered beyond belief that he would write what he did and, contrary to what he presumed, I truly hadn't thought he felt this way.

Of course, as I inched closer to the bar to order the largest gin and tonic on the planet, I went straight to Facebook to read the poem he mentioned in his letter. He wrote about a force that washed over him with unimaginable power, yet he felt powerless to hold onto it.

Before the bartender could hand me my drink, I quickly replied to him to not worry, that there would be no weirdness and that dinner with our friends was still on for the next night. He knew the score and admitted it. Because of that, I didn't foresee any issues with keeping our group dinner plans.

The rest of the night was kind of a blur. I kept replaying his letter over and over again in my mind while I made small talk with design divas until it was time to go. It was nice to feel appreciated after what I'd experienced the past two days. I went to bed thinking about the next day, which was filled with meetings with furniture industry CEOs and, most intriguingly, the dinner we'd all planned that was getting more interesting by the minute.

Morning came, and I shuttled myself from one meeting to the next, talking with many industry bigwigs about spokesperson opportunities. I was pretty much tapped out by 4:00 p.m. and ready for a fun dinner with my girlfriends and that handsome designer who'd proclaimed his love for me last night. The ladies and I grabbed a patio table and a bottle of wine at a local Italian restaurant. We laughed and decompressed from our busy Market day and waited for our fourth companion to arrive.

In walked Tony with a Fedora hat and custom kicks. No one could say he wasn't a style maven. And of course, he wore his usual charisma and charm as he sat down next to me at the table. We all laughed and talked about the industry and what was happening in our lives. Much to my delight, everyone rallied around me, knowing how much I worried about the future. All I could do was try my best at Market to strike up another deal, so why not enjoy a fun dinner with friends and forget about the stress of all that for a moment?

The next thing I knew, a text message popped up on my phone. I looked down expecting it to be Scott or one of my kids, but it was Tony. He was sitting next to me, yet texting me. He said two things: "You look beautiful tonight" and "I wish I could hold your hand under the table."

A rush of adrenaline coursed through me, making my heart feel like it was about to leap out of my chest. I was surprised by my reaction and equally surprised that he was writing those things to me. I shouldn't have been, based on the letter he'd written to me the night before, but his direct nature still rattled me. And I was wondering why he used the word "love" in the letter he sent to me. Did he really mean *love*? Whatever he meant, his words diverted my attention from all of the real-life heaviness that was my life at that moment.

We continued to get to know one another over the next three days. Each night, we would gather in a hotel room and drink wine—the four of us—and talk about life and love. When I looked at him, I felt chills run up and down my body. Based on that alone, I intuitively knew we were meant to meet. I could feel myself inching closer to him physically and emotionally. He even talked about how much he loved that I was intuitive and using that to help others. I told him about several of the cases I was working on, and he teared up listening to what happened to the children.

One night, after driving back from another group dinner, he sent me a very pointed text that said: *I wish I could spend the night with you.* This particular message made my heart stop for a second, and not in a good way.

Was he just trying to woo me to get me in bed? Was that ultimately what this was all about? I definitely felt a connection to him that was magnetic...deeper than some ploy to get me in the sack. I felt drawn to him, yet scared at the same time. I knew I shouldn't be feeling any pull to him—after all, I was married—but it was stronger than anything I'd felt in a very long time.

He later clarified that "spend the night with you" meant just spending as much time with me as possible with no expectation of sex. He just wanted to soak up time with me while we were in High Point. I believed him—he'd been respectful and caring, and the fact that both of my friends adored him made me think I had nothing to fear.

The more we hung out together, the more he continued to make his feelings known to me. It was intoxicating, to say the least. He was take-charge and direct, something I was unknowingly needing at the moment.

Four nights after we'd met, I asked him to accompany me to an industry dinner. We had a blast, but I could tell everyone at the event wondered what was happening, including my friend Katie, who asked me later what was up. She said our chemistry seemed electric, and she hadn't seen me that happy in ages.

She was right—our chemistry was on fire, and I felt completely drained of all motivation to make everything okay for everyone. I couldn't push away my feelings anymore, and I didn't want to. We ended up having a full-on affair that week, which was not something I planned, nor something I ever thought would happen when I boarded the plane for Charlotte.

I was always incredibly controlled in every part of my life, but not this time. This time, I gave in. It was a rush like I'd never felt before. Even my personality changed a bit—I was becoming more direct, less responsible, and more adventurous. It was as if I were morphing into him, but I didn't see it at the time.

It felt like I reverted to teenage Kiersten's state of mind—only, teenage Kiersten never stepped out of line or did anything to warrant disapproving looks. I just didn't care anymore; I had blinders on, and Tony was all I could see. I was free-falling.

We talked for hours over meals and while walking Market, sharing intimate details of our lives. He talked about his marriage to the mother of his kids, from whom he said he was separated but living in the same house. We also talked about a woman he'd fallen in love with online five years prior, but he said his feelings were waning, especially after meeting me. Tony reiterated that I was the one he'd been searching for all over the world—a soulmate he was destined to meet.

I shared more about my own childhood abuse revelation, and how I was done trying to ignore the problems in my marriage. He talked about the abuse and neglect he endured as a child and how it shaped him. He told me he loved me, and I reciprocated, even though common sense said this was all way too fast. Not to mention, wrong.

Not only was Tony trying to show me that he had fallen in love with me, but he was also trying to show me that he cared about my company, too. He volunteered to help resurrect my furniture brand, which was now in limbo because of the dead Stanley deal. It felt good to have someone want to help take over, especially when I was tired of feeling like it was all on my shoulders. If there was such a thing as soulmates, this is what I believed it felt like. Unlike Scott, Tony was an abuse survivor, too, and he understood what I was going through like no other. I kept moving my return flight to stay longer.

At one point, while Tony and I were driving to a music venue, Scott asked over text if I was having an affair. I'm not the only intuitive one in our family, that's for sure. The sheer fact that I kept delaying my return was a big sign that something was wrong. I denied it through text, not wanting to deal with anything but Tony. I was used to denying much in my life, although I felt horrible lying to Scott. The high I felt was a powerful drug, and Scott couldn't compete with that. No one could compete in that moment.

The next day when Tony was busy with meetings, I called an intuitive friend of mine who volunteered as a professional medium at the Little Light Project.

"I can't believe what I'm about to tell you because I never thought I'd be in this position, but I met someone here at Market," I started. "Would you mind getting a read on him and the situation? I don't feel like I'm in a position to read anything clearly but I keep having chills when I'm around him."

"Oh wow, Kiers, that's big," she replied. "I don't pick up any bad feelings on him or the situation. Maybe you were meant to meet him?"

I sat back in my chair, relieved that intuitively it all looked to be happening the way it should. And it was, but just not for the reasons I believed when I heard her give the green light.

Seven days after heading to High Point Market, I was on my way home thinking about this beautiful man who seemed to have floated into my life like an angel. I didn't want to lose him, but my head was spinning. He told me he cried on the drive home because he didn't want to let go of me and didn't know if he would see me again. He even helped me navigate some rental car issues—taking charge, as usual. He showed me he wanted to take care of me. I boarded the plane in a daze, wondering how I would handle the next few days.

The dreaded homecoming was just hours away. Each mile closer to Flagstaff meant a heavier pit in my stomach. I'd done something I didn't expect to do at Market. I chose a different sliding door after eighteen years of marriage.

I returned home and acted like everything was normal while I frantically tried to figure out how to handle it all. It was not an Academy Award performance, that's for sure. Scott could tell I was far from normal, but I maintained the façade. I felt scared to turn my life upside down on top of what had already happened career-wise in High Point, but I also thought I was in love with another man after knowing him for one week.

To make matters worse, when Scott and I were talking about next steps—now that I'd lost my job and my licensing deal—he made a comment about being sad that he could no longer play around with furniture design. With a level head, I would have heard it as intended, but his comment only fueled the fire for me. Here I was, again, feeling like I had to fix everything all on my own. He wasn't saying, "Kiers, I started pounding the pavement looking for extra jobs, doing everything I can to figure out how I can help us financially." As I heard it, he simply felt sad I lost my job because it meant he couldn't mess around with furniture anymore, and he was still waiting for me to spearhead the fixing of everything.

I was acutely aware at that moment that I was the one who always reinvented herself and who, at times, took menial jobs just to make ends meet. He never showed me that he was the kind of guy who would do anything for his family, including jobs he didn't want to do. It felt like it was okay for me to do those things, but not him. Even the radio station job seemed to be a good gig. After all, it wasn't like he was cleaning houses, taking care of other people's kids, slinging a hammer, or offering to do anything outside of what he had always done.

We grew up differently and there's nothing wrong with that, but our backgrounds definitely affected our marriage in ways I never imagined. I grew up the daughter of two teachers with a dad who roofed during the summers, and he grew up with a father who was high up in the corporate world. Money wasn't a problem for them. He is and has always been a hard worker, but wasn't taught to think three steps ahead or take any job available.

Right before we were married, Scott was jobless for a bit before landing a great gig with HBO. My parents and sister were worried about his ability to provide as if it had been some kind of foreshadowing. I didn't see it, and I made sure my family knew I wasn't worried.

He didn't have to scrape a bunch of jobs together to help pay for college like I had—just to make ends meet—and in this moment, I wanted him to show me he could. His plan was to spend more money and get his real estate license, which infuriated me. It could potentially be a long-term fix, but it wasn't the short-term help we needed. Rent needed to be paid and real estate school wasn't going to pay it. I was already contemplating what to sell and how to bring in more money working multiple jobs.

In comparison, Tony was also a scrappy doer like me who slung hammers, painted walls, and delivered pizzas just to make ends meet, and I held all of that in high esteem. Scott was in a losing battle but didn't realize it yet.

To make matters worse, like most husbands whose wives were gone for a week, he wanted to be intimate. I was struggling with it but was not ready to tell him what had happened in High Point.

Instead, I went right into smoothing and accommodating mode. I gave in. In my mind, it was just something I had to do to give me more time to figure out how to tell him the truth. Unbeknownst to him that night, I silently shed a few tears, all the while feeling that oppressive, claustrophobic energy I felt when the memories of abuse were coming back. I was having another panic attack, and I couldn't make it stop. I didn't know exactly why the sudden attacks started, but they came on shortly after we moved to Flagstaff. After it was over, I blocked it all from my memory and plotted how to get to the next moment when I could connect with Tony again.

About a week after I'd been home, I finally mustered the courage to talk to Scott. It was the perfect, imperfect moment—we were home alone in the living room. He was fixing the blinds on the bay window.

"Hey, can we talk?" I asked in a very matter-of-fact tone despite the fact that my heart was racing.

"Um, sure," he said while continuing to fix the blinds.

"I don't know how to say this, so I'm just going to say it. I want out of our marriage…and I did meet someone, like you suspected, in High Point. I'm sorry I lied to you."

There was no noise. No movement. Only silence for a minute as Scott processed what I'd just dropped on him.

He started to speak after the color drained from his face. While visibly choking back tears, he said, "I knew it…. It's that Tony guy, isn't it?"

"Yes, it is," I quietly confirmed. "I'm so sorry, but I just want out. I can't do this anymore."

Walking towards me, he pled, "Come on, Kiers, I know things haven't been easy for us, but please, please, would you consider therapy with me?"

"Scott, I don't think it will help," I said.

What I really wanted to say was, *No, I won't do that because I'm in love with another man, and I just want you to let me go. Please, let me go.* Even his pleading made me feel suffocated like I wanted to run. Fresh in my mind was the fact that I felt free with Tony—free of panic attacks, too.

I felt horrible hurting Scott but I still couldn't see anything but moving toward a life with my new love. Or rather, I couldn't imagine living without Tony. The choice was clear.

Scott walked into our bedroom, where he sat quietly sobbing on our bed for a few minutes before I followed him into the room. I felt a dagger in my heart seeing him like that; I didn't want him to hurt this way. He pled with me, again, to go to couple's therapy. I relented, wanting to give him some relief, but it still felt like I was just checking a box, hoping that my therapist would help him understand I was leaving.

A few days later, I shared what was happening with a few close friends and family. Some friends were as shocked as Scott was, but those closest to me said, "Well, it's about time. We thought this would have happened a long time ago, after all you've been through." Others said they always suspected that I felt suffocated in the marriage.

That same week, Tony also told his wife that he finally wanted to go through with the divorce they'd talked about for years. He told her about his feelings for me in addition to finally coming clean about the five-year online affair he'd been having with another woman. According to Tony, his wife had already asked for a divorce a while back. They had simply been waiting until the children were a bit older to formally split up.

He also told me that he had a heart-to-heart with his hidden online girlfriend after we got back from North Carolina, confessing that he had fallen out of love with her and in love with me. Over and over again, he made sure I knew I was the one he'd been looking for his whole life, and nothing was going to stop us from creating a blissful future that was meant to be.

We felt like we'd found one another because our love was written in the stars. This feeling was more powerful than anything I'd ever experienced. He adored everything about me, even my medium-ship work, and he, too, was an abuse survivor. We understood one another, which contributed to the feeling of finding a fairytale love. While we both loved being with our kids when we were in our respective hometowns, the reality was that we were still trapped in our old relationships thousands of miles apart.

I did all I could to give Scott space, other than when we went to therapy. And that was something I was doing in order to soften the blow of splitting up. I focused on the kids when I was home. Scott and I tried to keep up the façade around Grace and Noah, but when we were together in a family setting, we would make space for one another. I took a lot of walks around the neighborhood, allowing for time to think and to talk to Tony on the phone.

Thankfully, our counselor also reiterated to Scott that I wanted out. She could see that I had tunnel vision. I was seeing her with the goal of helping Scott move on, and he was seeing her with the goal of fixing our marriage. She let him know that wasn't going to be possible based on what she was hearing.

Scott was none too pleased with our couples' therapist, leading him to seek out his own individual counselor who told him that what Tony and I had would likely blow up in about six months. From what he said, she wasn't all that kind when it came to me, but she was right about one thing—things would eventually take a turn. It just wasn't at the six-month mark.

* * *

Six weeks after High Point, I was grateful that Scott had set out for a weekend with friends in LA. He craved the space as much as I did. In fact, I didn't even realize how much I needed distance until I started bleeding profusely. I'd been so wrapped up in trying to figure out why a child in spirit who hadn't crossed over yet was making herself known that I didn't even realize my period was late. Normally, when

I got an intuitive hit about a child, they'd come in, I'd help them or pass along messages, and then they'd head out. Not this girl—she'd been giving me signals on my right side for a week, yet I couldn't get a clear message. All I could decipher was that her name was Emma.

Emma would have to wait a bit because I was clearly not well. This was the worst period I'd had in, well, ever. I spent most of the weekend going from the bed to the bathroom because I honestly couldn't go anywhere else. I was bleeding through everything I owned and the cramps were almost unbearable. I had no choice but to tell the kids that I thought I'd come down with a stomach bug so they wouldn't worry about me. They didn't need to know the gory details.

Toward the end of the weekend, the bleeding and cramping finally stopped. Sitting at my desk writing on Messenger to one of my intuitive friends, I mentioned that I'd had a helluva weekend dealing with Aunt Flo. Just then, Emma came into view. She was beautiful with gorgeous curly brown hair that draped her shoulders. I guessed her age to be around nine.

As I typed the following, my entire body chilled from head to toe: *Oh, hey...I forgot to mention that I've been channeling this little girl for a week or so by the name of Emma, but I'm not really getting a clear message from her. I can tell by the fact she's on my right side that she hasn't crossed into the light yet.*

I waited patiently for my friend to type back. A few minutes went by before she wrote replied.

Kiers, is there any way you could have had a miscarriage this weekend...rather than a bad period?

Once again, I was covered in chills. Every bone in my body knew her question wasn't really a question. It was a statement. My mind flashed back to that day in 2009 when Sophia said she saw three souls attached to me—and one had long curly brown hair.

Emma. Emma had curly brown hair. I saw her smiling in my mind's eye—she could tell I was putting it all together. It wasn't unusual for a spirit to show me what they needed me to see so I could make sense of a message. Some children who died at birth or were miscarried or aborted did not present as babies but rather, as older children. Sometimes, all I would see and hear were the messages they wanted me to share with their parents but I couldn't see them in my mind's eye.

Emma's message was clear—she wanted me to know that she was the soul whom I had just miscarried. *But why did I need to know? What exactly was she telling me?* I continued to sit alone at my desk, quietly thanking her for her message. The more I conversed with her in my mind, the more clarity I gained. Within thirty minutes, I channeled two reasons for Emma's visit.

The first had to do with the fact that I had channeled (and would continue to channel) messages from many souls who never made it full-term. I learned that some of them would come back into the same family through full-term births down the road, while others would remain on the other side guiding and watching over their families. Many times, these souls told me that their journey was about learning and growth—for them and for their loved ones.

The second reason Emma made herself known wasn't as clear as the first.

"It's about Tony," she said.

Obviously, Tony was the father. That part wasn't a mystery that needed to be solved. Having just turned my life upside down at the age of forty, I was relieved to know Emma was not meant to come into this world at this time. Much to my surprise, Tony didn't feel the same way. He seemed upset that I wasn't pregnant, and it baffled me. I honestly couldn't understand why he would want a baby at this point in our lives. Between us, we had four children already.

Emma knew why he reacted the way he did, but it wasn't her job to tell me. I'd have to figure that out on my own.

* * *

A week after what I'd come to learn was a very early miscarriage, I put myself on a plane heading to the East Coast. New York City was a place I'd always loved visiting, but this time it felt even more electric, despite my red-eye grogginess. The last four weeks had been anything but easy. Living in the same home with a man you care about but are divorcing is heartbreaking and tension-filled. Hopping on a plane to see Tony meant I could breathe again. The sun was just starting to come up as the wheels touched down at LaGuardia.

Get off that fucking plane, he texted as the plane taxied to the gate. *I'm waiting right outside of security. I can't wait to see you!*

Ha-ha, okay! I replied. *These people aren't moving fast enough. I'm so excited! I can't wait to see you!*

I practically ran to the arrivals area. Through the crowd ahead of me, I could see a tall, handsome, dark-haired man with a smile from ear to ear. Our embrace reinforced that he indeed felt like home. I exhaled for the first time in days, and we walked hand-in-hand to his car.

We had lots of business meetings that made the trip seem legit, but in actuality, the work-related appointments were secondary to the fact that we were dying to see each other again. We hadn't stopped texting and talking since we met in North Carolina. I'd never texted anyone more in my life.

Our visit was everything I thought it would be, minus the threat of having to pay $200 for smoking in the hotel room. Tony talked his way out of it while I waited in the lobby, thank goodness. Even though I had broken the biggest rule of all—the infidelity rule—I was still a rule follower at heart and hated that the hotel rules had been violated. I wasn't accustomed to or in favor of smoking inside, but Tony didn't think twice about it. He knew all the tricks—he'd been a two-packs-a-day smoker since he turned thirteen. I knew he smoked—it was one of the first things he did when we met but, thankfully, he talked a lot about wanting to quit. He said Flagstaff would be a great place to stop smoking.

I smoked occasionally in the spirit of rebellion and fun, but mostly, I learned early in the relationship that when you sleep in a cloud of second-hand smoke—whether it's pot or cigarette smoke—a Virginia Slims Menthol or two isn't the worst thing one could do. I'd always considered myself lucky because I never developed an addiction to cigarettes after having an occasional one while out with friends over the years.

I knew it was a lifetime habit for Tony, but I was ready to help him quit whenever he felt ready. I also learned early on that he smoked pot to help with his ADHD. He called it his *medicine*. While I wasn't a pot smoker, I'd tried it a time or two over the years, and I didn't think of it as a crime, either. After all, he preferred it to prescription medicine that had the potential to make matters worse with all of the nasty side effects he talked about. And he needed it in order to calm his brain enough to design furniture, so how could I possibly attach something negative to what he did to self-medicate? As usual, I didn't judge even though it wasn't my cup of tea. I simply cared and wanted him to feel the best he could feel, even if it came with the name Mary Jane.

* * *

Around noon on one of our last days in New York City together, we stood outside with lit cigarettes in hand waiting for Mark Pucci, retired NYPD detective, to arrive. Mark and I had been working together on a missing persons case. We were connected by a mutual friend when both of us volunteered to see if we could help.

Not unlike the other detectives I'd been working with on missing children's cases, Mark believed in intuition. I felt comfortable with him over the phone, so I figured meeting him in person to go over case details would be easy and relaxed. Still, I was nervous. Furniture was my forte. This mediumship thing was relatively new to me, and the stakes were high.

"Kiersten, right?" the tall, gray-haired man asked, with a grin, as he walked toward us on the sidewalk.

"Hi, Mark! Yes! It's nice to finally meet you in person," I said as I offered a firm handshake. "Mark, this is Tony, who I told you about. Tony, this is Mark."

They exchanged handshakes and pleasantries as we made our way into the diner that lived below the hotel. I gave Mark a heads up before our meeting that Tony would be with me, and that I was separating from my husband. He didn't seem fazed in the least. In fact, he seemed happy for us.

We talked for close to two hours while Tony sat quietly at the table when he wasn't taking a smoke break. Mark brought a manila file folder with him that contained all of his "boots on the ground" detective notes. I brought a notebook that contained all of the details I'd channeled intuitively from Flagstaff about what happened to the missing person we were hoping to find. Much to my surprise, what I'd been able to channel matched what he'd dug up through good old-fashioned detective work, and then some. We were picking up on the same people and places without talking with one another. Mark looked stunned and amazed while Tony wore a prideful grin on my behalf. I was winning points with a decorated NYPD detective, yet I still felt completely out of my element.

Mark told me that in all his thirty years in law enforcement, he'd never met someone like me. He'd worked with psychics before, but he said I was different. Obviously, this wasn't something I did for a living, so that was the lens through which I processed his comment. I reiterated that I didn't ask for any of it and that I wasn't sure what to do with my newfound gift other than what I had already been doing helping grieving parents, passing messages when I was guided to do so. And in this case, hopefully finding the missing person.

When it was time to go, we all made our way to the door. Mark leaned in, gave me a hug, and thanked me for my time. I thanked him for believing in me despite the fact I wasn't a professional medium or psychic. Then we watched him disappear into the crowded New York sidewalk. Not only was I thrilled to validate his findings, but I was over the moon that he was helping validate for me that this was very real. Even after three years of channeling spirit, I still sometimes questioned how and why I knew what I knew.

While I was feeling good about being steps closer to helping a family find their loved one, Tony was in a different headspace.

"See how he went in for a hug, there?" he asked.

"Um, yeah, he must be a hugger," I replied. "I'm just relieved that it looks like what I channeled matches what he is getting, and even fills in some holes. I think we're getting super close to figuring out what happened."

"I think he wants to do more than solve cases with you, baby," Tony shot back.

My brow furrowed as I tried to hide the feeling of disappointment that, clearly, he wasn't reading the situation the way I was. Somehow, he wasn't at all focused on the fact that I'd just left a meeting with an NYC detective about a missing persons case, and what I shared actually helped. Never in my lifetime did I think I'd be in this position, or that someone like Mark would actually value my intuitive weirdness.

"Nah, he just believes in me. And I really appreciate that—there aren't a lot of cops who trust intuitive information. Plus, he just met you...I hardly think he's trying to make a move on me."

"Whatever you say, baby," Tony said as he grabbed my hand.

We walked hand-in-hand, looking like carefree lovers, but I was left with a pit in my stomach I couldn't shake. I felt anything but carefree at that moment, thinking about what just went down after one of the most significant meetings of my life. In true Kiersten fashion, I quickly buried the uneasy feeling deep down that way I could get back to feeling high with Tony by my side.

Groomed

Leaving New York wasn't easy. I was a mess, and I didn't care if anyone saw me bawling. We were both choking back tears as I entered the security line. I didn't want to lose the euphoria I felt when I was with Tony. I knew going back home meant awkwardness, pain, and isolation. But it also meant spending time with my kids, which was all I tried to focus on for the time being.

A day earlier, while standing in line to get our badges at New York's modern furniture trade show called ICFF, Tony said to me that he'd like to help me grow Mod Mom as an official member of my company. He offered to come on board for free to help me navigate the treacherous waters of the furniture world. After all, I'd just been burned by Stanley, and he knew I needed help figuring it all out. I was elated that he would offer to help, and it meant we would be traveling together.

I naturally assumed when he said he wanted to help, that he would come on as a consultant. After we said our tearful goodbyes—as I settled into my seat for the plane ride home—we texted back and forth. Lots of *I love you* and *I miss you* preceded one last message exchange about how excited we were about building Mod Mom together.

"How about if we name me President," appeared on my message screen.

I sat stunned for a split second. President was different from consultant, and I felt that all-too-familiar sensation in my gut. It was similar to what happened after the meeting with Mark. I held my breath until I could block my unease enough to rationalize that he loved me, and wanted the best for Mod Mom. While it wasn't my first choice, I thought maybe it was a smart move. As a novice in the industry, naming a veteran as president made sense. And not just any veteran, a well-respected designer who happened to be my soulmate.

"President Tony, it is," I typed out as the plane taxied to the runway.

* * *

Back to uncomfortable life in Flagstaff, I went. Regardless of the fact that Scott and I had jointly gotten to this place in our relationship, I was the bad guy in this scenario. I was the cheater. Some of our new friends took a side, and it wasn't mine. It was hard to swallow because they didn't know what had transpired over the past eighteen years. One of my new friends, Jules, didn't take sides at all and offered to take walks with me around our neighborhood. I am forever grateful for her kindness at a time when I felt completely alone.

Scott and I moved around one another, careful to not stir up trouble. Thankfully, in spite of the pain, we still respected each other as people and parents. Our main concern was how and when we were going to tell our kids that we were splitting up.

I started sleeping in the guest room, and we told Noah and Grace we just needed a little space as we worked through some marital stuff. Because we never really argued during our marriage, I'm sure that seemed odd. Scott didn't battle it out with me; it's not in his nature. It's not in either of our natures to fight.

Plus, he lived all the years of layoffs, bankruptcy, and more layoffs, leaving him feeling responsible. He could see why I'd come to the end of my rope. Life didn't change much for the kids because we argued only a few times during those first months after High Point. Yet, I knew they were sensing how off their world felt. Scott and I were always a good team—two people facing hardship at many turns but always working together to make it okay. For the most part, the kids still saw that in us.

Unbeknownst to me at the time, Scott also went to see a shaman in Sedona who gave him insight into how all of this would play out. On occasion, before I left for a business trip, he would say, "Make good choices." And at other times, "I know how this will end." Both infuriated me because I could have said the same thing to him about his choices and what the future held.

We continued therapy sessions, and I continued to make it clear that I was in love with another man and wanted out. It always broke my heart to hurt him in this way, but I knew in my soul I couldn't live that life anymore. I couldn't go back to feeling like I was holding the weight of the world on my own, to feeling smothered and tired. I finally felt free again, excited for the future.

Tony was helping me figure out the next steps with Mod Mom Furniture, and I couldn't get enough of the feeling I had when we were together, or when I was thinking about him. I genuinely wanted Scott to have the opportunity to be with someone who looked at him the way I did at Tony. I cared for him that much.

Being physically far from Tony was hard, but thanks to modern technology, we could see one another. Skype made it easier to be 3,000 miles away. I'd never been this connected to someone electronically before, but it was the only way to stay in touch. We talked and texted on Facebook Messenger almost constantly. He was always sending me music and love notes, and even crafted his own sign-off for me: "I love you then, now, and forever" or "I love you, TNF." He was a poet, after all, and I was his muse. We couldn't get enough of each other, no matter the time of day.

When *Baby* would pop up on my iPhone screen, my pulse would quicken. I would immediately text back, feeling that teenage-like, new love adrenaline spike.

Hi, baby? What's up? You okay?

I just fucking love you, he would write almost daily.

We talked for hours on the phone—about our dreams, our plans, and our newly formed business partnership—when he could scoot away from the house he lived with his wife and kids. The nearby park was one of his favorite spots from which to call me.

One evening in May when Tony called me, I knew it was time. I had to tell him about what happened the week I came back from High Point Market.

"Baby, I want to share something that happened before I told Scott I wanted out."

"Okay...what happened?"

"I didn't want to do this...but a few days after I got home, Scott wanted to be intimate. I didn't know how to tell him no because I knew it would lead to me having to tell him I was done. I was struggling with what to do, so I just did it, but I cried."

Silence filled the air.

I continued, "It didn't mean anything but I felt like I had no choice. I needed time to think about how to tell him."

Finally, he spoke. "I don't even know what to say, Kiersten. How could you do that? I mean, what you're telling me is that you cheated on me."

"No, no, it wasn't like that at all!" I pled. "I just didn't feel like I had a choice."

"Kiersten, you always have a choice. I can't believe you did this to me...I can't talk anymore."

Click. He'd hung up on me.

In one fell swoop, I managed to ruin the high we were on. Afraid to call him back, I sat weeping about what I'd done. And how if the roles were reversed, it would have been hard on me, too. I didn't understand, at that point, that I had always unconsciously done that when it came to sex: accommodated.

After all, I had just made the discovery that I was programmed to please a man from as early as age three. Still, no matter how I tried during that phone call, I couldn't get through to Tony. Sure, he'd slept with his wife, or so he said, the day before traveling to High Point, and right before he wrote me the letter telling me he was in love with me, but because it was *before* we met in person, it wasn't apples to apples in his mind.

He didn't talk to me for a full day. I knew he needed time to process, but the silence felt like punishment. When he finally texted, he said that he loved me but was taking time to think about how I'd cheated on him. Guilt washed over me like a tidal wave, and I recognized I needed to talk to someone about that. And I desperately needed Tony to forgive me.

My therapist said what I did was a natural response to smooth and accommodate given the fact that seven days prior, I wasn't even looking to get out of my marriage but was struck by a lightning bolt strong enough to unhinge me. He quite literally cracked open a vault of unconscious pain I'd unknowingly hidden away for years. I'm sure she also made the connection to the past childhood sexual abuse I endured, but we really didn't talk about that then.

I felt guilt and pain for hurting Tony and Scott—and for not being able to feel like I had control over any of it. I prided myself on my ability to control things in my life, making me feel safe and valued. To that point, I did recognize that what went down in High Point was about as far from controlled as you can get. And no matter how much guilt or shame I felt, I was still happy to let fate take the wheel. After all, it brought me my soulmate.

I knew in my soul that, soon, Tony would understand that I did what I did because I was in survival mode. That day finally came, but it came with a comment about my age, and how he knew our age difference might be a hindrance to our happiness. He said he forgave me, but he made sure to tell me that he would never hurt me the way I did when I slept with Scott after Market. He was older and wiser—and he now, privately, held all of the cards knowing that I would do anything to make up for what I did.

* * *

Publicly, Tony wanted to shout our love from the rooftops—or rather, the social media newsfeed. I was hesitant. Out of respect for Scott, I wanted to wait. I was lucky that my kids weren't into Facebook, so I didn't have to wrestle with that, too.

It didn't take long for me to come around, but I still didn't feel comfortable. I was public with my life, but never consistently gushy about my love life. Tony wasn't either, as he pointed out, but since he finally felt like he'd found his true soulmate, he wanted to post about us. A lot.

Facebook became the main vehicle for outing our electric romance, both behind the scenes on Messenger and in public posts. I was flattered he wanted to share that we'd found one another, and he had a way of posting the most romantic sentiments. Five thousand of his closest Facebook friends ate it up. Most of them were women in the design industry, and many of them gushed about what a great guy he was—how romantic, thoughtful, and committed he was to me. I felt lucky that he was indeed mine, even though I still secretly felt awkward with his posting about us all the time.

Baby, you'd tell me if men were writing to you privately, right? Tony asked one day over Messenger.

You mean like a male friend? I questioned. *I have a few who write to me, but they are and have always been just friends. Guys haven't approached me romantically, except for you, because I've been married for eighteen years.*

Well, if they're writing to you privately, there's likely a motive.

Um…I'm not so sure about that, I explained. *I can count on one hand guy friends who've reached out with questions about spirituality…and I've never felt they were hitting on me.*

Diving deeper into my memory, I continued:

There's one friend from high school who wrote me recently joking that he didn't realize I was splitting from Scott or he would have lined up. He's funny that way and has always said stuff like that since high school. I laughed and told him I was flattered, but that obviously, I'm madly in love with you. He's super happy for us and loves your furniture.

He was silent for a minute or two.

The visual quiet was deafening, and my heart started racing. What did I say that would cause his silence?

Then the little dots started up again. I exhaled—he was writing again.

Did you have to say you were flattered?

Isn't that what everyone says when someone says something nice like that? I wrote back, feeling my pulse quickening. *He was just saying he thinks highly of me. He's in a committed relationship, after all.*

How would you like it if I told a friend that I was flattered she said she wished she could have gotten to me before you did? he continued.

I sat stunned, frozen in my seat.

Oh my God, I thought. *Were we really fighting about this? How had I not seen it coming?*

Maybe he was right. I'd never thought of it this way, but maybe I was wrong to use the word flattered. I mustered the courage to type.

Well, I would expect you would be nice and do what I did—and then tell her you're in love with me, I typed, holding my breath again.

I can't believe you don't see how disrespectful this is to me, he responded. *For the first time in my life, I got totally honest with you when I met you. I'm an open book, and I want to share everything with you. In fact, I was about to tell you about a woman who wrote to me but maybe I shouldn't be that open.*

I stared at the screen not knowing what to say or do.

My brain couldn't figure out how one word—flattered—had caused such a ruckus. *Didn't he get it?* I loved *him*. Period. In fact, I was getting out of my marriage because I couldn't bear the thought of not being with him. We were soulmates destined for one another, yet we were fighting about a guy I hadn't seen in twenty years who wasn't a threat at all.

I wasn't a jealous person by nature, so this was foreign territory for me. *Did he want me to feel jealous? Why would he feel this way about a guy who has no shot, who connected with me once every couple of years, and who didn't really mean he wanted to be in a relationship with me?*

I want you to feel like you can tell me anything, I typed out on the keyboard. *I know you love me and only me. I'm not worried about the women who are reaching out to you. I mean, should I be? I'm sorry that what I said to him made you feel this way. I promise to share when I get messages from guys, but it isn't something that has happened much in the past, nor do I expect it in the future. We did just announce we're a couple on Facebook*, I pleaded on Messenger.

The air was getting heavier while I waited for his response.

I gotta go. I love you, TNF, he wrote, abruptly stopping the conversation.

Bam. There it was. That kick-in-the-gut feeling I hated. Couldn't we just go back to the *I fucking love you* texts from an hour ago?

After a few hours of the silent treatment, he wrote that he missed me. I replied the same, and the heaviness started to lift. I apologized again for hurting him, which seemed to help him move back to a state of equilibrium.

We were on our way to rainbows and butterflies again, and I couldn't wait to get there. One day, he would realize that he didn't

have to worry. It was just going to take some time, and I was determined to do whatever I could to minimize his insecurity about us.

* * *

Aside from the drug of new love, leaving my marriage, and figuring
out the next steps for Mod Mom, most of my life remained the same.
Money wasn't as tight because Scott did something I'd never seen
him do: he took odd jobs and signed up to drive for Uber, in addition
to his salaried job at the radio station. I was grateful for his willing-
ness to do whatever it took to keep a roof over our heads.

The Little Light Project was expanding, and I was not only
helping grieving parents by passing messages, but I was also in
charge of day-to-day operations for the nonprofit I founded. I didn't
want to admit it, but I was in over my head. I shouldn't have leaped
into building a 501c3—I should have kept it personal, the way it had
started. It was my own personal mission and path but I didn't realize
it at the time. On the other hand, it brought folks like Yvette and
Jason to me. Maybe that in itself was the whole purpose.

Yvette sent a message checking on me in June of 2014. She'd been
following the love story on Facebook and seemed very happy for me.
We talked about how we hoped we'd all meet up one day and how
Tony and I could possibly help her design her healing centers. It was
fun to dream up our future get-together, and I was excited for her to
meet him.

Out of nowhere, she told me Jason just popped in. Chills raced up
the left side of my body—one of my familiar spirit signs that what was
coming next was real and true, and from a spirit on the other side.

"Kiers, Jason wants you to know that this thing with Tony isn't
what you think it is."

She then went on to say she didn't understand what he meant
and it shocked her, but that's all he was willing to say just then. I was
supposed to figure it out on my own, but I appreciated the heads up.

I thanked her for passing the message, but of course, I felt major resistance to what Jason said. I knew what the relationship was—kismet, twin-soul, once-in-a-lifetime love I was grabbing by the horns. That's what I knew it to be.

We had a few things to work through, and the distance didn't help quell insecurities, but we'd figure out a way to be together soon enough. Tony told me the week we met that he'd move to Flagstaff to make us work, despite the fact that his kids were back East. He traveled so much that it actually didn't surprise me that he was willing to go back and forth to see his children. He knew that I needed to be close to my kids, and he agreed that it was important for me to live full-time in the same town as Noah and Grace. This declaration was one of the reasons I let myself fall for him. We dreamed up the homestead we'd build in Flagstaff and talked about how fun it would be to get all four of our kids together for extended periods of time.

Jason's message was seared in the back of my mind, but I didn't want to give it much attention because I was hell-bent on trusting that I knew what I was doing. In my mind, I was in control and making good decisions, and I truly couldn't fathom any other reality.

* * *

As Mod Mom opportunities popped up, we took every chance we could get to see one another. While I was still working on cold cases, I wasn't giving them the attention I had prior to meeting Tony. On occasion, I would work on them on the road, but mainly, I was completely wrapped up in Tony and getting Mod Mom off the ground again.

Typically, I flew to the East Coast or to wherever the latest furniture trade show was being hosted. This time was different. Tony flew to me in June. We were about to road trip from Flagstaff to Sedona to LA to Las Vegas for business, and I was beyond excited.

At this point, my kids knew I had a new business partner, and they were rolling with the changes in our family. They didn't ask many questions, and Scott pleaded with me to withhold telling them that we were splitting up until around the six-month mark. I disagreed with waiting but honored his wishes, knowing he was receiving professional guidance. Maybe this therapist knew what she was talking about, or maybe I wasn't ready to have that discussion yet either. It was easier to go on as we were because we were all still living in the same house, Scott and I weren't fighting, and I traveled most of the time.

Our multi-state road trip was eventful, to say the least. All was going well until I found myself being driven to a drug dealer's house in LA because Tony had run out of his *medicine*. He offered to drop me off at the place we were staying in downtown LA, but I thought I'd feel safer just sitting in the car while he ran in to get the goods. Upon pulling up to the salmon-colored rundown apartment in a pretty bad part of LA, I decided that maybe the safest route was going in with him. It was pretty late at night. God knows what would happen if I was noticed sitting in the car by myself.

Long story short, this straight and narrow forty-year-old mom from Flagstaff went into high octane small talk mode the minute John, the drug dealer, opened the door to his second-floor apartment.

"So, John, how long have you been here in LA?" I started. "Was it hard to move from the East Coast? Does your dog try to bite a lot, or is it just me? Dogs normally like me."

I surveyed the small living room, which was barren except for a desk and a cot. I kept going. I couldn't help myself.

"Clever use of this cot as a couch, I'd say! I know it's hard to furnish a home, isn't it?"

John, the tall, slender, twenty-year-old dealer, mumbled thank you while he was packing up Tony's order.

Just then, a young mysterious woman in her twenties with medi-um-length blonde hair walked through the living room/drug room without saying a word as she glided by a guy passed out on the hard floor. He looked to be in his twenties, too.

"Is he okay?" I asked. "He's okay, right? The mom in me wants to put a pillow under his head."

As I became more uncomfortable, the pitch of my voice climbed higher and higher. By the time I asked if the dude on the floor was alive, I was likely only heard by the dog that was trying to bite me. This whole scenario went on for a bit because, of course, they had to test out the batch together.

"Do you want some?" John asked.

"No, I'm good! None for me, thanks!" I chirped, almost gleefully.

A cloud of pot smoke engulfed me and the guy who was passed out on the floor.

My mind started listing what I knew I had and what might be in my future.

Inhaler. Check.

Scary "Mod Mom Busted in LA" headline flashing in my head. Check.

"Oh, you make edibles, too, John? Where did you learn to cook?" I continued.

I was an unstoppable question machine that night. Just plop me down in the middle of a drug deal in LA, and I will make everyone feel valued and comfortable. Accommodating and smoothing was my coping mechanism, especially when I felt powerless.

And I sure felt powerless that night. Tony apologized like crazy for putting me in that situation. I told him it wasn't a big deal—that it wasn't my norm but I was happy he had access to meds in LA. And I really meant that. I wanted him to be okay, but I wasn't comfortable enough to tell him that being mixed up in all of that actually scared the shit out of me.

Later that night, Tony succumbed to a horrible flare-up of self-di-agnosed Crohn's disease. He had his *medicine*, but he was doubled over in pain, sweating like crazy, and I couldn't do anything to help him. He said the marijuana would help ease the pain, which made me grateful for our stopover in drug land.

Unfortunately, I didn't catch how he helped me convince myself that the whole situation had been a good thing. Even worse, this would be a pattern that would continue to chip away at my good sense.

CHAPTER 10

Playing It Small

Tony seemed like a new man the next day, after the flare-up was over. We headed off to our next stop: Santa Barbara. After staying with friends there, we made our way to Las Vegas for Vegas Market—the West's version of High Point Furniture Market.

It was our first market together as a couple and we made the most of it. We had friends to see and folks to talk to about Tony's line of furniture, as well as the future of Mod Mom. It was starting to look like the possible manufacturing deal for Mod Mom, with a company in Greensboro, was not going to manifest. It was too expensive for them to produce my designs.

At that point, talk shifted from kids' furniture to upholstered goods because Tony and I were together. I was in love with an internationally known furniture designer who just so happened to have a binder full of rendered designs, and he was excited to share them with the management team at the North Carolina factory.

A quick phone call confirmed that the team was indeed interested in Tony's line.

"Baby, do you know what this means? We can build a Mod empire!" Tony came at me with one of his famous hugs.

"I'm so excited that they want to build your designs!" I held tight to him. "You've worked so hard for such a long time. It's about time you get a break like this!"

We were both beaming with excitement over possibly making this happen together, and I felt good about my contact opening doors for the production of his line.

"Baby, we should call the line something related to Mod Mom," he suggested as he stepped back to look me in the eye. "After all, we're in this together—this is all for our future and our dream. We can use the revenue from the upholstery line to help rebuild Mod Mom!"

"That would be amazing!" I replied with a huge grin on my face.

We were on our way to creating the life we wanted. Together.

I had full faith in the plan we'd concocted. It didn't matter if Mod Mom took a backseat now that the Stanley deal was dead. What mattered was that we could grow his upholstery line and then turn our attention to Mod Mom, as he'd suggested.

We strolled the Las Vegas Market hand-in-hand, proud as could be that we'd risked everything to be together. We met with many of Tony's industry friends and ex-colleagues who told us over and over again how happy they were for us. Some even said they were envious of what we had, and they'd never seen Tony this happy. It echoed what I'd heard from Tony's family members back East. The high I felt was at the stratosphere level, which helped me bury the pesky gut-punch feelings from before.

But that would soon change. Enter gut-punch number five.

After strolling the market, we sat down to check our emails.

After a few minutes, Tony put his phone in his pocket and turned to me. "Baby, do you know you look at guys with a lot of eye contact?"

"Wait, what?" I replied with genuine interest in what he meant. "What do you mean?"

"I know you're an open, loving person, but when you walk down the hall here, you look every man in the eye who walks past, and you smile."

Moments earlier, I was floating on air, and now I was flat on the floor. Again.

"Really?" I questioned. "I'm not trying to get anyone's attention. I was taught to look people in their eyes when I walk past them. But maybe I'm doing something from a subconscious place."

I'd successfully blocked memories of being raped as a child, so it was easy to believe that I wasn't aware of this behavior either. Maybe he was right, but no one had ever told me.

"I've noticed it for a while," he said. "I just wanted you to know because I don't think you realize how it comes across."

Beads of sweat started forming on my forehead as the gut-punch feeling settled into my stomach. My body was heating up and I wasn't sure what to do to calm myself. I could barely catch my breath.

"I really didn't know I did that...I wonder if it's a subconscious thing I do to protect myself."

Clearly, it was bothering him, and I had no idea I was coming across this way. Nothing was intentional—my eye contact wasn't the least bit premeditated. He knew I considered him the love of my life. Why did he notice and why did it matter when we were this unbreakable, twin-flame, soulmate duo?

For the rest of the Market, I became hyper-aware of where my eyes were directed. Changing my behavior became my first priority. I certainly didn't want to give off an unintentional vibe that bothered Tony. Besides, I wanted to talk about our future and our plans, not my eye contact. I did everything in my power to make it a non-issue. Keeping my head down was the easiest way for me to fix the whole situation. The sooner I fixed it, the sooner we'd go back to bliss. And I desperately wanted bliss.

* * *

I was lucky my friends—new and old—were rallying around me in spite of any hidden worries about my sudden life shift. Many knew the financial struggles Scott and I had weathered. They were naturally supportive but also curious about the guy plastering his love for me all over social media. My parents were apprehensive but soon showed their support after being impressed with Tony after talking with him on the phone. After all, he was well-spoken, charming, and funny—the perfect combination. Even more than that was the fact that my happiness was their priority, always. They made themselves open to accepting him into their lives.

In June, we made the trek to my parent's house in Ohio. Tony picked me up at the Detroit airport so we could spend some alone time together before the big introduction. Luckily, my parents liked him, and my beloved cousin, Andy, felt a good connection to him, too. She loved seeing me happy after hearing him gush about finding his true soulmate in me. I, of course, didn't tell either of them about the eye-contact incident, the warning Jason gave, or the other not-so-pleasant moments in our otherwise perfect relationship.

Tony and I spent the week on a love high, enjoying every minute before we had to part again. We took care of some Mod Mom work and lined up production with my Amish manufacturer in Ohio— the one that stepped aside when I inked the now-defunct deal with Stanley. Every bit of the trip felt like forward movement on all fronts, just the way I liked it.

We arranged to meet with Andy, her husband, and their son for lunch on our way to the airport.

I thought lunch went well, but I noticed Tony was on his phone quite a bit. It wasn't really anything new. He was famous for taking photos of his food and posting them on social media.

We said our goodbyes and headed toward the airport, an hour away. I ended up missing my flight due to traffic, so I called Andy.

"You're not going to believe this...we didn't make it to the airport on time."

"Oh no! Where are you now?" Andy asked.

"I'm still in Cincinnati, but I'm wondering if Tony and I could maybe crash at your house tonight?"

"Oh Kiers, I'm so sorry but we've been renovating our guest room and don't have space for you right now."

I was a little bit surprised but understood.

Later on, I found out that Andy's husband got very bad vibes from Tony—to the point that he didn't want him in the house. Her husband is a very open, loving person. It was shocking to Andy that he didn't like Tony. At the same time, she recognized that he is normally a very good judge of character.

I ended up booking a different flight out of Pittsburgh. We made the best of it with an Italian dinner and a cheap hotel stay near the airport.

As we said our goodbyes at the airport, I could barely see through my tears. Each time, it was getting harder and harder to let go. Pain filled every space in my body, thinking about how long it might be before we were in each other's arms again. Knowing that I was going back to my kids helped, but at the same time, I knew I was going back to a solitary, lonely existence without him.

* * *

Back home, Scott and I continued to follow the advice of his personal therapist, which meant we had one more month to go before telling the kids about our splitting up. I knew I was the only one wanting to talk openly with them because I was ready to move on, and I'd always had a very open relationship with both of my kids. Noah and Grace seemed okay knowing that we were sleeping in separate rooms while we figured some things out about our marriage. Unlike other couples in similar positions, Scott and I still rarely argued. When we did have a disagreement, we tried to keep it out of earshot. The kids saw us caring for one another the way you do when you've been best friends for eighteen years.

I made good use of my time in Flagstaff, diving back into helping grieving parents. One day during my daily walk in the forest, a small boy came to me. He told me his name was Evan and that his mom had written to me asking that if her son ever came through to me, would I pass on his messages. I was relieved to be connecting in this way, again. It seemed to happen more when I was home than it did when I was on the road with Tony.

Evan showed me a vision of a child's room with pink blinds, then showed me the symbol for love. He wanted me to pass on that he loved and missed his mom, and he wanted me to describe the vision of the room.

After returning home, I sat down on the couch with my laptop to craft the email to Evan's mom. I did exactly as he asked. She wrote back an hour or so after I hit *send* saying thank you and telling me she didn't recognize the room I described. I was shocked but chalked it up to the fact that I'm not 100 percent correct all of the time. No one is.

Months later, she wrote to me again to tell me that she was pregnant and they found out she was having a girl. She connected the dots—the pink window blinds were a symbol for a baby girl on the way. As I read her note, I sat stunned at how all of this works. How sometimes messages are glimpses of the future that our brains can't comprehend at the time. It was comforting to know that I could still count on my intuition, even when it seemed nonsensical.

When I wasn't channeling or taking care of the kids, Tony and I planned our schedule, which consisted of a lot of travel in September, October, and December. We were desperate to get back to one another as well as build the foundation for his new upholstery line—the ticket to our Flagstaff homestead and financial freedom.

In September of 2014, we celebrated my birthday in Las Vegas at the ABC Kids Expo, a trade show for manufacturers and buyers of kids' products. I arrived first, happily getting settled into the hotel before Tony's plane even took off. With a few hours to kill, I planned to head to the pool for a little sunshine after I checked in with him back on the East Coast.

"Hi baby, I'm here! I just got to the hotel. When do you start boarding?"

"I'm so glad you made it safely, beautiful! I board in about half an hour."

"Awesome! Since you don't get in till late tonight, I'm gonna relax a bit at the pool," I replied.

And then came the deafening silence.

What felt like three minutes of nothing ticked by until he finally spoke up. As expected, my body began to feel like it was on fire.

"Baby, I thought you would wait for me?"

Did he just get mad at me for wanting to go to the pool?

"Well, you don't get in until dark, and frankly, sitting in the sun with a magazine sounds pretty damn good right now."

"Baby, would you like it if I went to the pool without you, and women were hitting on me?" he kept on.

Oh my God. Here we were again. My body froze while my eyes darted back and forth trying to figure out how to navigate this unforeseen yet familiar minefield. I could feel the panic rising in me, even heating up my physical body.

Ever since I could remember when I was traveling on business, I would sit at the pool alone, and it was never a problem for anyone. I enjoyed having time to myself in the sun. In my old life, Scott even encouraged it. While I still wanted to go to the pool, my desire to squash the fight that was brewing trumped my longing to lounge in the desert heat.

I was unknowingly getting really good at back peddling. Almost immediately I responded in a way that I knew would put out the fire I was feeling. "Oh yeah, I see what you mean, hon...on second thought, I'll just walk over to the mall for a bit because I need a few things, anyway. And we can hit the pool together while you're here."

"Thanks, baby," he said. "Of course, I'm not telling you what to do, I was just surprised you would put yourself in that situation alone without me."

I resisted the urge to stick up for myself, thinking it was far more important to keep the peace than explain what I'd always done as an independent woman. I was becoming used to this routine and even recognized the pattern, but I had my sights set on the road ahead and getting that high from being together. I didn't recognize it as a high at the time; I just missed him.

"Well, I can't wait to see you!" I said. "Can you get on that fucking plane already? Sheesh!" We both laughed.

After our call, I walked to the mall in 110-degree heat. I was on a mission to find stuff I didn't really need but had convinced myself I did because I chose not to go to the pool. Once he arrived, for the most part, we had a great trip together. Laughing, loving, and talking with my industry friends at the show was the norm. That is, until my birthday on the 9th.

A mutual friend of ours sent a silly happy birthday photo over text. As a joke, he had his girlfriend take a photo where he mooned us with my cardboard cutout next to him. The only reason he sent it was because of an earlier joke when my friend rescued my Stanley Furniture life-size cardboard cutout from the company's headquarters after I lost my job. Some pervy stranger might have snagged it and hid it in his basement. I knew the intention of sending the photo was to make us laugh, and boy, did I laugh. I didn't think beyond the joke.

Chuckling, I showed the photo to Tony, doing some work on his laptop in our cheap hotel room. His reaction was the antithesis of mine. He was livid that our friends had sent such a photo and that I laughed at it. I spent most of the night trying to hold it together after being shamed for thinking it was funny. In his mind, my friend's boyfriend was clearly sexualizing me.

Here we were...*again*. God, why couldn't I rewind the clock and not laugh? Or turn the ringer off on my phone? Or do anything but do what I did? I stopped my emotional tailspin and went deep into myself, trying to figure out why I laughed. It brought up memories of the time when I was a four-year-old child playing the role of topless cheerleader for the high school football booster club fundraiser. Back in the 70s, that type of thing was considered a silly stunt. I knew my parents didn't think of it as anything but innocent fun. My dad was the football coach, which led the booster club to ask him if I would be willing to run across the court to him shirtless, wearing a cheerleading skirt and pompoms. No top. They innocently figured it was no big deal for me, of course, not realizing that it was during the same time period I was being abused by my uncle. As a shy kid, I ran to my dad's arms while the gym erupted in laughter.

Throughout the night, I replayed that cheerleading event in my head, and I offered it up as proof of why I laughed at the photo our friend had sent hours earlier. It was starting to make sense. In my mind, that had to be it—I was conditioned to laugh at my own objectification. He held me for hours while I soaked his t-shirt with my tears. Unbeknownst to him, I was only partly sobbing about the memory of what I endured as a child. The truth is, my unraveling intensified because, yet again, we were fighting over something I did that was completely innocent in nature. And yet again, I immediately felt shamed by him for it. Where were the good old days when we just had fun, laughing, joking, and loving together without judgment? I desperately wanted those days back.

I started to feel as if I couldn't do anything right, and that I was always disappointing him. Thankfully, in the wee hours of the morning, he quickly reverted back to praising and adoring me and telling me how it hurt him to see me so upset. He just wanted the best for me, and for both of us to get some sleep. Exhausted, we drifted off for a few hours before he needed me to take him to the airport.

He seemed much lighter as we both gathered our things before checking out of the hotel. Once again, we said sad goodbyes at the airport and told each other how much we loved one another. He reiterated that I was his then, now, and forever love. And then he disappeared down the security line.

It was time for me to drive back to Flagstaff. On my three-hour drive home, I did everything I could to block the memory of my horrible birthday. Deep in my heart, I took comfort in knowing I'd soon be back in the house Scott and I still shared with our kids. Despite the situation, they all still loved me and knew who I was as a person. Not one of them would think I was out of line if I laughed at a silly photo that tied into a running joke. Despite that, I still felt shame. I started to question myself. *What if he was right and I was blind to it? Had I been doing it "wrong" all this time?*

Only a few short weeks passed before I was back in the air again, flying to Tony for a road trip down to our first High Point Market since we met there in April. Thank God for that new credit card of mine. Traveling was becoming expensive, even when I was determined to pick the cheapest red-eye flights. The "Mod Squad," as he coined us, was back on the road to Market, and we had big plans.

We met with the manufacturer who would soon be producing Tony's line of furniture and ironed out the details. They would foot the bill for producing samples for Market in April, and they'd give us a section of their showroom where we could debut his new upholstery line. It was an absolute dream come true for both of us. Even Mod Mom got in on the action. We planned to produce a few upholstered toy storage bins and introduce the new additions, as well as original Mod Mom designs alongside the new upholstery line designs. We were over the moon and had a magical Market revisiting old spots where we first fell in love. Of course, I remained conscious of my eye-contact while at the trade show and seemingly did a good job because we didn't have any misunderstandings. In fact, we cherished that we still had a few more days to spend together after we left High Point.

The sounds of the 70s band, Foghat, played over the fierce wind whipping through our open car windows. Half-burned cigarettes rested between our fingers as we made our way back up north. Out of the blue, our friend, Lori, called to chat a little more about Market. All was well until she questioned something that Tony said. When we hung up, his whole demeanor changed. He said he couldn't believe she treated him the way she did on the phone.

"Maybe she said that because she's looking at it from another angle," I said, believing I was talking to someone who could rationally look within the way I thought he could.

I could feel that he thought I was on her side.

"Why would you say that, Kiersten?"

I knew when he used my full first name, we were not in good territory.

"I'm not giving her a pass," I said in my most convincing voice. "I was just trying to say that I know I tend to look at things through my own lens of experiences, so maybe that's what she was doing and didn't realize she was hurting you."

The rest of the ride fell quiet, with mounting tension replacing laughter and ease. I nervously opened a new pack of cigarettes as we both sat in silence. It was much later than we wanted to be driving and we were both exhausted. We agreed we should find a motel on the side of the highway and book a room for the night. He was still quiet and brooding as we unlocked the door to the motel room.

Two quick tugs on his boots, and he was ready for bed wearing exactly what he'd worn all day. He laid down on top of the worn-out bed cover, no less.

There was no *goodnight*.

There was no *I love you*.

I was left sitting on the bed next to him, feeling the familiar sting in my throat that preceded tears I didn't want him to see.

Because of the time difference, I knew I could call the kids back home. I composed myself while quietly settling into crossed legs position on the bathroom floor and called Noah. He had no idea just how wonderful it was to hear his voice. Tears started streaming down my face, but he couldn't tell by my chipper voice and manner.

After we hung up, I continued sitting on the bathroom floor, staring up at the corner that was not only covered in mold but had a few spiders. The one-star shithole was the personification of the last two hours of our night.

I finally pulled myself up off the floor and climbed into bed. Sleep was my escape, just like it was his. I just knew things would be better in the morning, and he'd see my true intention. That's how it worked in my world.

Darkness still painted the room as I woke to the sound of boots being jammed onto feet and the forceful rustling of a jacket. I realized he was about to walk out the door, and it wasn't just to smoke a cigarette. He wanted me to wake up and hear him banging around. He opened the door to leave as "Baby?" quietly came out of my mouth. My question was met with a slamming door.

I immediately felt pain in my chest. I clutched my hands, thinking the motion would help me catch my breath. Full panic-attack mode had set in and there was no stopping it for roughly ten minutes. Over and over again in my mind, I thought about how I had no idea what had just happened or where he was going, and he sure as hell wasn't going to tell me.

After what felt like hours, he finally came back. In truth, it had only been about thirty minutes. Though visibly calmer, his razor-sharp edge was still evident. He told me that he had a dream about his dad and one of his sisters, whom he didn't get along with, and in his dream, I went to both of them behind his back. I told him how sorry I was that he had that dream and sympathized with how awful that must have felt. I begged him to just lay down again. He did, and I made sure to not say anything that could be misconstrued in any way. I told him I loved him before we both fell back asleep.

He didn't respond.

In my past, things always looked brighter when the sun came up—tempers calmed and love took over. But that morning, in the crappy motel off of I-70, I sensed the same amount of tension as the night before. I pleaded with him to talk more about his dream, and he admitted that he thought I didn't have his back. He wanted me to be a pit bull for him like he was for me. I did my best to let him know that I had his back and that I loved him. I would never go behind his back to his sister or father. From stories he told of abuse he endured as a child, I instinctively wanted to protect him from all of that…and from nightmares about me going all turncoat.

After loading up the car, we slid into our respective seats. He grabbed my hand and told me he loved me. Slowly but surely, the heaviness started to lift as we made our way closer to his hometown. We had one more night to simply enjoy each other without any misunderstandings—this time in a clean, modern hotel I booked by the airport—and I was hell-bent on making sure that happened.

I went down my mental checklist:

- Watch eye contact. Check.
- Don't laugh at anything slightly inappropriate or objectifying. Check.
- Make sure my ringer is on silent in case Scott calls or texts about the kids. In Tony's mind, I was either talking to Scott too much or too little. It was best to avoid a notification. Check.
- Focus all of my attention on Tony. Check.

It worked. Everything went back to normal, and I was on cloud nine again. We tearfully hugged at the airport and counted the days until we'd be in each other's arms again.

He went straight to bed for a nap while my plane carried me across the country. It was about halfway through the flight when I decided to reach out to Scott to ask about the kids. We hadn't talked much as of late, so he was surprised to get my Facebook message.

We chatted about the kids for a bit, and he even remarked that it had been a while since I'd really talked with him like this. Prior to this conversation, we mostly shot texts back and forth about pick-ups and drop-offs. At the end of the back and forth, he said, "See you later, alligator."

"After a while, crocodile," I replied.

It felt natural and easy as it had always been with Scott. I took a deep breath and exhaled, finally able to let out all of the tension I'd been holding onto over the past two days. I finally drifted off to sleep for the remainder of the flight.

CHAPTER 11

Eggshells

The day Scott was dreading was finally here. It was October—time to tell the kids we were separating. We talked about how we would break the news to them and, of course, I was in the point position. I felt nervous but also ready to fully come clean with them. Hiding the reality was agonizing because I'd always been very open with both kids about everything in life.

We all gathered in the living room for a family meeting. It became quite apparent that I would be the one leading the talk. And frankly, it should have been my responsibility because I was the one demanding that we split. I sat on the edge of one of the chairs, while the kids sunk into the couch with Scott.

Scott remained quiet with his head down while I explained that we had grown apart as a couple, but we would always be a family. Nothing was changing in that department. Both kids continued to check on Scott, knowing that clearly, I was the one leading the charge. Noah looked visibly sad and shook his head, while Grace got up five minutes into the talk. Standing in the middle of the living room with clenched fists, she screamed at the top of her lungs and ran crying to her room. My heart was on the floor, but I knew to expect this type of response. We comforted both of them as best as we could, but I remember knowing that my words forever changed them and the way they viewed marriage.

After it was over, I felt equal amounts of relief and shame. The only bright spot was that finally, I could be honest with the kids even if they didn't like that their dad and I were splitting up.

Not long after our family meeting, Tony and his wife told their kids about their split. The boxes had been checked on both sides now. It wouldn't be long before we revealed to our children that Tony and I were more than business partners.

Before we knew it, we were back on the road for the fabric trade show in High Point called Showtime. It was his favorite trade show because of his love for coverings.

We booked a room in a lovely new hotel in Greensboro and planned out our days. Tony's Crohn's disease started acting up, on top of what seemed to be a respiratory illness. I offered to go to the hotel store to ask about medicine before we drove over to Showtime. I left my phone on my side table and headed to buy medicine for my love.

He was grateful and talked about how he wasn't used to someone taking care of him that way. I puffed with pride at being that person for him. I'd always been a caretaker—it felt natural for me to help any way I could. That's just what you do for loved ones.

Showtime was exciting and hectic. We were picking out fabrics for his new upholstery line, making sure we were using our time well. Dinner at our favorite Italian joint near the hotel made for a beautiful way to end the day.

Back at the hotel, we slipped into bed taking full advantage of the fact that he was feeling better. We laid together, reveling in the warmth of our bare skin against each other.

"Baby?" he asked. "Has that guy named Josh on Facebook ever written to you privately?"

I knew who he was talking about because that guy, who I really didn't know but had accepted as a follower on Facebook after *Shark Tank* aired, was "liking" a lot of photos and pictures.

I immediately started to panic. And out of nowhere, I saw Jason's face in my mind's eye for a split second before I was pulled back into the hell that was my reality at that moment. Josh had indeed recently written to me, but the last time I told Tony about my other two real-life friends who wrote me directly, my world went pear-shaped, and I was made to feel like I'd done something wrong.

Not only had this guy Josh written to me, but he'd sent a doctored photo of me to my inbox, and then played it off like he was drunk when he did it. I deleted the photo immediately because if Tony saw it, there'd be a misunderstanding. I didn't know this random fan, nor did I talk to him, but he did write to me. Laying there at that moment, I had a choice to make. Based on past history of feeling like no matter how I responded to other men, I wasn't right, I chose to lie.

"No, he hasn't written privately."

Silence hung in the air for a few seconds until he said, "Baby, I saw it," while still holding me in a tight embrace.

My blood pressure shot up, and I started to sweat.

"What do you mean?" I asked.

"I looked at your phone when you went to get medicine this morning. My intuition told me to look and it was right. Also, I saw a message from Scott, too. Um, what was 'see you later, alligator' all about?"

I started having a full-on panic attack, worse than I'd ever had. I hadn't done anything wrong other than not telling the truth, but I feared he would be mad at me for not bringing it to his attention before he asked. Lying to avoid more fighting about stuff that didn't matter to me had, ironically, thrown me into probably an even tenser spot.

Sitting up in bed, my body started shaking uncontrollably, and tears spilled from my eyes. "I'm sorry, baby, he has written to me, but

I just deleted the message because I was afraid it would be another situation like before. I lied to you and I'm sorry, but there's nothing to fear. I just didn't want any misunderstanding."

Unfortunately, that did nothing to assuage his worry or anger. He sat straight up in bed and hurled question after question at me about Scott and Josh, the interrogation escalating to the point that I was in a full-on, can't-catch-my-breath panic episode. He demanded a moment-by-moment account, refusing to accept that I was telling him the truth because he assumed there was more I wasn't telling him.

It was now one o'clock in the morning, two hours into the back and forth, and the thought finally occurred to me that he'd known this information all day yet chose to question me while we were lying naked in bed. I couldn't have felt more vulnerable.

I didn't have a password on my phone because I never felt I had anything to hide—then or in my previous life. I felt ashamed for lying and sad that I couldn't make him understand that there was nothing to fear or worry about.

I knew none of this felt right or safe but I didn't know how to make him feel that I was 100 percent invested in us. In addition to not being able to breathe, I started to feel a buzzing, pulsating sensation on my right hip that I couldn't explain. It only subsided when things calmed down.

The night felt long and painful. I was worn out in the morning, having not slept much at all, but I did have the strength to make a mental note before we checked out of the hotel to add one more thing to my "keep the peace" list: get rid of or block any guy I suspected could write to me out of the blue. Oh, and if I wrote to Scott about the kids, delete the message in case it could be misconstrued. My mode was hyperdrive fix-and-smooth—it was the only way.

I was relieved when he dropped me off at the airport to fly home. Even though he was visibly sad to see me go, I could still feel the undercurrent of rage from the night before. It was the first time I was happy to be going home for a bit. We both needed time to process what happened, and I needed to get to a place where I could block it all from my mind and focus on the good that we had.

Jason and Carrie did not make that an easy task. Both came in spirit while I was on the plane-ride home telling me to trust my intuition. They came in as quickly as they left. I hadn't heard from Carrie in a long time, so I was shocked to see her sweet face staring back at me. I took their message to mean I needed to tap into my intuition more, something I wasn't doing as regularly anymore. The kids and the cases felt separate from my life with Tony, so I compartmentalized their message that way, too.

Despite my big fat lie to Tony, life went back to normal in Flagstaff with a few episodes here and there whenever I did something to make him question me. Like a private detective on a case, he watched my every move from back East. I was doing everything I could to avoid the cycle, including pulling back from friends and family he wasn't keen on and policing my social media accounts and my time spent online. This was a point of contention on occasion because he was clearly watching when I jumped online and keeping track. If he posted something and I didn't "like" or comment right away, he would later say I didn't care about him the way he cared about me.

I started to notice that holidays and important events always turned volatile. Valentine's Day. Christmas. My birthday. Our Market debut. We even talked about it, but I, of course, still dutifully took the blame for all of it. Some of the blame, I believed was truly mine, and the rest was part of the routine. It's what I had to do to get back to the good, Facebook-able times I could post that convinced everyone that I really knew what I was doing after taking a giant sledgehammer to the life I'd known for eighteen years.

When I did something to tick him off, I could pretty much predict that a meme would show up on his social media, and the Tony fan club of mostly older women would clap and cheer him on while I sat alone in Flagstaff wondering how to make it all better. I hoped above all hope that it was only getting worse because we were apart. That had to be the reason we were having so many misunderstandings.

As luck would have it, July brought an opportunity to be together for an entire month. Tony was hired to work as head of production design for a low-budget film being shot in Florida, and he wanted me to help. Without hesitation, I said yes. I wouldn't see my kids for four weeks, and that would be super hard, but this meant we could be in the same place for a bit. In my mind, it was a sure-fire way to ensure nothing could be misinterpreted, and we could return to the honeymoon days I was craving. All I had to do was wait a few more weeks until I was scheduled to join Tony on the movie set.

* * *

Since meeting Tony, mediumship and nonprofit work were slowly taking more of a back seat to preparing for the new upholstery line and my new jet-setting life. And honestly, I wasn't feeling all that down about it, desperately needing the escape from that heavy responsibility. On the other hand, I knew that the channeling work I did was meaningful and appreciated, so I didn't divorce myself from it entirely. I wasn't sitting down weekly to channel anymore, but I still kept in touch with the intuitive friends I'd met along the journey.

One such medium named Necole Stephens came into my world because of the Little Light Project and blew me away with her compassion, skill, and strength. Like Yvette, she was a grieving parent. She also happened to be an experienced medium who had been channeling since she was very young, long before her son Zachary passed away in his sleep when he was eleven years old. At the time, she focused on helping grieving parents understand that their sons and daughters were still with them in spirit. I knew instantly that she was gifted and her intent was pure.

We clicked because we didn't fit the stereotypical psychic medium profile. We also connected because I could see her heart and she could see mine. There were no agendas at play, just two caring people who wanted the best for one another.

I quickly learned that I wouldn't have had the strength to get through the month-long movie shoot without her guidance and support. She became a lifeline for me—a true angel.

While in Florida on the film project, I did something that would haunt me for years. I left the door unlocked in a dorm room where we were staying alongside the rest of the production crew. One night early on, Tony went out with one of the other guys on the crew to buy marijuana, and I stayed back to watch a movie on my laptop. I plunked down on one of the two twin mattresses we placed on the floor to make a king mattress we could share. The bunk beds just weren't going to cut it. Content to be where I was, I rented the movie *Safe Haven* and settled in for a few hours of entertainment watching a story about how a spirit helped save a domestic abuse survivor.

An hour or so into the movie, Tony came back to our sterile beige room to find that I hadn't locked the door. Immediately, I could feel a shift in the energy of the room. I couldn't put my finger on it, but I knew it wasn't a good feeling. I waited for a sign to confirm that the air being sucked out of the room was indeed due to my failure to bolt the lock, but he wasn't giving me real clues even though my intuition knew. To fill the space, I talked nervously about how much I loved the movie I was watching before he announced he was heading to take a shower down the hall. His declaration doubled as a test to see if I'd lock the door. Of course, I didn't realize I was being tested—and about to fail, again.

I was looking forward to his return yet still on edge because I knew in my gut that shit was about to hit the fan. Minutes later, the door opened, and my world changed. It became very apparent that he was not happy with me in that moment. Over the next few minutes, much of what he said was escalating in both condescension and volume.

"How can you be so stupid as to not lock the *fucking door*?" he yelled as the door closed behind him.

I looked up at him, stunned. "Baby, I didn't think I was in danger. I feel safe around everyone on this set, and the main outside door is locked," I explained, hoping he would immediately get it.

"You *want* other men to come in, don't you?" he screamed, pacing around the room. "I can't figure out why you would be so stupid as to not lock the fucking door if you're not inviting other men in!"

"No, no, that's not it at all!" I continued to plead, tears streaming down my face as my voice trailed off. "I simply felt safe, is all."

He stared at me in silent rage as the room started to spin. I began internalizing the shame that was being heaped on me, but I didn't identify it as shame at that moment. My go-to mode had always been to look inward. All my life, I took constructive criticism well. Sitting back and really thinking about what I'd done wasn't foreign to me. While he continued to stare silently at me, I frantically searched my mind for answers, hoping I could connect the dots and see for myself just how idiotic I'd been to not lock the door.

Now, should I have locked the door? Sure, it made sense. I didn't know the rest of the crew all that well but I figured if anyone did harm to another on the floor, there would be hell to pay by the producers. Did I think chancing it by leaving the door unlocked would cause a massive fight? No way. I never for a minute thought I was committing the crime of the century.

Like a hawk swooping down to snatch its prey, Tony grabbed his pillow and blanket on our shared bed and climbed atop one of the remaining bunk beds in the 4-person room that still had its mattress. It was clear that the king bed we'd made on the floor would be a bed for one that night as my punishment.

The angry silent treatment was the worst. Not only did I hear and feel it, but I swallowed it whole. I literally absorbed every bit of what he was putting out. Sleep did not come quickly, nor did it bring calm the next morning. I stared up at the ceiling wishing I could turn back time...again.

Like the time in the bug-infested motel a few months earlier, Tony left the room in a huge huff when the sun came up. He didn't look at me nor did he seem the least bit rational when he grabbed his jacket and boots and slammed the door. I laid there stunned until I couldn't take it anymore—I had to get out of that room, too. I knew he'd be gone for a while. I set out on an early morning walk without any idea where I was going. We weren't due at the set for a few hours.

Despite my attempts to hold back tears, more fell. With each step, I felt more confused—more lost and isolated than I'd ever felt in my life. As I made my way to the main drag in search of solace in a cup of coffee, I saw his car on the street perpendicular to the one on which I was walking. My heart stopped, and I wiped the tears from my eyes in a fruitless attempt to pull myself together.

For a split second, I thought maybe he would just keep driving as his car came barreling toward me. When he was close enough, he jerked the wheel, stopping the car abruptly to the left of me. He got out and bee-lined it to where I stood frozen in fear.

In a full-on rage, he screamed, "You are sick, Kiersten! You want men to come in and that's why you left the door open. I can't do this anymore!"

I could barely see through my tears. Heat once again rushed up and down my body, and I felt the familiar buzzing sensation on my right hip. I knew I wasn't "sick," and I was cut to the core hearing those words come out of his mouth. How could he think that I purposefully left the door unlocked because I wanted other men to come in? I was a rape survivor, for crying out loud!

My protective instincts finally kicked in. I screamed back, "I'm not sick!" My courage surprised me because I finally stopped trying to make him understand. I was so angry and hurt that I yelled again, "I am *not* sick! Why would you say that to me?"

He didn't answer; he just stared back at me with the blackest of eyes. He wasn't done punishing me, and I knew it. Before he could call me sick again, I mustered the courage to speak.

"I'm gonna look for flights home," I said with less ferocity in my voice.

Part of me thought I could snap him out of this tirade, and the other part knew I didn't have that kind of power. Yet I stood still holding my breath, waiting for him to respond.

He didn't. He got back in his car and squealed the tires, watching me get farther away in his rearview mirror. I had no choice but to walk back to the dorm room and start looking for flights home—and a way to get to the airport, which was over an hour away.

I miraculously made it back to the dorm and passed a few crew members getting their day started. I'm sure I looked as if I hadn't slept—and I really hadn't—but I had to keep it together to do the job I was there to do. I remember the makeup artist saw me on her way to the main meeting room and asked if I was okay. I told her I would be, that Tony and I had gotten in a fight. She hugged me and, for the first time in twelve hours, I felt a smidgeon of comfort.

Back in the room, I opened my laptop and found a few flights leaving that evening. But I still wanted to believe it was all just a bad dream. I pulled myself together as best I could and went to work, doing everything possible to fade into the background.

A few hours later, after passing me on set without so much as a glance, Tony walked up to me and said in a very matter-of-fact tone that he didn't want me to leave. A sense of relief washed over me because I could see he was calming down. It was totally foreign for me to feel both relief and fear at the same time, but at that moment, that's exactly what happened.

I immediately went into eggshell mode. I was mindful not only of my words but of my eye contact, my moves, the door, its lock, and everything in between. I wanted desperately for all of the tension to just go away. I knew the only way to make that happen was to tell him I'd given the situation a lot of thought and it was totally my fault. I was the idiot who didn't lock the door and he was right to be angry. It took a little while, but slowly, he was becoming the man I knew before he went all Hyde on me.

Six hours later, when he was telling me how much he loved me, how hard it was to see me upset, holding my hand, hugging me, and telling me he was proud of the work I was doing, I unconsciously blocked the intensity of the nearly twenty-four hours of hell from my mind.

In my old life, this same scenario would have been handled like this, if at all: "Kiers, hey, I know you probably feel pretty safe in this building, but maybe we should lock the door just in case." I would have responded, "You know, you're right. Better to be safe. I'll do that from now on." End of story.

But it wasn't the end of the story. While I was relieved to be "back to normal," I was still on edge. The weekend finally came, which meant we had a little time off. We decided to stay at a different location. It was an apartment in the city that the producers owned. I was happy to leave the scene of the crime where I'd witnessed the other side of Tony—the side I hoped I'd never see again, but deep down feared I would.

* * *

The first day of our respite in the city apartment was calm. I almost let my guard down. That is until more comments were made about me not locking the door back at the dorm. Thankfully, there were moments of peace when he napped. During one of his first naps, I took the opportunity to go for a walk, locking the door behind me.

The moment I stepped out into the fresh air, I couldn't contain my emotion. The waterworks started once again. Inside, I felt completely cried out but my eyes proved me wrong. I finally had the freedom to let everything I'd stuffed down come to the surface.

And boy, did it. I immediately thought of my friend Necole Stephens and sent her a text to see if she could talk. Thank God for angels like Necole—she called me immediately. I explained what had happened in the dorm room.

"Kiers, I'm so sorry, but this isn't normal behavior. What he's doing is controlling, abusive, and irrational. Being a rational person, you can't rationalize with an irrational person."

"I can't figure out why it's happening—why he feels so threatened."

"It's not something to figure out, it's something I'm afraid you need to leave," she replied.

Her words stung. "Where did the man go that I fell in love with?"

"I'm sorry, Kiers. He showed you what he knew you wanted to see when he met you, leaving out the controlling and manipulative part of his personality. They never show that side until you've fallen for them, hook, line and sinker. Abusive relationships never start out with abuse."

"I know you're right—I'm just having such a hard time coming to grips with it. I never thought he was abusive...but then I forgot to lock the door and all hell broke loose."

"Kiers, it's not your fault. You did nothing wrong. He completely flipped out on you."

"Now listen, you're smarter than he is," she continued. "For now, if you feel you can't leave because of the project or you're just not ready, think of it like a game you're being forced to play. And you can play the game better than he can, now that you know what's at stake and who he really is."

"Okay...you're right—it's a game," I said, trying to convince myself that I could get in this headspace. "I have to think of it that way until I figure out if I'm going to hop on a flight home. I can't let his insecurity get to me. I'll put on a happy, yet apologetic face, and keep going."

"He's going to continue to cycle in and out of the anger," Necole said. "The hardest times will come when he's being that man you fell in love with, and you're going to want to let your guard down, but you have to remember that it's a cycle. The good *always* leads to another moment of pain where he finds something wrong with something you've said or done."

She continued, "Your Grandma Pennington is here in spirit, telling me that you have to get out of this. Maybe not leave this film project if you don't feel it's right, but you will eventually need to leave this relationship. He's not going to change."

Grandma's message sent shivers up and down my spine. I felt grateful to hear from her through Necole, but deep down, I resisted what she was encouraging me to do. I didn't want to believe that Tony was abusive, even though I had just lived through a horrific episode. Some call that cognitive dissonance.

If anyone knew about getting out of an abusive relationship with an abusive man, it was my grandmother. My grandfather was handsome, charming, and incredibly cruel at times, and he remained that way his entire life. As an orphan and childhood abuse survivor, not to mention a prisoner of war during WWII, healing from the trauma in his life became a mountain he refused to climb. He sought validation and power as a womanizer who verbally abused his wife. Grandma, who was beautiful, smart, and independent, divorced him when I was still living at home with my parents, but I know she endured years of hell and disappointment before she put her foot down once and for all.

After hearing what both Necole and Grandma were saying, pain and confusion overtook me, almost bringing me to my knees. It was not what I wanted to hear but I knew deep down it was spot on. I gathered the strength to stand and continued putting one foot in front of the other while I kept Necole on the phone like a lifeline. She must have known to keep reassuring me that I had what it took to play the game as long as I needed. She knew exactly what was happening to me, and she did everything she could to give me strength.

We hung up the phone as I approached a bench overlooking a serene waterway.

I sat for a moment contemplating my next move. Ten minutes went by before I dialed a number I knew by heart.

"Hi Kiers," he answered. "Are you okay?"

It was as if Scott instinctively knew that I wasn't calling to talk about the kids. The strength I'd gained on the phone with Necole was now a salty, streaming flood of tears.

I choked out, "No, I don't think that I am."

"Oh Kiers, I'm sorry...I'm here for you. What's going on? Are you safe? Where is he?"

I started telling him what transpired back at the dorm and could literally feel his anger and pain through the phone.

"Kiers, I love you. We all love you. Just come home."

All I could do was cry. How could this man whom I'd hurt deeply still feel this way? I was grateful but scared; I'd never felt this out of control emotionally. It was like I was split in two. I still loved the Tony I met at Market—the one who oozed love and compassion. And yet I couldn't deny that I still felt deep love for Scott, my best friend and love for all of those years.

"I love you, too, and thank you."

And I did love him. It was a love that wasn't easily undone no matter what we'd been through. It was an eighteen-years-and-two-kids kind of love. I couldn't explain that, so I just let it be. I had mixed emotions because I felt a lot of guilt for calling him, but also a great deal of comfort knowing that he somehow knew what was happening and why I was going through it. He knew much more than I knew, that's for sure. I was starting to calm down just hearing his voice. Knowing that he didn't hate me was a gift, but I still didn't know what to do with it.

"I don't know what I'm going to do," I said. "I would feel awful leaving the project in a lurch, but I also don't want to go through what I did at the dorm again. I think I'll just wait to see how I feel."

"I understand, Kiers. Just let me know if you need my credit card to book a ticket. We all love you and want you to be okay. It breaks my heart that he's treating you this way."

I didn't want to get off the phone, but I was running out of time. If Tony texted and I didn't answer right away, there would be hell to pay. I also wanted to call my parents before I got back to the apartment. I needed to share the truth with them. I needed to hear that they, too, knew that what I was enduring was far from okay.

I started walking slowly back toward the apartment where Tony was napping, knowing I needed to make my way back soon.

As I put one foot in front of the other, my dad comforted me and said, "Kiers, this just isn't right or normal. I don't like this at all. How can we help you?"

This was a big deal because, like me, my dad also believed Tony to be a good guy who would never hurt me this way. He had all of us fooled. Well, most of us. Dad offered to help however he could, but again I told them I was going to wait to see how I felt. After my short call with my dad, I called one more person who was near and dear to my heart.

"Andy, it's Kiers," I said. "I don't have a lot of time but I wanted to talk with you about something that just happened with Tony."

Our conversation was similar to the ones I had with my dad and Scott, but there was more fear in her voice. Though Andy is my dad's cousin and therefore my second cousin, we grew super close over the years because our kids were the same age. Not only is she a strong, beautiful, loving person, she's also a very intuitive person whose faith in God is at the center of everything she does. We've been through some big stuff together, and I even helped her move a dark energy out of her house a few years back. She really liked Tony when she met him but was finally confessing that things weren't adding up for her.

"Kiers, I've had this horrible feeling about him lately, but I couldn't put my finger on it. I'm truly scared for you."

I was silent for a bit but then shared that I, too, was scared and confused. It was paralyzing. I didn't want to leave, but parts of me didn't want to stay, either. I didn't even know how to explain it because the old me would never put up with any of this, yet there I stood in the middle of the sidewalk actually feeling like a big part of me still wanted to stay.

Andy told me she would pray for me and asked me to send texts periodically so she would know I was okay. I quickly hung up and deleted all call records before I stepped through the apartment door. My plan was in place: I was going to play the game until it was time to leave or until I knew I couldn't stay any longer.

As I climbed the last stair into the living room—where I'd left him sleeping on the couch—I took a deep breath, anticipating that I was about to face the inquisition. Much to my surprise, Tony was still out cold with a baseball cap covering his face. I exhaled, knowing it wouldn't be long before I'd be forced to put on my game face.

CHAPTER 12

Spiraling

Aside from a few comments here and there about the things I wasn't doing correctly, Florida days turned to nights without much fuss. I knew my role was to resist getting defensive. Intuitively, I felt hyper-aware of things great and small. Most importantly, I made sure the door was locked at all times.

During that trip, I kept quiet about the work I was doing with a detective named Charles out of Chicago. I knew how Tony felt about Mark, the NYPD detective we sat down with that day in the New York diner, and I wasn't about to cause more tension by telling him about the work I was doing with a different detective. Charles and I silently passed email messages about an abduction/murder that had come to my attention. I knew enough to turn my notifications off on my phone—I didn't need more questions. Thinking back, working on the murder case with Charles grounded me and made me feel valued, which was something I wasn't getting from Tony.

Unlike Mark, Charles wasn't a big believer in intuition—although he had come around over the years. I reached out to him years earlier about a case, and much to my surprise, he wrote back. From that day on, we talked quite a bit about case work and life as a medium. At first, he seemed baffled by my abilities, yet I think what I shared was comforting, too. We met in person once while I was alone in Chicago on business—it was a day I'll never forget. We talked over lunch about all of the crazy and horrific stuff we'd both seen. He'd viewed it in full color as a Chicago police detective, while I viewed it in my mind's eye. Still, we had this in common. I was and will forever be grateful for his guidance on how to process all of the darkness. During my time in Florida, I quietly replied to Charles' messages when Tony wasn't looking. It made me sad to know that I couldn't share that part of my life with him anymore without it causing a huge blow-up.

One Saturday afternoon, we were hanging out in the production company's apartment when I got a silent text from Necole. She was checking on me, as usual. For the first time in days, I stretched out on the brown leather sofa for a much-needed respite and replied to Necole while Tony worked on movie props at the kitchen table.

Necole and I had a bit of a code going because of suspicions that he might be monitoring my phone. Naturally, there was no mention of what we'd talked about prior. Of course, she was right. He was always aware on some level of what was happening on my phone.

"Baby, who are you texting?" he asked. "Is it the kids? How are they?"

"No, it's Necole, my friend from New Hampshire who's part of the Little Light Project."

"Oh," he replied with a bit of hesitation in his voice as he continued constructing a prop.

I felt the tension immediately but decided to concentrate on what Necole was writing, rather than give more energy to Tony's paranoia. She was telling me about how she channeled flashes of scenes related to me, but she knew they were not present day.

She was seeing me as a child with a man she knew was not my father. She went on to describe this man in a room I didn't recognize, but I immediately knew she was channeling one of the instances of sexual abuse I endured as a five-year-old. She was seeing my rape.

Silent tears made their way down my cheeks as saw the scene in my mind. Parts of what she described had already been shown to me when I first started having flashbacks of abuse, but my mind blocked the scene in its entirety.

I didn't feel comfortable sharing with Tony what I was secretly learning. I didn't know if I felt strong enough to handle his possible Jekyll and Hyde response. Instead, I knew I needed to share what Necole had just channeled with my sister, Traci. She had an uncanny ability to recall details from our childhood that had vanished from my brain and knew the room in Necole's vision down to the bedspread and wall color. She told me she was blown away; there was literally no way Necole could have known any of it. Traci wasn't surprised that I couldn't remember that level of detail because, for years, I had a hard time remembering much of anything from our childhood. I could relate to photos in our family album but I couldn't remember them first person. I'd always just accepted my memory deficiency as part of my DNA: I was 5'10", had hazel eyes, and had a spotty memory.

Up until that moment, I was an open book with Tony about my healing journey from childhood sexual abuse. In fact, in the beginning of our relationship, we both bared our souls and shared intimate details of our lives prior to meeting one another. At the time, it felt safe and natural. Now I felt guarded on every level.

Beyond that, I still didn't want to fully believe we were past the point of no return. I clung desperately to the memories of our early times and the words he still spoke almost daily. He made sure I knew that I was the love of his life, and that he'd come into our relationship 100 percent authentic and honest. He frequently pointed out how our seven-year age difference made it difficult for me to see the wisdom of his actions and reactions due to my lack of self-awareness. As someone who had blocked memories of abuse and was always very self-reflective, I was still willing to believe that what we were going through was my fault...despite knowing the way I was being treated was not the least bit okay.

I managed to get through the entire month of the film shoot without leaving. It wasn't easy because, as one would guess, the good times were quickly followed by dark times. Questioning. Shaming. Controlling behavior. Toward the end of filming, Tony went off the rails right before we were supposed to be on set, screaming and yelling about God knows what. I knew I had to reel him back in or the producers wouldn't be able to film on time. I did it, making him look like the professional he was not. I played the game at times, while other times, I involuntarily disassociated from the trauma.

But one thing remained constant: I always looked for the man I fell in love with. I looked so hard, I was choked up again when we said our goodbyes at the airport. I didn't want him to leave. It made no rational sense, but I didn't care. I wanted the high I felt when things were good between us. My new autopilot was enduring whatever was thrown my way in order to get back to bliss. I wasn't proud, but I didn't know how to change course. Unbeknownst to me, he'd become my heroin.

We had made it a year and three months as a couple, and despite everything, I wasn't about to quit. Even if it went against my intuition and logic. I mean, shouldn't I be flattered that he cared so much? I rationalized everything because I couldn't explain why I was still hanging on.

The next year brought more highs and lows. When I took time for myself, whether it was visiting my dear friend Lorraine in California or taking advantage of a massage my kids bought for me for Mother's Day, he said I was being selfish and wasn't working nearly as hard as he was.

When I didn't tell him that a male furniture buyer sent me a LinkedIn request, there was hell to pay. When I was asked to speak at a women's leadership group gathering in Sedona, and I excitedly talked about a seventy-year-old audience member who connected with me because I reminded him of his late wife, I was shamed for not talking about other parts of my experience first. He was starting to criticize the way I dressed, and claimed that I wasn't dressing up for him but for others. Every time it happened, I fought back, only to eventually apologize and own whatever he threw at me. It was the only way to make it stop.

I started noticing my panic attacks becoming more frequent—I couldn't catch my breath. When I was being shamed, I would shake involuntarily. My whole body trembled, and I couldn't make it stop. And I couldn't wrap my brain around why my body was reacting violently, or why I still felt the buzzing sensation on my right side when he wasn't happy with me. I chalked my weird body signals up to overall stress, not intuition.

Still, I fought for us. I convinced myself that distance was our issue. As usual, the minute we reunited at various airports, we clung to each other for dear life. We didn't want to be apart. Living afar meant there was too much to worry about and too much for him to misunderstand. I was determined to fix that. I set my sights on securing a place outside of the rental home Scott and I still shared with the kids.

It was time to put a plan in place. Tony suggested I move part-time to North Carolina, near the factory that made his new furniture line. After all, he'd decided it was the place he needed to be full-time for the time being. While I wanted to spend time with him, I also knew I didn't want to leave my kids for weeks at a time. Based on what we discussed when we met, it never occurred to me that we would be setting up a home outside of Flagstaff.

Unlike the many times I ignored my intuition while I was with Tony, this particular time I trusted it wholeheartedly. I knew that if I agreed to live there for two weeks out of the month, and money was tight, I'd have a hard time getting back to Flagstaff. I knew that keeping a roof over his ex and their kids took priority, and I had even helped make that happen monetarily a time or two. As much as I wanted to please Tony, the quiet knowing inside made damn sure I would never make that move. Jason even came in spirit saying—*Do not leave Flagstaff. Stay right where you are, near your family.*

If we were going to give living together a shot, I'd have to make it happen on my own. That way, he could travel back and forth from his kids and to North Carolina when needed, but we'd still be anchored in Flagstaff.

I wasn't making enough money to support myself with Mod Mom, so I applied for a job at the local university. When I told him my plan, he supported me, saying how much my kids needed me near them. In the same breath, he also told me he was bummed that I was applying for jobs in town and that I wasn't seriously considering moving part-time to North Carolina. With all the mixed signals, I couldn't tell how he really felt.

Against all odds, I was hired into a public relations role in February of 2016. After signing the contract, I started looking for apartments. I was relieved and excited at the prospect of finally getting my own place in Flagstaff. I knew that I would be the one to secure a very small apartment with one bedroom because I was the one who wanted out of my marriage. By this time, Scott was dating other people and he, too, knew it was time for us to part ways. Living under one roof as a separated couple was extremely hard especially when he could see that, despite everything, I was hell-bent on clinging to Tony.

One of the apartment complexes in town offered a move-in special for university employees, which meant I didn't have to put down a lot of money for a one-bedroom loft that still had plenty of room for my kids to come stay. I was set to move in April 1, 2016. Scott was also informed that the house we were renting together was about to be sold. This meant that he, too, found a place with three bedrooms for himself and the kids. Our arrangement was that we wouldn't have an arrangement. We agreed to let Noah and Grace go back and forth as they pleased from our respective homes. Now, all I had to do was get through the heartache of moving day, and come to grips with the realization that I wouldn't be with my kids 24/7.

* * *

Weeks went by as I prepped the apartment, adding photos of Tony and his kids in anticipation of his arrival in late April. I felt more excitement than I had in months. I was finally on my own, and while I wasn't living 100 percent of the time with my kids, I saw them quite a bit. I now had what the parenting experts call "quality time" with them. I also enjoyed not feeling everything everyone was feeling all of the time—Scott included—when we lived under one roof.

I was the queen of my domain and I loved it. I even noticed the TV turned on and off on its own a few times now that I was on my own. It was as if the kids in spirit were saying welcome home.

As for Tony, we were hopeful that when he came to stay with me much of what we struggled with would fade away. We'd spent a full two years living thousands of miles away. Proximity had to be the answer. While I knew being away from his kids was going to be hard for him, and I didn't want that for him either, he told me from day one that this was what he wanted and expected. As we grew the new upholstery line, he planned to travel to his hometown to see his kids every three weeks or so, and he would talk to them on Skype nightly.

The first few days after he arrived in Flagstaff were bliss— we finally found a way for us to live together. It felt like forward movement. He was thanking me profusely for getting a job at the university and funding this life of ours. Living together seemed to be the answer to my prayers. He was back to being the man I fell in love with in High Point.

With excitement, I finally introduced him to Grace. She laughed at his jokes and talked easily with him as he showed her photos of his kids. I could tell she liked him but still had a look on her face that told him she was watching him closely. Noah was very open and giving with him, too. They both loved seeing their mama smile.

Homelife continued to be bliss even though the fuzzy memories of the ups and downs of our relationship were in the back of my mind. The only thing I knew for sure was that we needed to give this a shot, or we'd regret not knowing whether giving it our all would have made the difference. We were in make-it-or-break-it mode. It was going so well that I didn't want to breathe too much and jinx it.

That is, until May 18, 2016. A few short weeks after he settled into the apartment, he spiraled. There were small signs, but I was really getting good at ignoring those and doing everything I could to mitigate the chances of a fight. To make matters worse, he was smoking nonstop and refusing to smoke outside. I never thought I'd be living in a cloud of cigarette and pot smoke. When I brought it up, I was chastised for renting a place that didn't allow smoking on balconies. Sadly, I didn't know that was the case until the move-in day. As I was signing paperwork, I thought seriously about walking away but decided to press on. Everything was already planned. I figured he could just walk outside and smoke, but I was mistaken.

The morning of May 18, while I was at work, I received texts about how he felt I didn't have his back. He even let me have it for hanging pictures of his kids prior to his move in. Apparently, he wanted to hang them. The relentless barrage of texts felt like bullets cutting through my chest.

He'd been secretly keeping an invisible tally of all the ways he felt I wasn't a pit bull for him. Despite the fact that I got a job, moved out of Scott's house, and secured an apartment for Tony and me, I still wasn't "all in," according to him. Small things became big things. I noticed, again, that if I talked too much to Scott about shuttling kids, he had a problem with it. Conversely, if I avoided Scott, he would say we weren't doing a good job of co-parenting.

Nothing I did was good enough, but I felt trapped and paralyzed at the same time. Trapped, because of the choice I made to partner with him both professionally and personally and paralyzed because I still couldn't figure out why I was having such a hard time walking away.

I knew we needed to talk face-to-face. I told my colleague and friend, Theresa, that I was heading home for lunch to talk with him. On my drive home, I could feel the heat rising in me. It continued until I parked my car in a spot outside of our apartment building. I sat for a moment, gathering strength I knew I'd need. Just before I pulled the door handle to get out of the car, I saw a vision of a group of children in my mind. When I focused on them, I could see Carrie, Jason, Nate, and the many other kids I'd connected with over the years. They were staring at me with light behind them.

Then suddenly, I heard a small voice say, "Kiersten, you know what you have to do."

I recognized Carrie's voice as though it were my own daughter's. Upon hearing her message and seeing all of their beautiful faces, I felt both comfort and dread. Because of the hot and cold nature of my relationship with Tony, my head really didn't know what I was supposed to do. My heart was a different story—it wanted Tony to go back to the way things were just a day before.

I slowly opened the door to our apartment and walked upstairs to find him with his eyes closed, lying in bed with a plastic cup filled with water and used cigarette butts on the nightstand. The room reeked of Marlboro Red. I gently and nervously put my hand on his arm, and he opened his eyes. They were cold and black.

Chills ran up and down my body, but this time, they weren't comforting. They were terrifying. I told him how sorry I was for upsetting him, and that I came home to talk. He didn't look at me lovingly; he just sat up in bed and lit another cigarette. At this point, I was so incredibly stressed that I, too, reached for a cigarette.

He gave me a look that said *get the hell out of my way*. And I did. I moved to the other side of the bed and sat down on the mattress. All I could do was watch him smoke and pace the room while I endured an avalanche of vitriol. I watched my hope for a rational talk go out the window with the smoke. As he grew louder and louder, I realized he saved all his anger up for this day. And I was all out of armor.

In addition to whatever I'd done that triggered him, he started yelling that I was cheating on him with Scott. Again, I found myself in a puddle of tears, pleading with him to calm down and lower his voice. No matter how many times I explained that I was not cheating on him, he persisted. He ranted and yelled endlessly for thirty minutes while I sat silent, naively hoping he would see my side. Just then, we heard a knock on the door.

He went downstairs to answer, thinking it might be the manager of the apartment complex. I stayed upstairs wiping tears from my eyes, stupidly getting rid of cups of cigarette evidence—as if they couldn't smell the smoke that hung in the air.

"Kiersten, can you come down here, please?" Tony yelled up the stairs. "There are three police officers here."

I was frozen in fear and disbelief. My God, someone called the cops. Oh. My. God. With my heart racing, I did my best to pull myself together. After straightening my skirt and wiping tears from my face with my hands, I slowly walked downstairs. If I'd gone any faster, my legs would have buckled underneath me. I was barely hanging onto the little stability and grace I had left.

Three police officers explained to both of us that a call had been made because someone in the building heard yelling. One of the officers made a point to say he could hear Tony yelling at me from down the other end of the hall as they approached my door.

The lead officer asked to speak with Tony while the other two asked if they could talk with me in the hall. I obliged, of course. First, they asked if I was okay. Rattled and tearful, I choked out an unconvincing yes.

"Ma'am, has he ever been physically abusive with you?"

"No, not at all. He's just so stressed right now and upset because he's away from his kids."

I couldn't believe what was coming out of my mouth. I was *defending* him—making excuses for his horrific behavior. The detectives were kind and comforting, and one offered me a pamphlet about abusive relationships. Because they were there on a domestic disturbance call, one of us had to leave the apartment immediately or one of us was going to jail.

"Oh, yes...I'll leave," I said in a small, defeated voice. "I need to get back to work at the university. No one needs to go to jail. This was all just a heated argument, and he's really under a lot of emotional stress right now."

There I was again—defending him.

They warned us that if they received another call, one of us was absolutely going to jail. I later found out that the maintenance man had called the cops, fearing that Tony might get physically violent. He told them he heard a man yelling at a crying woman. According to the police report I obtained later, Tony was acting very agitated and defiant, telling the police officer that it was a private matter.

Walking to the elevator with all three officers, I felt embarrassed and scared, wondering if management would evict us. How would I explain that to my kids? To Scott? The officers watched me walk to my car and drive away. What they didn't see was the complete breakdown that happened in the front seat on my way back to my office. I could barely catch my breath. I sat in the university parking lot, trying to put myself back together before I opened the car door to go in.

As I walked back into the main office, I kept my head down and beelined it for Theresa's office.

Her face said it all—she could see the anguish on my face.

"Oh, no...Kiers, what happened?" she asked as I made my way into her office. "Are you okay? Please sit and tell me."

"Theresa...I can't believe this is my life."

She handed me a tissue as I went on to tell her what happened and how the cops showed up at my door.

Her mouth fell open. "Kiers, my heart breaks for you...I'm sorry you went through that." She put her hands on my knees as I sat blubbering in one of her office chairs. "I know how hard this is for you, and I'm really worried."

I will never forget her compassion that day. She's a true angel on earth—one of the best people I know. Theresa supported me when I told her I separated from my husband and was making a new life with Tony. She even came over to the apartment to meet him. He knew that she was becoming a dear, dear friend of mine. Naturally, he was on his best behavior that night as he dished out homemade meatballs and sauce.

The day the cops knocked on my door, she was there with her invisible wings, comforting me.

"I think I'm in shock," I choked out. "Never in a million years did I ever think I would be involved in a domestic disturbance call. Nothing like this has ever happened before. Ever. Scott and I rarely argued, let alone to the point that someone would call the police. How is this my life?"

My entire body started trembling uncontrollably. I stood, knowing I needed to let her get back to work, and I needed to figure out a way to calm myself. She stood to hug me, telling me she was there for me—whatever I needed, day or night, she was there. The tears continued to flow as I opened the door to my office.

I must have sat in my chair, staring at the wall for hours. At least it felt like hours. I contemplated how we'd gotten where we were, and how somewhere along the way, I became someone I didn't recognize. I always stood up for myself but would eventually cave and apologize, taking all the blame for whatever was being thrown at me. It was the only way I could restore peace. I did it, but I didn't like doing it—nor did I think it was right. But it was becoming my way of being.

After a few hours, I sent Tony a text telling him I was sorry. He texted back saying he was sorry, too. I felt my body stabilizing. I was thankful I still had a few more hours to calm myself before it was time to head home.

Theresa checked on me before she left, making sure I knew she was just a phone call away. I felt grateful for her friendship and support. There was no way I was going to tell Scott what had happened that day. Theresa was my only lifeline.

As I turned my key and walked into our apartment around fifteen past five, I was greeted with silence even though I knew he was home. I slowly trekked up the stairs to the loft bedroom where he was sitting. I expected him to stand up, hug me, and tell me how sorry he was. Instead, he sat in his chair and asked, "What are we gonna do, Kiersten?"

He used my full name. Not *baby*. I immediately knew he was not in a good state of mind. He wasn't going to scoop me up and tell me that it would never happen again. He lit a cigarette in silence. I went into the connected bathroom, turned on the exhaust fan, and sat down on the floor while I fumbled through my purse looking for my cigarettes and lighter.

He could see me and I could see him, but we sat silently smoking, waiting for the other to speak. After about ten minutes, we started talking about how we trigger one another and how never in a million years did either one of us want to hurt the other. As the night went on, we inched closer. He even started joking about the whole incident, making comments about how crazy the unknown nark must have been to have called the cops. He apologized for getting loud, and I apologized for making him feel like I didn't have his back. Tony sobbed that he didn't want to lose me. He promised he would make an appointment with my therapist to address his anger issues.

I felt such hope in that moment. He was willing to go to therapy for me. He was finally admitting that our issues were not solely my responsibility. Therapy was something he'd done when he was with his ex but claimed it was all bullshit. All I knew was that he was really trying more than I'd seen him try before. And he was doing it for me—for us.

CHAPTER 13

Full Circle

Tony did go to therapy once, but all he reported to me was that my therapist supposedly thought I was in the wrong. I ate up the blame, as usual, and felt the hope drain from me. Despite it all, we still had good days in between fights, but true peace only came when he traveled back to see his kids or elsewhere for work. Those times gave me space to think about things outside of our relationship.

It had been almost three years since I discovered the truth about my childhood and the reason I couldn't remember a lot of my early years. During one of Tony's trips to the Northwest, I had started thinking about my uncle. I never really intended to address him head-on. I focused on my own healing first, but there came a time in 2016 when I felt guided to write to him.

As I sat down to pen the letter, I felt the familiar buzzing sensation on my right hip. It stood out to me because, unlike other times, I wasn't being yelled at by Tony. In fact, it had nothing to do with him. I'd come to expect the sensation when he let loose, but this was entirely different. Eventually, I stopped focusing on the buzzing and continued writing, thinking what was meant to come out on paper would spill out similarly to when I channeled spirit. And that's exactly what happened:

Uncle,

I'm writing to you because I want you to know that I know what you did to me when I was little. Maybe you thought I wouldn't remember. Maybe you didn't care either way.

I remember.

And here's what I know. You sexually abused me and raped me when I was just a tiny child. Multiple times. The pain and damage you caused—the subconscious scarring—is something I've had to work very hard to recover from over the past three years. You see, I didn't remember any of it until I was 40 years old.

There were clues along the road of life, like having to endure vaginal surgery at age 19 due to scar tissue from you raping me. And many, many other telltale signs over the years told the story of what I suffered because of your sickness, but the dots didn't connect until three years ago. Until it all started to come back to me because I was ready to face it and heal from it.

Here's something else I know: I'm not the only child you abused.

When I ask myself how in the world you could do what you did to a precious little child, there is a part of me that actually feels empathy for you because NO ONE does what you did (and may still be doing) unless it was done to you in some shape or form. Or was promoted within your family growing up. Cycle of abuse. But that cycle stops here. You weren't strong enough to break the chain. I am. I'm not letting the abuse break me.

I pray to God you aren't still abusing children and that maybe, just maybe, your past is catching up with you. Your conscience is screaming. And I hope you will not turn down the dial on the noise. That you will really think long and hard about how you conducted your life and the wake of pain you left behind you.

Know this: you may have violated my body but you did not break my spirit. I am proud of the strong, confident woman I am today and I'm proud to help other childhood sexual abuse survivors reclaim their lives.

I've thought about whether or not I truly forgive you and, right now, I can't honestly say I do. I'm sure I'll get there someday. But not now. What I do know right now is that everything I've endured in my life has made me stronger. I am the person I am today because I overcame what you did, and I'm grateful for who I am and the light I bring to this world.

Kiersten

I printed the letter, then found his address. It was surreal to think about mailing a letter to the man who affected me to the point that I repressed memories. As I slid the letter into the envelope, I recognized the enormity of the moment. I didn't feel choked up, but as I sealed the envelope, I noticed tears running down my cheeks. It was unlike anything I'd ever experienced. I normally get choked up at anything remotely heart-tugging, but I always feel the burn in my throat before the tears fall.

This time, it was as if Little Kiersten was the one who was crying. Maybe she was. After all, someone finally stood up for her.

I never received a response to my letter, although I can't say I was expecting one. Thanks to Google Analytics location settings, I know he's been reading my blog over the years. I doubt I'll ever hear from him before he dies because in doing so, he'd have to face the truth that he is a predator.

* * *

I felt as if I closed a chapter when I mailed the letter. It was time to focus on the here and now: my precious kiddos and helping Tony feel secure about us. I was lucky my kids still wanted to spend the night with me when Tony was in town. But then again, he was fun and really tried to engage with them. The only thing Tony didn't expect was just how intuitively perceptive both kids are. They could feel things weren't always rosy. Like everyone else, they saw that I was riddled with anxiety and losing weight.

For most of their lives, until 2014, they knew Scott and me to be a couple that rarely argued. They rode the choppy waves of our separation with such grace. Scott and I knew they wanted us both to be happy and that was the place from which they operated. Noah and Grace supported the new life we were living, except for one thing: they didn't like seeing their mom change personalities.

Until 2014, I was always the happy mom—the mom who was silly and loved to laugh. They also saw me tackle the business world, forge paths in male-dominated industries, and win an investment deal on national TV. Noah and Grace knew me to be a compassionate mom who helped others, and who would also stand up for herself, her kids, and her family.

After the initial honeymoon phase of my relationship with Tony, I became a woman who walked on eggshells. I also carried the guilt of still hanging onto a relationship that was volatile, but I didn't feel strong enough to pull away for good. Sadly, my kids could see all of that. I noticed little things—like Grace coming to my defense when she perceived Tony was slighting me, even jokingly.

I will never forget one particular night shortly after the cops came to our apartment. Tony and I were upstairs talking about something that related to the furniture business, and I was clearly not living up to his expectations. In his mind, I'd let him down by not supporting him enough. This type of control had been escalating. If I posted something about his line of furniture before getting approval, he'd get angry because even though I was supporting him, he wanted complete control over everything. In these situations, I tried desperately to make him see how much I was truly supporting him. This time, it led to an argument.

My kids—ages eighteen and fourteen at the time—were downstairs. They'd come to spend the night with us and heard him yelling at me. I was trying, to no avail, to explain my side. After enduring ten more minutes of insults, I pulled myself together and went downstairs.

Without words, Noah got up from the couch, walked over to me, and opened his arms. All six feet and one inch of him just stood there holding me—his mom who always held and protected *him*. I felt such guilt for not being the strong mom they grew up with, and for exposing them to this type of abuse. I didn't see it as abuse at the time but I still knew it wasn't right.

After we hugged, I sat down on the couch between them. Grace and I held hands, and we just sat there watching God-knows-what on TV. I apologized to them for having to hear what just happened upstairs.

I'll never forget the shame I felt on every level. I couldn't figure out why I couldn't break away and why every time he would get angry, I'd go into explanation mode. Didn't I know it was pointless by now? Apparently, I didn't. While I never wanted to expose them to what I was enduring, I know it helped them decide very quickly that he was not who he made himself out to be.

At that point in our relationship, we'd broken up and gotten back together seven times already. Later, I learned that it takes an average of seven times for survivors to leave an abusive relationship. In fact, two of those times I packed up ten boxes filled with his clothes and belongings and prepared to ship them to where he was staying at the time. I'd had enough, but something inside of me—and the fact that I'd put my company and career in his hands—led me back to him every time. It made no rational sense, and it certainly didn't feel right in my bones, but there I was letting him back into my heart and my life. And I was doing it right in front of my kids.

In July of 2016, we were still riding the rollercoaster of bliss and torture, but we weren't doing the torture part in front of Noah and

Grace. I was firm about that never happening again, and it was obviously in Tony's best interest too. He wanted them to like him, and he secretly blamed me for standing up to him that night when Noah and Grace saw the truth. I was still blaming myself for letting it happen.

July also brought hope that a new manufacturer for Tony's furniture would bring financial relief all around. His first one didn't deliver the product on time; therefore, Tony lost clients and got paid by just a few of the ones who remained.

I was barely making enough to keep the apartment and food in the house and was ignoring mounting credit card bills I'd racked up paying for travel, marketing, and bills associated with the relaunch of the upholstery line.

Thankfully, our new manufacturers supported us in big ways, even giving us a showroom to use free of charge at the upcoming Vegas Market. In addition, they hired Tony to work in their West Coast store and let him live in the store while he was an employee.

We worked hard to get ready for the show and were lucky that the press shared our announcements about new products and manufacturing. I was writing the press releases and designing marketing for the event. In spite of the excitement of this new chance, I was already nervous that we were heading down the same road as before—remembering how trade shows and stressful events brought fights that came out of nowhere.

This show was no exception. I was uber-aware of eye contact and made it a point to mostly only talk to women. I thought I was doing everything I could to mitigate the chance of a fight.

One morning, a twenty-something photographer came by to snap a photo of us. We obliged, posing with arms around each other. The very next morning, he walked our hall again and stopped outside of the showroom while he was waiting to photograph our neighbors. I looked up from my phone to see him standing there. I waved.

That was all it took. One quick wave and my world turned upside down. Tony let me know he was livid that I was encouraging and validating the photographer. His energy changed for the rest of the day—he was suddenly distant with me. That night, we spent five hours fighting about the wave. Towards the end of the fight, I laid down on the bed crying, trying to catch my breath as he droned on and on about how I didn't care for him like he did for me.

"Way to make him feel good, Kiersten!" he screamed, standing near the window with his hands on his hips.

In that moment, my entire body started shaking uncontrollably. It finally hit me that this level of shaming was all too familiar. I couldn't believe I had the strength and state of mind to even come to that revelation. On top of the shaking, the weird buzzing sensation on my right hip returned.

He was blaming me.

Shaming me for making the photographer feel good as if I was purposefully trying to reel him in.

Still shaking, I sat up on the bed, staring at him as he stood by the bathroom door.

"Don't you *ever* say anything like that to me again!" I shot back with strength I didn't think I had. "You're blaming and shaming me for something that is not my fault."

In that moment, I finally realized the parallel between what happened to me as a child and how much I unconsciously blamed myself for what my uncle did to me. Tony was unknowingly helping me understand that subconsciously, Little Kiersten still blamed herself, even my though my conscious mind knew it wasn't my fault.

I did nothing to deserve what my uncle did to me. And I did nothing to deserve five hours of verbal abuse because I waved at someone I'd met the day before. It was a turning point, a moment of true clarity.

CHAPTER 14

God Help Me

We'd managed to make it back to Flagstaff after Market without calling it quits, although tension was still high. He was equally as good at heaping praise as he was at slinging mud—eventually, I let my guard down. All I needed was one moment of the man I fell in love with, and he had me right where he wanted me: controlled. On the drive home from Vegas, he quietly reached over to take my hand in his. I exhaled, knowing we were finally back to the good part again. It was the hit I needed, and he was the drug.

At home, we talked about the show. It seemed we did well, based on feedback and interest his line received. All we had to do was wait for the orders to come in, but they never did. Not one. No matter what we tried, no matter how much great press we garnered or how many people raved about the line, there was always an issue with either sales or manufacturing.

Our business was mirroring our relationship. Even Necole once said, "Kiers, it's never going to work because there's too much darkness. You're the light that's moving it forward, but it will never be what you hope." She was right, and I knew it. Failure seemed to be the only option.

Not only was the business part of our life one big disappointment, but I was also becoming known as the girl who cried wolf. Each time we broke up, I'd share the news with my inner circle. By this time, everyone could see the pattern clearly, and many were worried I'd never be able to leave him for good.

My family and close friends all checked in on me weekly, if not daily. They listened with a mix of fear and compassion, but I was starting to feel like I needed to keep my mouth shut about the bad stuff. I wasn't used to doing that; I've always been open about the good and the bad in my life. The sheer fact that I started making everything sunshine and rainbows made my family and friends desperately worried about me. Even Andy got to the point where she picked up the phone to have a "come to Jesus" meeting with me.

"Kiers, I love you beyond words, and I'm scared to death for you at the same time. It's incredibly hard to watch you get pulled back in time and time again."

"I know, Andy," I said in a quiet, defeated voice. "I just keep clinging to the past—to the man I met. To the man you met and initially loved. It's so hard to explain because I don't even understand it myself."

"But what if he has never really been that guy?" she said. "What if it was all an act to hook you?"

Unbelievably, it was the first time I'd ever really considered that perspective. As a woman who takes people at their word, I had a hard time believing it was all a lie. The chills, the instant connection, and the undeniable attraction couldn't all be bullshit. The signs were all there. There's no way he was that good of an actor, I thought. The only other person I'd ever dealt with like that, to my knowledge, was my uncle. He was definitely not who he pretended to be.

Andy is a straight shooter—she flat-out told me that she couldn't be this close to me anymore. She couldn't stand to watch me get repeatedly pummeled emotionally. I understood why she wanted to distance herself from me.

Sadly, I also felt relief when she told me she was backing away. Tony had come to hate her because he knew she had his number. Any time I mentioned her or she texted me when he and I were together, I would pay the price. We hung up the phone knowing it would be a long time before we would speak again.

By the end of 2016, I was more isolated than I'd ever been in my life. Tony made it clear that he wasn't a fan of many of my nearest and dearest, for one reason or another. I found myself hiding the fact that I was meeting up with friends when he was on the road. While I was still occasionally helping friends from an intuitive and Reiki space, the lack of kids in spirit coming to me for help was even more pronounced.

Deep down, I knew it had a lot to do with my relationship with him, but I really didn't want to acknowledge that part. Thankfully, not everyone in spirit had abandoned me: Carrie, Jason, and Nate were chiming in more and more. Jason was coming through quite a bit as a guide, telling me that I knew the answer to the question I was asking. He also said he knew it was something I had to come to on my own, in my own time. Lastly, he warned me about the drug I was addicted to: Tony. As someone who knew the pain of childhood sexual abuse and subsequently battled life-long addiction, he knew the subject well. Nate came through, on the anniversary of his death, with a message for his mom, as well as a message for me:

Kiers, pull yourself up by the bootstraps! You can do this. He's not right for you and you know it.

Carrie, Jason, and Nate had never been wrong in their interpretation of events, or shy about sharing messages with me, but it was one thing to get guidance from spirit and something else to see with my own eyes that things were indeed not what I thought.

I was groomed to believe that I was at fault in our relationship, and it affected my whole being. Even when I secretly reached out to his ex-girlfriend—the one he tossed aside when he met me—and she started sharing bits and pieces of what happened during their five-year relationship, it took more than a minute for my brain to recognize the actual truth. I'd known her for a while in a work capacity, but it wasn't until I asked about his controlling behavior that we became super close.

We helped one another come to grips with what was really happening despite wanting to believe otherwise. She and I talked about how and why we were drawn to him, and how shocked we were that it seemed he was using the same script with both of us. My heart broke for her, knowing that she'd been strung along for five years.

The first time she shared what he'd written to her during their relationship, I about fell off my chair. It was as if I were reading a letter he'd written to me. And he flat out lied to her about what happened when we met in High Point. He told her he would never stop loving her because they were soulmates. I sat stunned reading every instance of "baby" and "I love you then, now, and forever."

Anger consumed me as the puzzle pieces started fitting together. She admitted that because they had more of a long-distance relationship, and didn't live together like he and I did, she didn't see the controlling, abusive side of him—but she was starting to see that we were both played.

As we grew closer, I couldn't help but notice our similarities. She was also a highly intuitive, caring, creative person who celebrated others. We were both spiritual, too. While chatting with her, I remembered that I was encouraged by Tony to keep my distance from her, even though she and I were connected in the design industry. She said that he told her I couldn't handle being friends with her, which was far from what I felt and said.

In a fuming rage, I wrote him. It was Christmas day, 2016.

I never imagined what he would do when I told him she and I had been talking, and that she'd shared letters from their relationship. He contacted her and threatened to post intimate photos of her on the internet. He was in retaliation mode—an evil state I would come to learn had no limits.

I couldn't believe that the man I fell in love with—who was outwardly championing women's causes, and crying when he thought of what I endured as a child—would be capable of threatening such a thing when faced with the truth. Not only did I hear directly from her that he threatened her, but he admitted it to me. Tony wanted her to fear what she did to him when she shared private messages with me but claimed that he was never going to post her photos. He just wanted her to think he was capable of it.

Had I been under hypnosis this whole time? And why did I still feel love for this man who called me sick and threatened an ex? I couldn't figure out why I would feel anything but disdain and disgust for him, which felt like the beginning of the fog lifting.

Two things happened after my heart-to-heart with his ex-girlfriend: one, I was connecting the dots more and more; two, I noticed the window of time between fights was getting shorter. Before, we'd go months without a big blow-up. But now that 2017 was almost here, we couldn't even go a few weeks. As always, I was at fault for every argument, even though I was still doing everything I could to keep the peace.

We broke up on Christmas Day, 2016, after I confronted him about what his ex-girlfriend sent me—only to get back together in January and break up again shortly after. It was a rollercoaster I knew I needed off of, but I couldn't completely let go before wanting the drug that was Tony again. And I felt like I'd created this shit storm, and therefore, had to endure it.

During school drop-offs and pick-ups, Scott was clearly tuned into what was happening. He could see me whittling away to nothing, and he knew I was chain-smoking when I wasn't around my kids. On occasion, I would tell him that things weren't good, but for the most part, I still acted like I had everything under control.

Sometime between January and March, Scott pulled me aside when I came to pick up the kids at his house and said something I'll never forget.

"Kiers, I don't want you to live like this," he started, with tears in his eyes. "I don't want this for you. I don't want it for our kids. He is pure evil and he's tearing you apart."

"I know," I replied quietly, trying to choke back tears. "But I've made my bed."

I really felt that way. Aside from not fully understanding why I was still drawn to Tony, I made the decision to partner financially with him. It served me right for jumping ship the way I did, even though I knew love wasn't supposed to hurt like this.

"No, Kiers, it doesn't mean you have to live this way because of the choice you made. It's killing you."

I knew he wasn't saying this as a maneuver to try to win me back. He made it clear that if he wasn't the one for me, then so be it, but he didn't want me with Tony. Anyone but him.

Later, Scott shared that around the same time he pleaded with me, Noah prophetically told him, "Don't worry, Dad. This is the last time she'll go back to him."

I had no idea Noah sensed this, nor did I think he would say something like that to Scott. Despite what we thought we were doing to shield them a bit, both kids knew our truth.

They knew there was real love between us in spite of the fact that Scott was dating other people. They also knew Tony was at the core of my downward spiral. Unfortunately, the fog that cleared when Tony and I broke up for the umpteenth time had rolled back in, as usual. I couldn't go more than a few days without the irrational longing for him.

I went back to holding out hope that maybe when things weren't stressful financially, Tony and I would finally stop arguing. I even made up excuses for him, for all of his bad behavior, including threatening his ex. It wasn't all bad, I kept telling myself. And then I'd conveniently block the hurtful memories.

The truth is, hope was at the core of everything I did, and the memories of the good times we shared in between the pain reinforced that irrational longing. The draw to him was still magnetic, even though I was finally absorbing that he wasn't just in a bad mood; he was emotionally abusive. It felt hopeless—like I couldn't get out, and I didn't necessarily want to get out, yet I knew I would die if I stayed in it.

Twenty-four hours later, Jason came in spirit to reinforce what Scott said:

Kiers, you don't want to live this life with him. It will be hell. He will destroy you.

I remembered what he said about my addiction to Tony. I knew he was right, but I still didn't understand why I was having such a hard time severing ties completely.

* * *

Days later, I got a phone call that would change my life. Scott told me that the house he and the kids were living in was being sold quickly, which meant he had less than thirty days to find a new place. He'd already been looking for places around town, and for one reason or another, nothing was a fit. Either the houses were outside of the school boundaries or outside of the budget.

"Hey, have you thought about Aspen Place?" I asked. "They don't require a big deposit."

"Um…well, I had thought of that, but they only have two-bedroom apartments and…well, there's the smoking elephant in the room, too."

"Oh, right. Yeah, I get it…about Tony…and being in the same complex. That could be super hard for you both." After a beat of silence, I added, "But seriously, I'm worried that you won't have a place to go, and I like the idea of making it easy for the kids to see both of us. They could run back and forth between our apartments at a moment's notice."

"I think you and I would be just fine coparenting in the same complex, but there's still the issue of only two bedrooms," he said. "Wait...what if I helped upgrade you to a two-bedroom and Grace could take that bedroom? Then Noah and I could live in another two-bedroom."

I thought my heart might burst from the thought of having my kids close by—and Grace actually living with me again!—but I tempered my response.

"I like this idea a lot, if you're okay with it. I know for sure you and I can handle living in the same complex. This would be really good for the kids. Are you sure you can afford to pay the difference between what I'm paying now and the new rate?"

"Yeah, I can. It actually saves me money. I'll give the office a call."

This plan made practical sense, plus I would get my babies under one roof. A mighty big roof, but still one roof. Scott and I were good at co-parenting—I knew that wouldn't be an issue. We would respect one another's space, and I would pray that we wouldn't run into each other much when Tony was in town.

Oh, God. Tony. *Shit*. As the heaviness hit me like a gut punch, I realized I had to tell him what was happening. When I didn't immediately share any kind of news, he would get angry. I knew he was in meetings in the Northwest which meant I couldn't call him. I simply spelled it out in a message that Scott and the kids were being moved out of their house in twenty-eight days, and there was a plan in motion that might involve Aspen Place.

The moment I hit send, panic flooded my body. Surely, he would see this for what it was—a way to make sure our kids had a roof over their heads. If the situation were reversed, I wouldn't hesitate to welcome his ex into our apartment complex. We could all be adults—and this would be good for the kids who had already been through hell.

Two hours went by and it finally hit me: I was getting punished with the silent treatment again. I immediately went outside and lit a cigarette...or three...and sent him another message.

Baby, did you get my message? I really want to talk to you.

A response flew in quickly this time.

Yes, I did, he wrote. *I can't believe that you're okay with moving your ex into our apartment complex. This says everything. And it's fucking bullshit!*

I held my breath as I read his response, then I promptly went into smoother mode. I tried calling, but he didn't answer. By this point, I was ready to throw up.

As usual, I thought more explanation might help. I typed out that they only had twenty-eight days to find a place and move, and this seemed like a great option for the kids. I emphasized that if the shoe was on the other foot, I would do whatever was needed for his ex and his kids to be safe and sound. I didn't think it was a big deal from a rational coparenting standpoint. It wasn't like that they would be moving right next door—the place was huge.

When he finally called me hours later, we fought for what felt like eons. He would hang up, and I would call back. I couldn't stop myself, which made me feel weak. Who keeps going back for more yelling and berating? I did.

"Kiersten, you're a thick fucking brick!" he screamed.

That was one of the doozies hurled at me in what felt like a never-ending barrage of insults. Halfway through his tirade, I started having a panic attack. And the familiar buzzing sensation on my right hip reappeared. I truly hadn't imagined it would be this bad. I thought he would view the situation from a place of caring about the welfare of my kids. I was very wrong.

We broke up for the millionth time that night after he told me that I didn't have his back and that he couldn't believe I didn't come to him in a panic the minute I found out that Scott needed to move. He claimed he would have done whatever he could to find a house for us and the kids. Rationally, I still couldn't understand how that was possible given he wasn't making enough to cover rent for his own kids.

After the panic attack subsided, I started packing up his things. I couldn't bear to see them anymore. With tears streaming down my face, I dumped all of his hanging clothes into multiple boxes.

Unlike times in the past when I packed up most of his things, this time, I took the boxes to FedEx and slapped labels on them bound where he was staying in the Northwest. I had helped him get a job with a friend of mine doing sales for an equipment company in the Pacific Northwest. Like every other time we'd broken up, he blocked me on all social media. It was one of his go-to punishments. He even did this to my parents, who loaned him $8,000 years earlier. His blocking knew no boundaries—everyone was at risk if they ticked him off.

Days went by and, like all the times before, Tony started sending me photos of us in happier times, saying how much he missed me. No matter how much I told myself not to engage, I felt the magnetic pull. I knew we weren't over. The truth was I missed him, too. Or rather, I missed the high I got from connecting with him—but the fog wouldn't let me see that just yet.

CHAPTER 15

Broken Wings

Packing the apartment brought a plethora of emotions to the surface. I was beyond excited to have my kids with me, yet I was leaving the first place Tony and I shared. It was hard to think that it would likely be the last. I took time to remember the moments we lay in bed playing favorite songs, watching old TV shows, joking, and laughing. The moments that led me to believe we were soulmates. That's the thing about abusive relationships—it's not all bad, or we wouldn't fight to save what we think we have.

Moving day came and I heard little from him. It was just as well—he would have asked how much heavy lifting Scott was doing with me. Scott knew I shipped Tony's things but he also knew I was still talking with him and that he was recently in town. Scott had gotten used to the cycle, just like everyone else. He knew he'd done all he could to help me see the light without coming across as pushy, suffocating, or controlling. He knew part of the reason we imploded in the first place was because I felt like I couldn't breathe—like I had no space of my own.

One morning during moving week, Yvette checked in to see how I was doing. She knew all of the ups and downs. Yvette was there for me during the time that she, too, was coming to grips with the childhood abuse she endured. Despite our age difference, we had a lot in common.

My other supporter chimed in with a message in spirit.

You do not need a man to be whole, Jason said. *Everything you need is inside of you.*

Initially, I was perplexed, because I'd always been independent and knew I didn't need a man to be whole. I wasn't raised to believe I needed a man. My parents taught me to be a fearlessly independent, brave, strong woman, and that's exactly who I saw myself as…except when Tony and I fought.

I knew I loved being on my own, but I felt like Jason was urging me to dive deeper than my surface-level reaction to what he was saying. As usual, he was coming in with a message I needed to hear during the calm before the storm.

* * *

Grace and I were having a blast decorating our new place, and Noah was running down to hang out whenever he wanted. My heart was full because prior to 2014, it never occurred to me that a time would come when I wouldn't be down the hall from my kids, feeling them near even when they were busy doing what kids do.

Years prior, I'd built my world around making sure I was with them—as much as a carpenter building furniture in our garage could be. Aside from the $1,500 bill, I had to pay to replace the carpets in my old apartment—thanks to Tony's refusal to smoke outside—I felt things were going my way.

I was busy putting the last of the dishes away when my phone rang. It was Tony. He hadn't been as communicative as of late, so I was excited to answer his call. "Hi baby, how are you?"

"Well, I was just told the company wants me back on the East Coast permanently."

"You mean they're moving you? But what about your West Coast territory?"

"They're restructuring. They want me to cover the East Coast because they're bringing in a West Coast distributor."

The gut-punch/slight relief combo that came with his news settled in my stomach. I wasn't sure what to say, so I carefully chose my words in a walk-on-eggshells kind of way.

"Oh…wow…how do you feel about that?" I asked. "I mean, it's great you'll be close to your kids. I'm thrilled for them. I know how much you've sacrificed to come West."

"Yes, I'll be close to my kids again, and I love that. But it's another strike against us, Kiers. Even if we knew we had a future, and could get past all of our issues, how are we supposed to do this living three thousand miles apart? It just seems hopeless. Now that Scott is living with you again, I have no choice but to wait until your lease runs out in a year to even consider if we have a shot or not. And now I'll be doing that from the other side of the country."

I was glad we weren't having this conversation in person so he couldn't see the sweat forming on my forehead.

"I get it, but Scott's not living with me. You know I have my own place with Grace. But I get what you mean, and I know you're angry, and now this is happening. When are you supposed to head back East?"

"In a few days."

He was rarely upfront about his plans, like the time he surprised me during the snowstorm. It wasn't shocking that I felt like I was being led to ask if he wanted to see me.

"Are you planning to come through Flagstaff on your way back?" I asked. "I'd love to see you, if you feel you can. And you know you have a place to stay to break up the trip."

"It's going to be hard, Kiersten," he shot back. "You're in your new apartment, and he's in the building."

"I'm the same old me…and I'm still on my own—with Grace, that is."

"I love you, Kiersten. I'll let you know the plan as I figure things out."

* * *

While my internal voice quietly nudged that Tony's move back East was a gift, my heart was trying to wrap its head around the idea. Even through all of the ups and downs—and our attempts to fix our relationship—I never thought he'd be forced back to the East Coast. Tony always said he wanted to live out West. In fact, he said he'd rather live with me and deliver pizzas than live full-time back home. Our plan from the beginning was to buy a nice place in Flagstaff with room enough for all four of our kids to stay at one time.

On the seventh of April 2017, he showed me he was committed to trying to make it work—despite the fact that I was still living in the complex with Scott four floors up. He arrived at my new apartment on his way back to the East Coast, then posted a photo on Instagram about how three years ago that very day, we kissed for the first time. All of his cyber-world friends were riding the rollercoaster with us; he gave them everything they needed to believe he was indeed the romantic, caring man they thought they knew.

Tony showed the world just how committed he was to me even though, just a few days prior, he'd been posting memes about how, in real relationships, lovers don't lie. It was an effective passive-aggressive slam because he was frequently bringing up the fact that I lied to him about that random guy who wrote to me on Facebook.

Tony received a plethora of support from his female social media friends, especially the posts that painted him as the victim. Shortly after those posts were published, he'd go right back to praising me and telling the world I was his one true love. It became predictable.

He flip-flopped between loving me and shaming me, and it all played out on Facebook and Instagram.

On the day of his arrival at my new apartment, he pulled up to the complex and I jumped into his car to give him my garage parking space. He told me his car was supposedly scheduled to be repossessed because he hadn't been able to pay the bill for a few months. Hiding it was the only answer. We pulled into the spot and hugged for what felt like days before we lugged his bag into the apartment.

I told Scott and the kids that while Tony was stopping by, we were not back together again because technically, we weren't. I couldn't blame Grace for being standoffish with Tony. She didn't trust him one bit. Thankfully, she was already scheduled to spend the night at a friend's house while he was in town.

Tony and I were both careful to focus on just being in the moment. We took a day to tour Sedona, enjoying the lightness of being that made us remember the old days. I made him laugh; we were genuinely enjoying our time together.

At one point during our cruise around Sedona, I burst into tears. Out of nowhere, I was hit with the realization that this would be the last time we'd do something like that. He comforted me, remaining even-keeled and compassionate, reaching for my hand to hold. Of course, that made me want more time with him. That is until he thought he saw Scott walking down the hall when we got back to the apartment complex. He didn't see him, but it provided a great springboard into one of the final tirades:

> *"You have never been truthful with me. You've lied and 'hedged' with Scott. I never lied to you or hedged with my ex or anyone. I left my home and my kids for you—for us. And now you've brought Scott closer. If you look deep into your soul to find the truth, someday you'll see what you've done to me. I've walked in my truth this whole time, but because you haven't, you're losing me...the only man who truly loves you and who truly knows you.*

Kiersten, I'll wait for you to grow up and see the truth, but I won't wait forever."

Crying, defeated, and feeling like a broken record, I replied, "You're right. Maybe you're right. I'll look deep into what I've done. I'm so sorry I've hurt you."

I slid right back into apology mode, all the fight in me gone. I was so sick of this cycle and questioned if I'd ever have the strength to stop it. Still, I was incredibly sad thinking of what could have been— what I led myself to believe. I knew intuitively this would be the last time I would see him in person. We hugged and cried for a very long time before he drove away.

After he turned the corner and I could no longer see him, I went out to my patio and stared into the morning sky, thinking about how I could still smell his cologne. Instantly, I heard the song "Blackbird" in my mind and turned to see a blackbird flying close to me before jetting up into the sky. The song, which talks about taking one's broken wings and learning to fly again, played on a loop as I stared into the distance.

It took a moment but suddenly I understood the symbology of the song. It was quite evident to me after years of channeling that there were no coincidences. The sheer fact that he was being moved to the East meant I could take my broken wings and learn to fly on my own again. It was a gift I would fully recognize in the coming weeks.

CHAPTER 16

TNF

Tony and I kept in touch via text and phone during the time he was back in his hometown living with his ex and kids, but we both knew it felt different. Around the 17th of April, the toxic cycle started again. I felt powerless to stop it. He was slinging all the same mud at me about how I'd wronged him in a million ways.

He sent hateful, damning messages one after another until I finally blocked him. I needed peace. I couldn't take the sound of my phone pinging every few seconds. In that moment, I thought of Scott's "make good choices" line. I felt as though I'd made a good choice to stop the barrage of hatred being thrown at me.

Hours went by—light turned to dark—when I decided to unblock him. I still craved his attention, no matter the kind, and was feeling guilty for shutting him out. I reached out, saying I was sorry and that I wished we could stop the madness. A reply came back, only it wasn't from Tony. It was from his stepbrother.

Tony had suffered a heart attack and was in the hospital in critical condition. Heat shot through my body to the point that I thought I might pass out. Through tears, I thanked his brother for letting me know and asked him to please keep me posted. He said he would.

Then, out of the blue, I received another message from Tony's phone:

Hi Kiersten, this is Tony's mom, Kathleen. Please leave Tony and his family alone during this time.

I started shaking when I read what she'd written. Clearly, I was at fault for causing him unbearable pain that led to a heart attack. He knew it and his mom knew it, too. After sobbing uncontrollably, I thought of our mutual friends, and a client named Ross came to mind. I immediately reached out to see if he knew what was happening. Ross was naturally concerned and had apparently reached out to Tony.

I couldn't sleep. I couldn't eat. I couldn't do much of anything for twelve hours. When I wasn't checking my phone every five minutes, I lay in bed, watching the light from the outdoor street lamp project shapes on my wall. At 3:38 a.m., a message came in from Tony's phone:

Kiersten, please stop talking about my and our personal issues with my friends or anyone in the furniture industry. You just keep hurting me. You've been talking to Ross and God knows who else about our personal issues. Keep it in your own world, please! I don't talk about you to anyone! Please stop hurting me! Nobody in the industry can know this! I'm up for a huge job, and I have to get out of here to make the interview. Please, please stop hurting me!

I sat up in bed stunned, unable to move even though I immediately felt the buzzing sensation on my hip start up. He'd had a heart attack and was in critical condition and *that's* what he writes to me when he's finally conscious? It didn't make sense. It wasn't rational. While everything he said stung, I still couldn't make it all fit together. If he'd been in critical condition, he wouldn't have been in any shape to send a message like that. And what person comes out of a life-threatening heart attack without simple gratitude for just being alive? Ross was the only person I contacted because I was worried about Tony and wanted to talk to someone who knew him. There was nothing malicious about it.

"Dig deeper," Carrie said before vanishing in front of me. The irony that she was telling me to dig deeper was not lost on me. I'd done a lot of digging for her.

I called Andy, who immediately said, "Kiers, this isn't true. I bet you anything he didn't have a heart attack." Unbelievably, there was still a part of me that believed him. I was conditioned to believe him, but my intuition won this round. I did what any good investigator does—I called every hospital in his area. All twenty of them. Not one had a patient named Tony.

My dear friend, Cynthia Spiece, an incredibly talented and gifted medium and energy healer who was the first to help me with my inner child, wrote me back after I shared what happened.

"It's not true," she said. "He needed contact from you. He's desperate to have the last word. My advice is to cut off all communication immediately and never get sucked in again by any ploy he pulls."

"This is so fucked up," I said.

"He's addicted to getting a rise out of you...broken people do really broken things like this. Delete him from your phone or he will keep doing it."

In disbelief, I asked, "How in the world could someone who proclaims to love me do this? I mean, I've seen him at his worst, and I know he's wounded from his childhood, but it's unthinkable to lie about almost dying!"

She replied with one simple line: "He's a sociopath, Kiersten."

I knew she was right. I knew Andy was right. I knew I was right when no one by his name was admitted to any medical center within a thirty-mile radius, but that still wasn't enough for me to wipe the sliver of doubt in my mind that it might be true. It felt like

I was brainwashed to always believe what he said no matter what my intuition said. Feeling mad enough to do exactly what Cynthia suggested, I blocked him...for a little while.

I vowed never to connect again, but like many times before, I eventually unblocked him. His drug was too powerful. He sent a message about trying to get ahold of me and how much he loved me. He thought something horrible had happened to me and explained that while his heart attack was happening, he was silently begging for me to help him. Tony went on to say he needed me and loved me TNF.

Even though my intuition and my besties told me he was lying, I couldn't help but be a moth to the flame. I flat out couldn't stop myself from communicating with him. I was now a full-fledged junkie who had to get her fix, even though I knew he'd lied to me about his stint in the hospital.

Shortly after things calmed down, the cycle started again.

You lied, you hurt me, fuck you...but I love you forever, baby, I forgive you, and I have hope for us was coming at me almost daily.

Filled with shame, I kept it all secret. I didn't let anyone know I was still communicating with him. It wasn't as frequent as it had been, but we were talking. He tried to convince me that he was doing what he could, through new business connections, to help find a new manufacturer for Mod Mom.

This round of niceties felt hollow. I knew in my soul that the whole "let me help Mod Mom" stunt was just another way to gain control. And I knew intuitively I didn't want what he was proposing on a business level.

A few days after professing that he wanted to help Mod Mom, he brought me an overseas manufacturing offer. In fact, the offer was to partner with a European company that would produce both his line and mine.

The moment I politely declined the offer via email, the wrath began. I knew it wasn't good for many reasons, including the fact that I wanted to keep manufacturing in the US. As soon as he read my reply, he was livid. He called me selfish for potentially ruining the deal for his line.

I think it surprised him that I would turn down an opportunity like that because Mod Mom wasn't even being produced at the time. I'd put all my energy into trying to build up his line. Turning down a work opportunity that kept us connected was a huge feat for me.

When it was becoming clear to him that I was standing my ground without caving as much as I used to, he upped the ante. First, he blocked me on text but kept email wide open in order to inflict more pain.

He was throwing the usual punches as we went back and forth on Gmail one night in late June. I was proudly still standing my ground. Out of the blue, he wrote:

Kiersten, I'm ending my life. The pain is just too great. And even right now, your cruelty is just too much to take. And something I will never feel again. I'm going to peace now. Goodbye, my precious, precious love.

And then he left me dangling there in silence.

For hours.

I panicked, thinking he might actually be serious about ending his life given his current state of mind. He was floundering financially while living with his ex-wife in a city he proclaimed he didn't want to live in.

Over email, I begged him not to do it, not knowing if he was reading my messages or not. I assumed he wasn't getting them from his lack of response. My mind went into fix-it mode. I thought long and hard about who I knew was nearby to help him. Suddenly, it came to me—his cousin lived in the vicinity. I felt comfortable reaching out to her. Feeling powerless, I wrote Tony telling him I was about to reach out to her to intervene.

A few moments later, a text message popped up on my phone:

I'm standing on the bridge at valley road and I can't do it. I don't want to live anymore but I can't do this to my kids. I wish I never met you. You will never know the pain I've felt from you. I wish I never knew this love. Nobody will ever hurt me again.

I immediately wrote back, relieved that he was okay and not going through with it:

I'm so glad you wrote me! You will be okay. You will heal. I know you're hurting...in so much pain. Are you getting these texts? I'm so sorry for the pain. I just want you to move on, and focus on your beautiful kids...and building your life again.

I exhaled, thanking God that he didn't jump. Two seconds later came the crushing weight of responsibility for him being on that bridge in the first place.

Again, I reached out to Cynthia. She could hear the panic in my voice. In tears, I told her what had just happened.

"Kiers, this isn't real. Like the heart attack wasn't real. He's probably sitting in his car in his garage smoking pot." Her words snapped me out of my fog.

Looking back, that's likely exactly where he was when he told me he was going to take his life. He knew he'd put me right back where he wanted me—claiming all responsibility for his pain. I felt stupid for not seeing it.

Again, Carrie came in saying, "Dig deeper." About a year after the suicide threat, I learned that the bridge he mentioned in his frantic text message was not large, as I'd envisioned. Not even close. For the record, maybe he didn't think I'd go as far as to investigate, but I did, and I couldn't believe my eyes. Turns out, the bridge is featured all over YouTube as a family-friendly place for preteens to test their daredevil skills by jumping into the water below. Parents are seen applauding their kiddos who decided to take the plunge off the beautiful golf course bridge. The height of the bridge suggests that a jump into the waters below might possibly cause a bruise. Of course, I didn't know this at the time of Operation Suicide Ploy.

A few days went by after his supposed suicide attempt, and he started sending me photos of us from our early days accompanied by a declaration that we were once and for all over. He couldn't continue to be in a relationship with me when all I did was cause him pain. And he was posting about us on social media. He did a great job of making himself out to be the wounded one—the one who gave all of himself. He even posted this:

I'm picking myself up off the ground. It's time to finally heal this completely broken and devastated heart. Time for healing, learning, clarity, and never giving up hope for authentic truth and love. I'm proud I was able to give all of myself, all of my love, and all of my truth. And I'm grateful for the beautiful moments lived, the peace I'll now find, and gifts I know will be on the other side of pain. #MyTruth #TNF #Love #Pain #Healing #Life

The minute I saw it, I could hardly contain my anger. I questioned if I should go public about why our relationship ended. I ultimately decided it was what I had to do. But even then, I simply shared how we were two wounded souls who just couldn't make it work, but that there was real love between us. I still believed his behavior stemmed solely from his abandonment issues in childhood. I didn't know who would read my blog, but I felt better knowing I was able to speak my mind about it all.

He was shocked that I'd done it. I don't think he had any idea how much pride I would swallow, or how transparent I would be. Still, he told me I was his soulmate, and he hoped for the future we planned if I would just go to my truth. He needed me to see that I was indeed the problem all along.

In the middle of messaging back and forth, I heard a notification come through on my email. It was from a woman who knew Tony. She explained how she met him on a dating site a month prior. She felt compelled to write to me after reading my blog post.

This was the moment. The moment I needed to pull the virtual needle from my arm. Tony was still sending me photos telling me he loved me "TNF" when I learned that he had been with a woman when he left Flagstaff. Of course, to me, he was adamant about only focusing on his work and his kids. And waiting for me, the love of his life.

When I dug deeper, I found out that he was sending her the same songs and messages he sent to me, as well as to his ex-girlfriend overseas. Ben Harper's "Morning Yearning," Phil Collins' "Hold on My Heart," Gary B's "Life is Beautiful," and French Montana's "Unforgettable" were on the list of favorite songs he would send to women he targeted. The revelation that I was not loved—but *targeted*—brought me to my knees. I was glued to my phone watching message after message pop up. The more I asked, the more she shared. The room spun around me as my brain finally, once and for all, integrated all of the puzzle pieces. In one fell swoop, all of the blinders I'd been wearing for three years fell off.

She said he'd told her we were in an open relationship where I was parading men around in front of him. Tony said we had recently broken up but he left out the part where he was still telling me I was the love of his life, and he was trying to figure out how to get back to Flagstaff. I believed every word she wrote but I also asked to see screenshots of their conversations.

Seeing the conversation with my own eyes changed my life forever. I sat back in my chair, holding my breath as I read their first exchange on the dating site. It was a conversation that officially landed him in the smooth-talking, manipulative predator club. A club he eloquently said he wasn't a part of when he wrote to me that night three years prior in High Point.

You make me feel like a teenager.
I haven't felt like this in so long. My heart is racing.
Your eyes are beautiful, but it's more than that.

And then there was the line about being a tantric masseuse who typically wasn't attracted to his clients, but she was the exception. He told her he thought he might have a hard time not falling for her, and that after the massage, he wanted to make love to her for hours. She was intrigued and flattered and ended up spending time with him—only to be tossed aside and blocked after he'd gotten what he wanted.

I didn't puke but I came close to it. While I was busy reading about the escapades of a predator, he was texting me that he loved me. He wasn't waiting for me to go to my core after all—in reality, he was going after multiple women using a line about tantric massage that, according to news reports, was frequently used by convicted sex predators.

My new friend wasn't the only woman who reached out to me about how Tony spent his time after he moved from Flagstaff. I will always be grateful for multiple women who stepped forward to share truths about what Tony did to them. They were innocently looking for love and they found him. And then they found me.

Sitting at the bar counter in my apartment one morning shortly after receiving the ladies' messages, I had an epiphany. I was a woman who had been abused by a predator as a child, who also worked on cases involving kids who were targeted by predators and pedophiles, and yet I fell head first for a man who was, unbeknownst to me, a predator.

I couldn't move. I couldn't speak. I couldn't even cry.

How did I not see this before? I'd even been in therapy working through a lot of what was coming up from my childhood abuse. I was completely blinded on a conscious level. I believed what I wanted to believe about him for years.

After I told him that I knew he'd been lying to me since we met, he became frantic to reach me. I started blocking him on every communication channel possible. Before I could block all of them, he would show up on another, begging to speak with me. He was one step ahead of me, as usual. He admitted he sought out women because I lied to him in the beginning. In his mind, I deserved his disloyalty. He said he wanted me to feel the pain I caused him over the three years we were together. Of course, Tony vehemently denied that he took advantage of the women in intimate ways. I knew better. After all, I'd seen the screenshots. Nothing was as it seemed in the relationship I'd come to both crave and curse.

Once the truth revealed itself, I decided the only way to combat his clever slander on social media, and within the furniture industry, was to publicly tell the whole truth. I had to tell the whole embarrassing story about how we met and what I let happen.

When I told Scott what I'd found out from the women who'd bravely reached out to me, he hugged me. He knew me better than anyone on the planet. Scott understood how much pain I felt with the realization that I put my trust and career in the hands of a predator. He knew intuitively from the beginning that my journey was partly about my healing from unknown abuse and partly about what our marriage had become, but I just couldn't see all of that at the time.

Although Scott told me numerous times that he loved me and was there for me, he wasn't trying to pressure me to reconcile. I intuitively knew it was what he wanted, but I also knew that he understood I had to stand on my own. I had to embrace the fact that without either man, I'd be just fine. I needed to clear codependency from my world, and Scott was no exception.

Still, he seemed to know how the future would play out more than I did at the time. He told me that early on in our separation—around the two-month mark—someone recommended he see a shaman in Sedona. Of course, having had the experience of being part of the

Scooby-Doo gang and learning firsthand how trusting intuition led to validation, he set up an appointment. The shaman told him that what I was going through with Tony was indeed a personal healing journey that would take two to three years to resolve. There was literally nothing he could do except move on and keep the faith that, if we were meant to be together in the future, I would choose a way out of the cycle of abuse. She also mentioned seeing us both speaking on stage about what we went through as a couple.

Simply put, I had to choose healing and real love—not trauma-bonded love—above all else. He told me that he held onto this message because it resonated with his own intuition about my sudden exit from our life back in 2014.

While I was processing all of what I was learning, I thought back to what Jason said to me about fully embracing that I didn't need a man to make me whole. There was truth to it; I was finally starting to see that it just wasn't conscious truth. My subconscious was running this whole "you need a man/you need to please a man to be whole" program on a never-ending loop. I would soon learn about the long-term effects of childhood sexual abuse on the subconscious. What I did know without a doubt was that it was time to put pen to paper. I had to write my truth—the embarrassing, ugly, shameful truth about what happened.

I asked Scott if he would like to read the blog post I wrote entitled "I had an affair" where I outlined what happened when Tony and I met in person three years prior in High Point, NC. I knew it couldn't have been an easy read. After he finished it, he hugged me and told me I had his full support.

CHAPTER 17

The Restraining Order

The aftermath of publishing that particular blog post was unlike anything I could have predicted. Thousands of people were reading and sharing, and many were writing to me about their own stories of the cycle of abuse and the effect it had on their marriage. I was gaining strength, but I was also missing the good times I'd had with Tony. I didn't dare talk about that with anyone because it was shameful and confusing. Even I couldn't figure out why I still felt tethered to him and all the memories we shared.

One day, while getting ready for work, I saw a blond-haired boy in spirit run past me in my bedroom. I didn't recognize him. I said *hello* in my head and heard a quiet reply: "Hi."

"Do you need help, sweetheart? I'll help you if I can."

"No, I'm just saying hi. We've been waiting for you."

Tears came quickly when I realized what this precious boy was saying.

They've been waiting for me.

Aside from my core spirit support group that included Carrie, Jason, Nate, and my grandparents, the years I spent with Tony brought fewer kids in spirit. Far fewer than when I was hit over the head with all of it back in 2011.

They've been waiting for me, I thought. I had to climb out of the dark before they were able to come in again. It was no wonder they didn't come. I had free will, as we all do, but maybe they saw how it would eventually play out. Or maybe they just hoped I'd finally see the light again and choose love and healing over abuse and darkness.

They were back in view on a level I could recognize, even though I suspected many of them were flanking me the whole time. And I was forever grateful.

I wasn't only hearing from spirit and folks who could relate to my story; I was getting messages from Tony's old colleagues, clients who were awaiting payment from him, clients he'd done business within the past, his distant family members, and much to my surprise, many women who had claimed to have gone through what I did. My inbox filled up with supportive messages and heartbreaking notes from women who told me they were still scared of him and that he'd broken them in ways they never imagined.

Every time I read a new message from a woman who had been with him, I felt overwhelming compassion for them. I knew what they saw in him in the beginning. *But still, how could I have been this naive?* I was a medium and I still couldn't see through his facade. I let him in without knowing anything about him, except that he was a friend of two colleagues.

Working through the grief and pain felt unrelenting at times. I took solace in talking with friends and family and writing about what I'd experienced. With each new blog post I penned came a private message thanking me for speaking out because *she* couldn't. The collective "she" was made up of beautiful, smart, empathetic women who had fallen under his spell. I sought professional help from the therapist I'd been seeing for a few years as well as a new psychologist from the university where I was working. I needed a lot of help.

The pain and shame overwhelmed me, and I truly didn't understand how I could have been so blind. After all, I felt all of my intuitive signs when I met him. And more importantly, why did I hold on to him so tightly after the blinders came off? I questioned everything because I let Tony steal my sense of safety and security.

The more I learned from other women in his life, the more I was able to balance the grief I felt. I realized I was no different from the women writing to me except I was able and willing to speak publicly. I came to learn that many of his targets were married at the time they fell for him. Several women, married and single, were being pursued by him while we were together. One, in particular denied his request to meet while he was living with me in Flagstaff. Like the first woman who wrote to me, each subsequent woman described the same tactics, ploys, and come-ons. To illustrate that, I've included excerpts from messages I've received from roughly twelve women. They all came to me as online public comments or email messages. Here are seven of the twelve messages I received:

"I too am a victim of his abuse like you were. He just stole from me with the same promises he said to others. I am ashamed that when I was so vulnerable, he got me to sleep with him (my own fault) and also convinced me to lend him money. I have been reading your blog and you are truly a hero to all of us that have been deceived by this monster.... He disgusts me and I feel so stupid for falling for his BS. Karma as you have described seems to be waiting way too long to take effect. I know I should forget and forgive but it's just so hard. By your posts, you help ease my pain and the pain of so many others. As the tears are running down my face, thank you for all that you have done to stop this inhuman human. Your friend in spirit xxx."

"I wish I would have reached out a long time ago about him and what he did to me but I was sure you wouldn't believe me. In a weird way you were that girl you were writing about. I didn't

want to seem bitter or jealous by telling you what a total scum he is. I believe all the women you write about! but I also believe that half the ones against you are made up by him. He made my life hell when I finally couldn't take it anymore. I was threatened and abused on line. It's been a nightmare. Sad to say I was relieved when he moved on but I knew it would be only a matter of time. I don't know why you are so much stronger than most of us but keep it up. Every time you tell your story I feel like I get a little bit healthier and freer of his sadistic ways. Both physical and mental. So please continue to write your story and know that all of us caught in his web of deceit and lies are better off every time you do."

"He swept me off my feet with constant texting and messaging of love notes, songs, he called me 'baby,' he offered tantric massage. Then after he got what he wanted, he ditched me and blocked me on social media."

"I lent him more than I care to admit. I also know he ripped off a couple for tens of thousands. I don't know how many more but I'm surprised he's not dead. And the lies and BS. I don't believe a word he says. I wish I had the courage to warn you. I saw how much you trusted him. You were both so open about your relationship. I could tell you were sincere and I knew it was a matter of time. I can't believe you survived all those years."

"So, my friend in the furniture business told me to check out your blog. I asked why and she said just read it and tell me your thoughts! OMG this guy was walking around the Vegas market a couple years ago saying he was a big designer, taking pictures and telling me how beautiful my product was and that he could help me by making a website and through his contacts getting my products out to the masses. He wanted to discuss this over dinner and drinks but had to wait until the market was over. We connected on social media. How he knew I was the one and *wanted to perform tantric massage. He was sending me music and telling me I was an old soul. He sent me pics (you know those pics). He creeped me out and I blocked him. He blew up my phone until I had to change my number. This is the guy. What a dirtball. Glad you got out. Wow."*

"I am happy for you and I wish I could be happy but I can't. He has destroyed me inside and out. I hope he wasn't physically abusive to you as well. He made me feel like a piece of trash and then would tell me how much he loved me. I was so confused I didn't know what to do. I moved out of the country but it's not far enough. Your story eases me that's why I am writing. I see you in me but much stronger. He put me through hell. I could go on but I won't. I replay our time together from the poems and songs to the soulmate and I can't believe how stupid I was to fall for this abuser...I hope he will feel the wrath of my savior our Lord. He teaches me to turn the other cheek but it's so hard. I thank you for your writings it gives me some solace. I pray I can be like you someday and heal my heart."

"Do you know he now lives with his (still wife) and kids? Yeah, he told me he would leave her for me. How much money does he owe you? I lent him more than I care to admit I don't know how many more but I'm surprised he's not dead. And the lies and BS. I don't believe a word he says. I wish I had the courage to warn you. I saw how much you trusted him. You were both so open about your relationship. I could tell you were sincere and I knew it was a matter of time. I can't believe you survived all those years. One observation: to me this was the cruelest of all. When you became aware of your sexual abuse, he came out with a similar story to match yours. I don't believe any of his abuse stories because he never brought this up to me. Only after you found out is when he needed to match you in some sick way. Again, thank you from the bottom of my heart for exposing him. You are my therapy (Can't afford a real one) lol.

I know one thing; it takes a long time to get his disease (no pun intended) out of our system. Come on Miss Karma, it's your turn wherever you are. Love, Just one of many Xoxo"

As the messages came in one by one, I carefully documented them with corresponding IP addresses and cities of origin. I managed to piece together that he was literally with or going after roughly six women while he was targeting me.

As if those messages weren't hard enough to stomach, I received one that literally left me speechless. Sitting with Scott at a lunch café in Flagstaff, I heard my phone ding, announcing I had an email message. I looked down to see it was a comment on a recent blog post I wrote entitled "Breaking Bad." I casually started to read the comment, expecting it to say something like *You go girl*, or *I've been there, too*. Instead, it read:

"He did play you. I was duped by him and didn't know about you. You also need to know about the 15-year-old girl he was screwing (raping) while dating us. Do you remember him telling you he got mugged? That was the father beating him within an inch of his life. When I found out about that, I couldn't run fast enough. Then he rubbed you in my face and said he didn't need me. He had his soulmate. Thank God for that. Peace and good luck. – Another former victim"

As I mulled over what I'd just read, I felt my heart sink into my stomach. Chills raced up and down my body. Had I been standing, my legs would have buckled beneath me. Without saying a word, I slid my phone over to Scott. He looked perplexed for a moment but clearly understood when we locked eyes that what I was sharing with him was serious. While reading the message, his eyes doubled in size. He looked up from my phone dumbfounded by what he'd just read. I couldn't even speak other than to say, "Oh my God."

All I could think about was that poor girl. Fifteen. My God, fifteen. Then the full circle realization all but punched me in the face...again. I was a childhood sexual abuse survivor abused by a pedophile, who helped solve cold cases involving murderous pedophiles, who then unknowingly fell in love with not only a seductive predator...but technically, a pedophile.

After getting over the shock of what I'd just read, I made a plan to do some research. I did remember the story about how he got mugged one night while working in a pizza shop. He said it was drug-related—some junkie attacked him while he was about to close up.

I needed confirmation of this heinous crime, STAT. I didn't doubt what the commenter wrote—based on what I'd learned about Tony's fondness for young women and the story he told me about being mugged—but I needed to know more.

I couldn't get ahold of the woman who posted the comment because there was no email address attached to her comment but based on IP address info, I did know she was writing from near where Tony was living on the East Coast. Despite not talking to her firsthand, I started putting the puzzle pieces together:

- He worked at the pizza shop off and on when we met. He said it was because he needed to supplement his furniture design income since his manufacturer was ripping him off.

- Not long into our relationship, Tony stopped working at the shop and started painting houses for extra cash. I never really questioned why.

- I knew there were several young girls working at the pizza shop because I saw them when we stopped in one day. He wanted me to meet everyone.

Using my detective skills, I reached out to a few folks I'd met back East who I suspected would have information on the incident at hand. One in particular, who actually knew the fifteen-year-old, confirmed that what I'd recently learned was indeed true. Tony was forty-eight at the time.

After filing away screenshots of the confirmation I received, I realized I was never going to be able to get to the young girl directly. There was nothing I could do but continue writing in case more women or girls came forward.

As I continued writing and publishing what I endured for three years, I braced for epic retaliation. Once, he responded to a blog post I wrote about the door locking experience in Florida:

You are sick Kiersten. And you were sick in Florida. And you're sick from the abuse you suffered as a child not any from me. And the blindness from your parents for their own facade all your life. Being sick does not make you bad. But it sure keeps you blind. And, you've lost the only one with the insight, guts, and the true love enough to tell you. You've surrounded yourself with only enablers. Truth needs NO validation. What happened in Florida got to anger on both sides. And you helped big time! Just as you did all along knowing each button to push, when calm loving truth showed itself, you RAN again to projection and blame....

With love only,

Tony

It was clear he wouldn't take my standing up lying down. Despite all the proof I had amassed that he was indeed an abusive, controlling predator to many in his life, he continued to parade his victim story.

In August of 2017, while working in the university marketing department, I received a message from the Equity and Access Department about an incident that had occurred. Several incidents, in fact. Apparently, someone named Tony sent my personal blog post about having an affair to the Office of the President of the university, as well as about eighty folks who worked for the Institute of Human Development. I believe he thought they were the HR group on campus but he was mistaken.

He also posted the link to my blog all over various university Facebook pages using a little-known page he created called Question Mark. Clearly, he hoped that sharing my link would get me fired. His plan backfired—the university immediately blocked his email address and supported me fully.

Mark, Charles, and the rest of my detective friends told me to consider getting a protective order against him because he was sending me threatening emails that said he would never rest until he got justice. He was also sending me messages supposedly written by his fans, who were calling me crazy.

The detectives I knew urged me to learn to use a gun. It was a reality I wasn't ready to hear, but I knew they were right. I'd seen him lose his cool more than once, heard stories of walls being punched, and remembered the visions my friends shared about seeing me covered in blood from a punch. The more I learned in therapy about what I actually endured—and what this kind of abuse was called—the more I realized how much I risked being vocal. I was also acutely aware of domestic violence statistics as they related to breakups.

Not only were my therapists telling me what they saw from the outside, but friends who had endured similar abuse were sharing stories of almost identical experiences. Jane, whom I helped get out of an abusive marriage years earlier, was one of those women. It had come full circle; she was now helping me.

Camilla also shared her experiences with an ex-boyfriend that mimicked a lot of what I was enduring. And Stacey, who was supportive no matter how many times I went back to Tony, told me that I would be able to let go when he finally did something to wake me up. She knew exactly how it would go down because she lived through a similar relationship. Like many others, she also feared for my safety. Then Jason, in spirit, chimed in after Tony pulled his university email stunt:

Kiers, you have to get a restraining order. Please do it. Now! Please!

"Okay, J…I will. I promise," I reassured him.

I mean it. Go today.

I'd never before sensed this kind of urgency in Jason's messages. I took his advice and went to the police department with all of my evidence. The Flagstaff PD officer I spoke with agreed that I needed to take a legal stance. I went down to the courthouse with copies of what he'd done at the university, copies of the email message where he threatened to never stop until he got justice, and the police report from the domestic violence call in 2016.

I sat in the lobby waiting to be called. Upon hearing my name, I was ushered into a cold courtroom and led to a seat in the front of the room with a lone glass of water and a microphone. Much to my surprise, "you will meet with a judge" meant you will testify in a courtroom before a judge.

I sat nervously next to my pile of evidence. While I waited for the judge to enter the courtroom, I read over the papers for the thousandth time. I took deep breaths. My eyes welled with tears a few times as the weight of all of it covered me like a heavy blanket. I willed myself to be strong no matter what I had to go through.

After I nervously spoke with the judge and the court reporter for about thirty minutes, the judge agreed that an order of protection should be granted. I was surprised to hear that although he read the police report describing the domestic violence call that happened a little over a year earlier, the document wasn't admissible in court because it occurred over a year prior to filing for a restraining order. However, if the police had been called to my door within a year's time from when I was standing in court, it *would* have been admissible.

It seemed ridiculous to me because when someone is abusive, there's no magical change overnight. Or even over a year. Still, I was eternally grateful that he granted the order. I don't know about other states, but here in Arizona, it's not easy to get a protective order. After the judge announced his decision, he continued with a bit of advice:

"Ms. Hathcock, this order will not keep you safe. You will need to be vigilant about your safety and the safety of your family."

I agreed with him. The order was a piece of paper that would help me get him arrested quickly if he contacted me in any way, but it wasn't bulletproof. The onus of my safety was on me.

With mixed emotions, I gathered up my papers and waited for the order to be handed to me by the court reporter. In those moments between the announcement that the order would be granted and when I walked out the door, I saw his face in my mind's eye and felt the sting of emotion in the back of my throat. Welling up, I thought about how no matter what he had done to warrant a restraining order, I didn't want to hurt him further. It was as if my heart and my head were in a tug of war. I would later learn this is part of the conditioning I'd undergone over the past three years. Protect at all costs, even when you're being abused. And the fact is, I felt real love for him—for the man he pretended to be—so undoing all of that was beyond painful.

Now that I had the official order in my hands, it was time to have it delivered to him and the only way to do that was through a constable or a process server in his area. All of this was new to me. I ended up asking Mark if he knew anyone in Tony's hometown. He recommended a great guy who held my hand through the process.

It took four tries, hours and hours of surveillance, and close to $500 to serve him the order of protection. When he was finally served the document, he denied his identity, took the closed envelope in his hands, looked at it for a moment, then left it on the ground. Photos taken at the scene when he was served are included in the affidavit that the server sent back to me to file with the court and police. There's no denying that it was clearly Tony.

On September 14th, 2017, I requested that Flagstaff Police call him to reiterate the protection order was active. Jason validated that I was doing the right thing by saying: *Kiers, do this. It's all you'll have to do. And he knows it's from you already, but you need to do this, too.*

When Flagstaff PD called Tony, he again denied his identity and the fact that he was served. The cop emphasized that no matter what his thoughts were on the situation, the order was active now. She said that he'd been officially served and that there was a legal record of it. She reminded him that he could contest the order, but he refused.

This was such a big step for me on all fronts. My accommodate-at-all-costs conditioning was becoming undone as I realized I had to do this. I was finally standing up for myself. For my family. For Little Kiersten.

CHAPTER 18

Here's Why

My visits with both of my therapists became a weekly lifeline for me. I believed all of the evidence and messages that were coming in about Tony, but I was still having a hard time reconciling why, at times, I missed him. It made no sense.

To make matters worse, he was also trashing me both behind the scenes and publicly on his blog. One such post was entitled, "If you leave me, I'll ruin you." As usual, he wanted to paint the picture that he was the victim. In the same post, he flipped the script, calling me an abusive woman with borderline personality disorder/narcissistic personality disorder.

I learned from both my therapist and my psychologist that this maneuver is par for the course with folks like him. But still, reading his post made me question myself slightly. I marched into my psychologist's office and flat out asked if I could possibly be who he was painting me to be and not recognize it. Dr. Botello calmly said, "Kiersten, you are not the things he's saying. You are a survivor of narcissistic and sociopathic abuse, based on everything you've shared with me." In that moment, I exhaled while tears ran down my cheeks. They were the same kind of tears I experienced when I sent the letter off to my uncle.

"One more question…is there any way I could have multiple personalities based on what I endured as a child?" I asked.

"No, Kiersten. Your personality is fully intact; you just have some inner child healing to do because of the abuse, that's all. You do not present with alters."

This explained why I would feel a buzzing sensation on my right hip when he yelled at me. And why, prior to the first appointment with Dr. Botello, I felt that buzzing sensation all day long. Little did I know that she specialized in helping heal the inner child. I never again felt the buzzing sensation on my right hip after making the connection that it was a physical way for me to recognize when Little Kiersten was speaking up. I finally stood up for her.

Hearing that I was not dealing with Dissociative Identity Disorder felt right to me. I didn't feel as though I had different alters that would come out at different times—I only felt numbness when I tried to access Little Kiers or think about my childhood. My memories consisted mostly of what I'd seen in our photo albums, but nothing first person until the memories of abuse started to come back.

Dr. Botello and my therapist, Deanna Vance, both explained that not only was I dealing with the trauma of abuse, but my body had become addicted to it. Endorphins and oxytocin would rise and fall during extreme highs and lows, and now my body craved the high.

It made my head spin but felt 100 percent spot on. It explained one of the reasons I still craved his attention at times. He felt like a drug from day one. Aside from the nasty smoking habit I'd developed during our time together, I was clean; however, I was trauma bonded to him. It would take some serious work and patience to fully recover. I knew it would be much harder than quitting smoking.

In between therapy appointments, I read everything I could get my hands on about recovering from this type of relationship. I didn't know it existed before I found myself smack dab in it. Worse yet, because I repressed memories of childhood abuse until just months before I met Tony, I didn't have any understanding of the term *wounded attachment*.

Psychotherapist Valerie Kuykendall Rogers shared an article online that describes how sexual abuse survivors frequently fall into abusive relationships based on wounded attachment without fully recognizing what's happening. She described wounded attachment as the unconscious way of being attracted to or attached to someone or something that reinforces the childhood wound/trauma.

Ultimately, by finally standing up to the abuse I endured with Tony, I was healing Little Kiersten—the one who couldn't stand up as a child. I just didn't know what I was doing because it was happening in my subconscious. It was finally all making sense on a conscious level.

* * *

Thankfully, after the restraining order was served, I felt like I could finally make more space for myself, for the kids, and for Scott and me to reconnect. He wasn't the least bit suffocating, which was admittedly a fear of mine. Scott had been working through his own codependency tendencies, which was critical to our relationship.

Scott knew I needed time to come to a decision about whether or not we would try to give it a go as a couple again. He made it clear that he wanted to reunite but that things would be different this time. By some miracle, neither one of us ever filled out the divorce paperwork. I carried mine around in my computer bag for close to a year but never formally filed. We couldn't bring ourselves to do it for various reasons. We were separated, but not legally separated.

Over the next few months, we spent time together as a family and we spent time alone just hanging out without any pressure. He saw me through what I know were PTSD reactions to the abuse I'd endured for such a long time.

One night, we went to one of our favorite Italian restaurants. As I sat down in the booth, it hit me that I was still unconsciously choosing the side of the booth that didn't face the door. In an effort to be fully open with him, I shared my revelation.

"I didn't realize I was still conditioned to pick the seat that doesn't face the door."

"Wait, that was a thing?"

"You know how the eye contact thing was a big deal to him? Well, one time, when we were traveling, I took a seat in a Mediterranean restaurant that faced the door. The sun was kind of blinding me every time the door opened, and I would instinctively look up."

"Don't tell me...he thought you were scoping out other men," Scott said, shaking his head.

"Yep, exactly...if I wasn't being accused of checking out other men, then I simply wasn't present with him. I was too busy looking at the door, apparently."

He grabbed my hands across the table.

"I'm so sorry you went through that...and that it's still haunting you."

"I just can't believe I'm still doing it. I mean, I know you're not him, but I'm still doing it."

Still holding my hands, he said, "It will ease in time, I'm sure."

He wanted me to give myself a break because of all I'd been through. I'd always loved his sensitivity and kind heart. It was one of the reasons I married him in the first place. While the love we had for each other was still very strong, he knew I needed a friend in that moment.

I intuitively felt we were on the precipice of an even better relationship than we had during our first eighteen years together, but I still had to focus heavily on my own healing. The words Jason said played over and over again in my mind: "Kiers, you don't need a man to be whole. You have everything you need inside of you."

I also didn't realize at the time how much I feel other people's energy without them saying a word. I knew I was a sponge who felt overwhelmed in crowds, but I didn't get the depth of the sensitivity. I didn't want to be a pleaser anymore.

I had to work hard to rewire my programmed responses, as well as ask myself: *Do I really want to do this or that?* My therapist, Deanna, taught me this little trick. Once I became conscious of my unconscious patterns, I was able to change them.

I didn't let fear or guilt rule me anymore when it came to my relationship with Scott. Now, don't get me wrong—I still felt huge amounts of guilt and pain over what I put him and the kids through. But I knew our only shot at creating a better tomorrow as a couple was to be fully honest about everything. Thankfully, Scott understood this better than anyone because he admitted and understood his part in the demise of our marriage. He even wrote about it and asked me to publish it on my blog:

"Here's Why" by Scott Hathcock

The story goes like this…

There was a Zen master by the name of Hakuin. He lived in a village where he was praised by his community in having achieved a pure life. Enter a young Japanese girl of the same village. One day, her parents discover she's hiding her pregnancy. They were a prominent family in the village and served as the main food store owners. Ashamed, they demand that their daughter confess and identify the man that made her this way. Knowing it would only hurt the young fisherman to reveal his identity, she remained quiet at first. Ultimately, the pressure is too great. Rather than telling her parents and the village the truth, she reports it was Hakuin. When they confront the Zen master with her accusation, his response is simply, "Is that so?"

Once the child is born, it is delivered to Hakuin to raise. By this time, Hakuin had lost his reputation with the villagers—now vilified, he is no longer celebrated. Neither seemed to bother him. He accepts the baby as his own and cares for the child as if it's his own.

Eventually, the young Japanese mother can no longer bear the weight of her lies and being away from her child, so she tells her parents the truth—the name of the real father. The mother, father, and the girl all rush to Hakuin to ask for forgiveness. They apologize at great lengths and ask to have the child back.

Despite raising the child for a year, losing his reputation, and receiving ridicule from the villagers, Hakuin was willing and responds only with, "Is that so?"

I share this only to say that in the past three years of my personal journey and separation from Kiersten, I found great solace in NOT reacting and taking it personally. Of course, it was difficult at times. She said some harsh words my face. I would listen and with verbal or non-verbal cues respond with, "Is that so?" Intuitively, I somehow knew this was HER journey. I felt as if I even knew how the story would end. Once, I even confidentially stated that to her, but in that particular moment, the declaration only fueled a stubbornness within her. I learned that she needed a good listener and a friend, not a consultant.

As time passed, I would find her at my door. These visits would be under the premise of dropping off or picking up the kids, but they usually allowed for a bit of lingering on her part. And, in these moments she would exhale, give me a sweet smile, and through non-verbal or verbal cues, tell me how she was doing. I knew my place was just to listen, not to fix. I saw her struggling with things that had happened to her in her new relationship that I recognized as abusive. It was hard to witness. I remember her asking me if I ever thought she had too much eye contact with men, because she was being told that she does. Being made to feel *like she was doing something wrong. I told her no, that's not who she is. She's a kind, open-hearted woman but not a flirt. In addition to dealing with losing her, it was hard to watch the woman I love becoming a shell of herself due to an abusive relationship she didn't understand.*

Finding this Zen space did not happen for me overnight. In fact, I would suggest I spent the first 4-6 months operating out of a very raw and emotional space. I was reacting. I was working from a headspace of mostly "taking it personally."

Don Miguel Ruiz's book The Four Agreements *started me on this path.*

The Four Agreements are:

1. *Be Impeccable with your Word*
2. *Don't Take Anything Personally*
3. *Don't Make Assumptions*
4. *Always Do Your Best*

These rules have a way of resurfacing in my life; they are similar to when you exercise and are reminded to work on your core. To me, these agreements make up the mental core.

I can by no means say I have mastered any of them. But, for the purposes of addressing the common question I receive from friends and family who have read or heard about our love story (and it truly is a love story), I answer here...

"Scott, how are you able to take Kiersten back?" or "How did you manage?"

...I defer to the second agreement. I never took it personally.

But I can also honestly say that because I tried my best in our 18-year marriage to not break the other three agreements around issues of integrity and intentions when it came to her specifically. I do feel like you could take the second agreement too far if you set out to do harmful things to others, not caring for others in general, and then becoming offended that you are not personally liked by those people. So, one does have to have a working moral compass when abiding to the agreements; otherwise, it's like playing with chess rules when your opponent is playing checkers.

When Kiersten surprised me with her new direction in life, I did not immediately go to this centered way of thinking to process what she was saying. I was a raw, emotional mess. It felt as if I had entered a completely new universe and was now living in a body I was familiar with but a life that was unfamiliar and strange. I couldn't grasp the "why" of it. Why this? Why now? Why us? Why him?

Because I was asking her these questions, she was giving me hard-to-hear answers. Some of her answers flowed out like personal attacks on me, some were more introspective, and some came from a place of matter-of-fact reasoning. To her, they all had to be convincing since she was changing her path in life.

There have been many times in my life when I need to justify a decision I'm about to make or have made. The higher the stakes and impact my decision makes on others, the greater the sales pitch. It's human nature. We've all done this. That inner monologue is a great motivator for action in ourselves; the more self-convincing we can do betters the chances of being able to start doing that thing.

Over the course of months, as she tried "selling" me on her new path, I learned to distance myself from the more negative justifications ("Is that so"?) and provide support to the "child" within her that needed a supportive "man" role. Before I continue, I may need to also inform you that just four months prior, Kiersten and I started coming to terms with the fact that she had been sexually abused by a male family relative as a young child. With that realization, I knew there was a chance that I would take a few "hits" if something I said or did triggered that "little girl."

I say all of this because intuitively I felt as if I understood. Despite the personal pain it was causing me to potentially lose the woman I loved, I knew I was witnessing the process of healing. In the big picture, these were chapters of self-discovery and healing in her life book that she needed to experience that had very little to do with me.

Were there lessons, healing, and improvements that I needed to make? Of course. I'll tell you what they were.

1. I needed to grow-up
2. I needed to take more responsibility of my life and my career
3. I needed to learn patience
4. I needed to be a better father
5. I needed to be a better husband
6. I needed to be more of a listener and less of a fixer
7. I needed to appreciate staying in the moment

I could go on, and the list continues to evolve, because I do, too. For the most part, one could consider the improvements I needed to make cliché when it comes to relationship breakers. Only from experience and life come lessons that move the needle forward and continue self-growth. But, for many of these, you don't ever actually stop working on them until you are in the ground. There will always be areas for improvement.

I recently read another book called Designing Your Life by Bill Burnett and Dave Evans. In the book, they have the reader create a dashboard that measures (0-5) the fullness of one's life in four main categories—love, play, work, and health. Essentially, in designing a life you will make unknowing sacrifices to one of these four pillars at any moment in your life IF you are unaware that they exist and can be measured. A balanced life is a happy life and one with complete fulfillment and all 5's in each category.

Let's look at a car. If cars were built without gauges to tell the driver they had no fuel, were almost out of oil, the tires were running low on air, or there's little to no coolant left, you would have a lot of bewildered, surprised and possibly angry drivers sitting in cars that don't work. Throw into the mix a surrounding condition that exists outside of the car (like weather) and you'll have further levels of complexity generating even more confusion. With a car, you need a dashboard that helps you understand what you are doing to the car. And, with life, at the very least, you need an understanding of a theoretical dashboard that brings awareness.

Do you know what also brings sudden awareness? A divorce, a DUI, being fired, and a stroke. With Kiersten's latest news, I was about to check the box for 3 out of 4 of those. While a DUI had personally never happened to me, it would have not been without effort, so for arguments sake, let's say all four boxes had now been checked. If that's not an awakening slap, then I don't know what is.

The irony is that in my dashboard "love" reading, I would have felt it had always been steady in the 4-5 scale. Kiersten's sudden announcement that she now wanted a divorce should have killed me, but instead I went inward.

As I look back on this time in my life and with the lens of this dashboard—love, play, work, and health—I can guarantee that I had too much weight in the love area. I had lost focus in managing the play, work, and health pieces. I had become too reliant on Kiersten in helping me stay "happy." She did an awesome job of that for years as she is a pleaser by nature, but maybe her work on me had resulted in a deficit in her scale of fullness.

With her news, I woke up. I started reading. Two books found me—The Four Agreements and The Untethered Soul. Both books allowed me to "escape" from the day-to-day of still living under one roof with her but at the same time stay emotionally grounded while being spiritually elevated. I also started meditating, walking in the woods, and briefly stopped drinking. I started listening to my body. I noticed that when I had more than two glasses of wine,

I could feel the weight of depression add a layer. I started bringing fun experiences to my children that we could share. I made it a point to just be present for them and keep smiling. Eventually, I was strong enough that I no longer worried about what the future brought but instead created this sense to be in the moment and float. To float, however, did not mean I couldn't manifest good things in life, so I also got really good at manifesting opportunities. Those opportunities included all the areas of love, play, work, and health. In other words, I got my mojo back.

But, in the end, you've asked some variation of the question, "How did I manage to stay with Kiersten through all of this?" You can clearly see it was a mix of borrowed things I had read and perhaps experienced through observation of others. I created very little of this, only absorbed it. There really is no simple answer.

Well, I take that back. There is. I love her.

And, to borrow from someone else's teachings, I know what love is. Thank you, Forrest Gump.

—Scott

CHAPTER 19

Like a Phoenix

The ride down to Phoenix felt easy and fun, which was in such stark contrast to how I'd been living. I hadn't gotten away for a weekend vacation in a long time. If anyone needed it, Scott and I did. We were inching our way back to one another, spending more and more time together while I was living in my own apartment with Grace.

Talking about what we endured during our time apart wasn't all that hard. He was and has always been my best friend. We pledged to be completely open. He told me about the women he dated in Phoenix and Flagstaff, detailing some of the crazy escapades he experienced, and I slowly revealed all of the details of what I had lived.

He knew I endured a lot of emotional and psychological abuse, but I don't think he understood the escalation of the abuse. After all, I didn't tell him about the cops coming to my door until after I finally broke free from Tony. Many times, he would listen with tears in his eyes and then swoop me up in his arms and hug me tight. I was having to learn to trust all over again, even though I knew I could lean into Scott. My triggered reactions to closeness created panic attacks at times. I made sure he understood that I wasn't reacting to him, but rather, anything that felt confining or controlling. Everything I'd buried deep for forty years was right at the surface. Thankfully, he didn't take it personally. He simply wanted me to feel safe again.

After two hours of talking, laughing, and singing on the way to the hotel, we finally arrived ready for some fun in the sun. Our weekend was beautiful and I indeed felt free to be silly again for the first time in a long time.

Scott said he could see the joy in me that had been lost. Being together again was both familiar and new, exciting and comfortable. Still, he could see pain and sorrow in my eyes at times, even though my light was returning. As we were driving home, we stopped at a P.F. Chang's restaurant just north of Phoenix. We were on cloud nine, almost not believing where we were in our lives after all we'd been through. We still marveled at the fact that we never filed for divorce.

Over appetizers, I asked, "Hey, what would you think about getting rings again?"

"Seriously? Yes!"

Back in December of 2014, I had to sell our wedding rings, my engagement ring, and a few of my grandmother's rings in order to pay rent shortly after we told the kids we were splitting up. At the time, I knew selling the only valuable things we owned was some-thing I had to do to provide for our kids. I did it without hesitation, but it was still a very emotional moment for me.

After we talked about where we could get rings, we went back in time remembering how we met and the story behind our first set of rings. I was fresh out of Ohio University in 1995 when I made my home in Charlotte, NC, and met Scott at the not-so-classy Vinnie's Sardine Bar. He got a call that night from a friend who invited him to join her and her new friend from Ohio—me—at the dive bar. He decided to pop by, even though his fellow housemates had other plans. He walked in looking strikingly handsome. I knew instantly there was something about him. We talked and laughed as if we'd known each other for years.

When we said our goodbyes in the parking lot, we promised to see each other again soon. He tells the story that when he got home, his roommates asked where he'd been. Without hesitation, he said, "I just met the girl I'm going to marry."

Four months later, we were sitting in his parents' den in the sleepy town of Tallassee, Alabama. We were about to end a wonderful weekend with the seven-hour drive back to Charlotte when he whispered in my ear, "Can I please tell them what we did? About looking at rings at the mall last week?"

I chuckled because I knew he couldn't keep it a secret, even though he was the one suggesting not telling anyone. I smiled and nodded. Immediately after Scott announced that we were looking at rings, the room erupted in squeals, clapping, and hugs. Lots of hugs. Laughing, I said, "Whoa, hold up a minute! He hasn't even asked me yet."

Before we knew it, both sets of Scott's grandparents and his aunt and uncle were on their way over to the house to celebrate. Scott and I were sent to the grocery store to buy champagne, but for what? Because we'd looked at rings? It was comical and fun so, naturally, we were both all in.

Loaded with bags of snacks and champagne, we made our way up the front stairs of Scott's parents' gorgeous southern home. Suddenly, he stopped me. He placed his bag on the step and got down on one knee. "Kiersten, will you marry me?" A smile spread across my face and without hesitation, I said yes. Now, we truly had something to celebrate!

We decided to spend one more night at his parents' house while we celebrated our news, but it wasn't lost on us that we were missing an important, traditional component of a proposal—the ring.

As it turned out, the only jewelry store in town was the same place that sold two generations of Hathcock men their wedding and engagement rings. We knew the perfect place to go in the morning.

Fast forward twenty-one years to Phoenix, Arizona, and here we were again needing new rings. We knew what we needed to do and it didn't involve a jewelry store. After shelling out $250 at the nearest Kohl's, we walked to our car wearing new silver wedding bands and a cubic zirconia engagement ring. Even though we paid a fraction of what we did for our first set of rings, our new rings will always be priceless symbols of our second chance.

* * *

Back home, the restraining order made me feel like I'd done everything possible to protect myself. Still, I resided on the first floor of the apartment complex, and Tony knew exactly where I lived. Given what I'd endured, I worried he might try to confront me in person. After all, I was the only woman who ever publicly stood up to him.

This led me to knock on the apartment manager's door to explain what had been happening—that Scott and I had reunited, and that I had a restraining order on Tony. Jennifer understood my situation all too well because she had dealt with a similarly abusive ex, and had—at one time—woken to him hiding under her bed in her first-floor apartment.

During our talk, Jennifer was not the least bit timid about telling me that other tenants frequently called the office to complain about the yelling they heard coming from my apartment. The maintenance man who'd called the police wasn't the only one concerned about my wellbeing.

She also informed me that my official restraining order against Tony for domestic violence legally allowed me out of my lease. That didn't apply to Scott since he wasn't on the order. Leaving us with only one option, we decided to make his two-bedroom apartment our home until his lease ran out.

We sat down with the kids at dinner to tell them about our plan. They'd been through the wringer, but we had a feeling that this move would be welcomed, especially because we let the kids have the two bedrooms and we put our bed in the living room. Loft-style living for seven months sounded like a fun adventure for all. And who could argue that placing your bed just inches from the kitchen is a bad thing?

Grace and I scooted out after our dinner conversation to run errands. When we came back, part of our apartment living room had been moved up to Scott's place. It was fun to see the excitement on Noah and Scott's faces when we walked into his apartment.

We had a blast making our tiny home work for us and took pride in our innovative interior design ideas. Being under one roof again was a dream come true and a financial godsend. Having hemorrhaged money when I was with Tony, it was nice to feel like I wasn't drowning anymore.

But mostly, I was just relieved to feel like I could actually breathe again. I've never been a person who likes to cuddle, but the first few months that Scott and I were back together, it's all I wanted to do. I felt safe and happy nestled in his arms while we watched movies in our living room bed. Life was beginning to normalize, thanks to Scott and the kids, my therapists, my friends, and my resolve to undo the subconscious programming that kept me locked in the cycle of abuse.

It took about six months for my body to calm down from the addiction to the abuse and trauma bonding. I was so used to cortisol rushing through my body when I lived on pins and needles that I had to get used to feeling even-keeled. Normality and awareness were the cures.

Then it came time to kick the cigarette habit that had spiraled out of control toward the end of my time with Tony. Intuitively, I knew I could do it and it wouldn't take much effort since I was out of the abuse, but it did take two tries to get there. On the second try, I quit cold turkey. Shockingly, I didn't even relapse when I was thrust into a triggering situation a month after I quit smoking.

I didn't know this man named Scott Tullman, but I decided to accept his private Facebook message out of curiosity. I wasn't sure what to expect, but it sure wasn't something scathing and shaming.

Mr. Tullman told me how horrible I was for talking openly about the abuse I endured and added lots of other lovely digs. It didn't even occur to me at the time that this man could be my ex in disguise.

Just like old times, my body was heating up and I felt the flood of stress hormones coursing through my veins. After a few deep breaths, I replied that I thought it was strange that he was writing me about something he had no experience with. That maybe he should support women who report abuse rather than shaming them. Naively, I still didn't think it was a fake profile. After I replied, I blocked him.

About an hour later, I received another message request from a woman named Karen, claiming to be Scott's wife. My jaw hit the floor. *Who were these people who were invested in shaming me for sharing my journey? Did they know my ex?*

Hours went by when suddenly it hit me: they weren't real people. They were one person disguised as two fictional characters in order to get the last word and circumvent the law. After my revelation, Jason popped into my consciousness confirming this truth and asking me to trust it.

Thankfully, working with law enforcement on cold cases helped me hone my detective skills. I investigated Scott Tullman and Karen Marie, starting with Google image searches that revealed both profiles were using photos of other people. Scott's photo was a well-known photographer named Lee, whom I let know that his photo was being used on a fake profile.

Karen's photo was of a bartender in New York City. I dug deeper to connect more dots. Karen and Scott lived in different areas of the country, yet both had reviewed the photography business of a woman named Kay on Facebook. Kay was connected to—you guessed it—Tony. Kay had reviewed Tony's Houzz profile, yet when questioned directly by a friend, she denied knowing Tony or Scott, her supposed client. The connections were pretty clear to me, but getting Facebook to give me the IP information proved impossible.

I remembered what the detective at the Flagstaff police department said, "You can pretty much bet that he'll try to get around the order by sending messages somehow." I immediately sent her all of the evidence I found.

Violating the restraining order should have sent him to jail, but Facebook never released the critical IP info. This is just one of the ways abusers can break restraining orders regardless of how much evidence piles up. It was beyond frustrating, but not something I wanted to dwell on once I realized I had no recourse.

The only thing I could do was help others in similar positions. I wrote a blog post about how to research fake profiles. Maybe, just maybe, I enabled one person to put their abuser behind bars for breaking a protective order. I know I reached Kay and Tony because Scott Tullman's profile photo disappeared quickly. Someone had been reading my blog.

CHAPTER 20

Conduit

Healing continued to be my top priority, but I took the time to do fun things, too. Feeling free to do whatever I wanted without fear of judgment or shame was liberating. As I looked around the crowded ballroom filled with Flagstaff's biggest creative enthusiasts, I smiled. I was sitting with my dear friend, Tracie, who invited me to be her guest while Scott sat a few tables away as a guest at the Mayor's table. Scott and I made goofy faces at each other, then met at the bar pretending like we didn't know one another. We laughed about doing the very thing we'd seen in a million cheesy romantic comedies.

Back at my table, I sat next to Tracie who hadn't told me that she was secretly considering a big career change. That is until one of her loved ones in spirit decided to pop in during a beautiful choral number that raised the vibration of the room ten-fold. As I immersed myself in the gorgeous sounds of the Flagstaff Master Chorale, tears welled up in my eyes. The message was clear and beautiful—one that I had to pass on right at that minute. I leaned over to tell Tracie that her relative was there in the spirit and wanted her to receive a message. Minutes later, she, too, was in tears telling me about a big decision she was about to make. The reason spirit wanted to chime in was clear—she needed a nudge to take the leap of faith.

Shortly after I shared the messages, my phone lit up. I hadn't touched it nor received a call or message that I could tell. I was perplexed but picked up the phone anyway. I unlocked it to find a note open, one I'd stored months prior when I wanted to remember what spirit shared with me. Because there was no logical way for that note, which was farther down on the list, to be open, I knew spirit had made it happen.

When I read it, my jaw hit the floor:

K, everything you are going through was laid out long before you were born. You will be a conduit for others but not until you're healed or on your way...this is still tough for you. –Jason

He came through with that particular message six months prior to me sitting in the ballroom with Tracie, but I knew exactly why he'd opened the note for me to read again.

It was time.

I was helping my friend by passing messages to her.

I was on my way to being fully healed.

I was, in that moment, a conduit for another.

He was confirming that I was indeed on my way, and I couldn't have been more grateful. I blinked back tears while I read the message over and over. Chill bumps appeared on my left arm—another sign that what I was experiencing was divine truth.

Healing from abuse is the hardest thing I've ever done. And it's very confusing at times because, on a human level, I felt every emotion. Anger. Sadness. Grief for what I'd endured and for the loss of what I thought was real. As an intuitive medium who knows there's a bigger picture than what we see, I also had the knowledge that maybe meeting Tony was indeed planned for me. After all, when I met Tony, I experienced all of my intuitive signals including chills, encouraging me to press on with him. Apparently, I was supposed to endure what I did to get where I was going. I had never thought of it that way, but Jason validated that it indeed was part of my soul journey in his message.

I was getting my own mojo back. I was helping others the way I did before I met Tony and I was, most importantly, helping myself heal. I knew the road would be longer than I wanted, but I could finally look back and see just how far I'd come.

* * *

"Hon, when do you think we should start looking for another place?"

"It wouldn't hurt to put feelers out even though we still have a few months left on the lease," Scott said.

One week later, we were signing a lease for a house in our favorite area of Flagstaff. It felt meant to be on all levels, and the entire family was beyond thrilled to leave behind the apartment complex where I lived with Tony. We cherished our time in Scott's apartment, but it was time to close the chapter and move forward. It was time to have a bedroom with doors again.

I was noticing things were falling into place in a way they hadn't for a very long time. I left my job at the university and inked a licensing deal for Mod Mom one week after receiving an email from a manufacturer asking if I was looking for a new partner. This kind of thing did not happen when I was locked in the cycle of abuse.

One day, while searching for an email about Mod Mom from 2015, I happened upon a message from Tony to his wife that I was blind copied on while we were together. He was explaining a *situation* in writing, or rather putting his false truth in writing in order to gaslight and instill fear in her.

Almost immediately, I felt a lump in my throat that grew to full-on tears as I read the message. I'd read this particular email back in 2015 but completely dismissed her. I chose to believe the bullshit story Tony had made up about why the cops were called to their home.

I hadn't believed her.

How could I have not seen what he was really doing back then? I was already dealing with his abusive behavior in 2015 and I still didn't see that she was speaking the truth.

Wiping tears away, I immediately started writing a letter to her. I'd never apologized for all of the pain I caused her. I could never take that away and I needed her to know that I was wrong to not believe her. And most importantly, I believed her now.

A few hours later, I was almost ready to send the message—but I hesitated out of fear that it would cause her more pain. After more thought and a nudge from spirit in the form of head-to-toe chills, I clicked *send.*

Dear D,

I have wanted to write this for a long time but was afraid it might make things worse for you on a number of levels. First, I want to say how sorry I am for my part in your pain. There's no excuse—I'm truly so sorry for not honoring you. I understand more about why I fell for Tony, but that's not important. What is important is that I caused you pain, which I will forever regret.

Yesterday, I was searching for a document he sent years ago and an e-mail message trail jumped out at me. I didn't remember it. Tony blind copied me on messages he sent to you—and you responded to—after you called the cops on him for abusive behavior. Of course, at the time, he wove a story about you that is completely contrary to who you really are...and I naively believed it. All I can say is that I was under his spell. I regret believing his lies about you.

I can't believe I didn't see the truth in what you wrote back in 2015. I have endured similar abuse from him resulting in a domestic violence call to my apartment when he was here in

Flagstaff in 2016. I have a police report documenting it. I'm not sure if you know, but I did file a restraining order against him. He is everything you stated, but I know I don't need to tell you that.

I hope so much you are on your own, now. Please know I have heard from ex-clients, ex-girlfriends, ex-colleagues, and received confirmation about the testimonies of abuse (financial, emotional, sexual), violence, drugs, and predatory behavior.

Again, I'm so sorry. I hope so much you and the kids are well.

Sincerely,

Kiersten

I sat in silence for a while hoping that I did the right thing. I thought about how much she'd endured already and, as the mother of his children, how much she still had to endure. My heart broke for her. I could get out, but she was forever tied to him. Guilt washed over me for hurting a woman who was already in more pain than I could ever imagine—and partly caused by me. Not only was I the one he left her for, but I and the Universe sent him back to her.

Flashes of what I remembered him telling me came to my mind like real-time visions. I recalled when he was back home living with her during one of our break-ups. She had to be taken to the ER because she was having heart attack symptoms. Turns out, it was a panic attack. I, too, was having panic attacks when I was with him. She finally got some distance and space despite how much I know it hurt her initially, only to have him come back.

He was abusing her, and she was stuck. Stuck financially. Stuck physically. Stuck being the only rock for their kids. He told me during their marriage that he threatened to start looking around if she wasn't going to give him what he needed emotionally. He painted her as a cold person, and all along, he'd been cheating on her and abusing her to the point that she called the cops. He told me she was irrational and called the police because he was opening her mail. I stupidly believed it, or rather, didn't want to look any deeper.

Shortly after I wrote to Tony's wife, I was making plans to pay back my childhood friend, Eddie, who bought a $3,500 sofa from Tony only to never receive it. Eddie bought the couch from Tony because of my connection to him. Eddie was telling me that his attempts to get repaid were being shoved back in his face. He tried everything short of small claims court but, as Tony put in writing, *you can't get blood from a stone*. Then, he told Eddie to stop asking for a repayment plan because he wouldn't be responding again.

Eddie and his wife were more than understanding and accommodating. They didn't hold me accountable but appreciated that I wanted to get them repaid. And I did. The more I learned about all of the people who were swindled by Tony, the more I understood that no one, not even my parents, was going to see a dime of what they loaned him. Ever. It would be up to me to see that my parents recouped their investment. I wasn't the only one who'd paid the price for being in Tony's orbit.

CHAPTER 21

Light

Light was flooding back into my life again. Ironically, all of the boxes you check on the *most stressful events in life* checklist were checked—a new job, a new home, healing from abuse, trying to make amends for what I'd done, and public speaking in the guise of a terrifying stint on stage called a TEDx talk—yet all I could feel was excitement. Excitement that I survived a relationship that had been killing me physically, emotionally, spiritually, and financially.

On second thought, I felt both excitement and serious anxiety about the TEDx talk. At the core, an inner peace came with my whole TED experience, but there was also sheer terror and frustration. It all started in October of 2017.

Kiersten, you're going to do a TEDx talk, declared Jason in spirit.

I answered him in my head. "Um, no I'm not...TED doesn't want to hear what I have to say about intuition. It's crazy talk!"

Remember when you found Mom's lost cat near her home while you were sitting in Flagstaff and she was in Connecticut?

You didn't think that was possible but it was. Listen to me, he insisted. *You're absolutely going to do a TED Talk.*

"Fine, you win...I'll start thinking about what I'd like to share and look into how to

apply."

During the little downtime I had between work and family, I started formulating my talk. I knew it would encompass healing from abuse using intuition, but I wasn't quite sure where to start. I poked around on the internet and found an application for TEDx Las Vegas. I applied but didn't get selected as a speaker.

Then I saw that Sedona—a town only thirty minutes from where we live—was holding one in November of 2018, and they had just opened their application page. If Sedona, land of "woo-woo," didn't accept my application, who would? This time, my intuition told me to reach out to Mark to see if he would write a testimonial. I figured his endorsement might help provide proof that scientific TEDx needs. Thankfully, Mark quickly wrote the testimonial shown opposite.

I carefully crafted the synopsis of my talk, included the endorsement from Mark, and hit the *Apply* button. Much to my surprise, I received a message from the event producer asking for more information. I had apparently made it past the first round. Now, I had to videotape myself talking about my TEDx talk, which would be limited to eighteen minutes, as all talks are in TED land.

I did that and jumped through a few more hoops, revising a bit of the structure based on their feedback. They even put me in touch with an outstanding TEDx talk coach who helped me craft the title to be more suitable for the event. I wanted it to be titled, "Healing from Abuse Using Intuition." They pushed back, asking me if the part where I talk about seeing visions of other kids in spirit was really necessary. I had to reach deep down into my soul and ask that very same question.

Each time I did, I got the same answer: Keep it in—it's part of your journey. My intuition was loud and clear. I told them that I wouldn't have known to trust the visions I received about my own abuse had I not trusted the ones that came in about other children

NEW YORK PRIVATE
DETECTIVE SERVICES

275 7TH Avenue
7th Floor
New York, NY 10001

Tel: (888) 691-3313
Fax: (815) 425-8891
www.nypdservices.com

February 9, 2018

Kiersten,

It was great to hear from you, and I am more than happy to provide you a with my personal endorsement, and I look forward to the time that we have the opportunity to work together again.

Kiersten and I got to know one another when we each volunteered to work on a missing person's case in the NYC area. I knew the minute we started talking on the phone that Kiersten was the real deal. As the case progressed, I was blown away by the amount of detail she shared; it matched what I had in my hard-copy file.

She was channeling all of this from 3,000 miles away without any tie to the case, or way to validate details. She had no stake in the case other than the drive to want to help her friend's friend whose loved one was missing. I have to say, as a retired NYPD Detective and the current *Founder & Chief Investigator* for: **New York Private Detective Services**, with over thirty years of crime solving experience, it is rare to find someone like Kiersten.

She is truly one of a kind, and I'm honored to work with her. I truly believe she has a "very big purpose in this life . . . one that will help many people globally."

All my best,

Mark Pacci *NYPD Detective (Ret.)*
Founder & Chief Investigator

during my intuitive awakening. In addition, every narcissistic abuse survivor I've ever met has said the same thing: intuitively, they knew early on in the relationship that it wasn't normal, but they refused to believe their intuition. I did the very same thing. TEDx backed down after I shared why I felt it was important to keep it in. It was not lost on me that I went through something similar with *Shark Tank* producers. If I'd learned anything since being on that reality show, it was that I had to keep trusting my own gut.

Finally, I got the news. I'd made it! They let me know about three weeks later than the rest of the speakers because they'd forgotten to tell me that I made the cut after deliberations.

After I stopped jumping up and down with excitement, I went into nervous as hell mode. *How in the world was I going to be able to memorize an eighteen-minute speech when my memory was shot?* An unfortunate side effect of abuse is memory loss, something that got worse after enduring three years of relationship abuse. Still, I was determined. If I practiced four or five times a day, I could make it happen.

I had to give Jason his due—he was right, again. It was silly of me to doubt his prediction because he had never been wrong. Ever. Even when I wanted him to be wrong.

I had a month to prepare before I stepped onto the TEDx stage in Sedona to give the toughest speech of my life. Not only was I concerned about my ability to memorize it, but I was also nervous about putting it all out there. My uncle, my heightened intuition, and Tony were all key elements of my talk, in addition to sharing how I was able to rebuild myself and my life after abuse.

I was overcome with emotion the day of the event. My husband and kids proudly sat in the front row, and Theresa, my friend who let me cry on her shoulder after the domestic violence call, made sure she was in the audience that day, too. In addition to all of the love I felt, I was acutely aware of a friend who had passed away earlier in the year shortly after leaving a twenty-year-long abusive marriage. She and I talked about founding healing centers for trauma survivors before her death. I felt her on stage with me alongside Jason.

Despite some tech difficulties with sound and a temperamental slideshow clicker, I managed to give the hardest talk of my life without forgetting much of what I'd practiced. Much to my surprise, I got choked up during my talk.

When I left the stage, multiple teary-eyed people thanked me for being vulnerable and open. Some of them were abuse survivors, too. I was in tears hearing their stories. Many hugs were exchanged between random strangers. And then there were the hugs from the organizers thanking me for not giving in to their suggestions to take out the whole first section of my talk. I felt vindicated and proud. I'd done it!

Shortly after I finished my TEDx talk, I checked in with Jason's mom, Yvette. She reminded me that it was Jason's "angelversary," otherwise known as the anniversary of his death. As soon as I told her I was sending her hugs, I felt full chills from head to toe. I heard Jason say, *I've got your back, Kiers.*

He sure did. I knew in my soul that it was not a coincidence that I gave my TEDx talk on the anniversary of his death.

Grace asked if she could stay with us that night, making me a happy mama. As people approached me after my talk, I watched her expression. She knew that by telling my story, I was helping them tell theirs. She teared up a few times listening to others talk about the abuse they endured as well.

As for Noah, I knew it was better for him to head back home after I finished my presentation. Events like TEDx are an introvert's nightmare—there was an incredible amount of energy in the room that day. After a while, I wanted to hide under something, too.

The next day after the TEDx presentations, the audience members who wanted to dive deeper into our TEDx topics partic-ipated in a round table discussion. Grace and Scott came with me.

During the discussion, the most incredible thing happened. People asked Grace how what I endured affected her.

"I knew it was my mom's journey to go through," she replied. "It was hard to watch, but I knew I just had to wait until she was ready to stand up to the abuse."

With tears streaming down our faces, Scott and I watched her answer questions. There wasn't a dry eye at the table, actually. We've always known our kids are old souls and wise beyond their years, but we also recognized that what they endured affected them greatly. And that was part of what I felt I needed to help them with, one way or another.

As the instigator of too much change in their lives, and the person who brought an abusive man into their world, I knew my main role was to be there for them. I needed to listen to them, no matter how hard it was to hear.

One day about a month after the TEDx event, Noah and I were out running errands together and Noah took the opportunity to share his feelings.

"Mom, I don't want to feel resentment toward you, but I do," Noah said.

I felt a dagger pierce my heart. "I don't blame you for feeling that way. In fact, if I were in your shoes, I would feel the same way. What I did caused a lot of pain."

"But you know I love you and it doesn't change that," he said.

"I sure do, and I love you and Grace more than anything in the world. I want to help you heal the pain you feel anyway I can."

After that, several very hard conversations were struck up over the dinner table when it was just the three of us. Even though I knew they were proud of me for my TEDx talk, were happy Scott and I were back together and understood what led me to do what I did, they both harbored a lot of deep pain neither had really processed.

In anger one day, Grace said, "Mom, I wish he'd never been in our life—he's an abusive asshole."

"I know, honey, and I will regret letting him in until the day I die. You have every right to feel angry and hurt by all of it. I wish so much that I could change the past."

The conversation went on like that for about an hour. Noah and Grace talked about the painful years when Tony was in their life, and I intuitively knew my only job was to listen. I knew all I could do was own all of the hurt and pain they buried. It was humbling, painful, and beautiful at the same time. I was grateful they were willing to talk it out with me. I could have lost my relationship with both of them, but because they opened their hearts, we moved through raw, emotional talks with a lot of love and tears.

* * *

After the TEDx talk was over, I had to wait for the professional video to be edited together. The organizers managed the whole video editing process, letting us know that speakers wouldn't see the video of their talk until it was published by TEDx headquarters. Based on last year's schedule, it would likely take three months for the videos to be uploaded to the TEDx site.

I waited with excitement in my heart.

Two months.

Three months.

Four months.

Five months.

Other talks in my taping group were being uploaded, yet I heard nothing about mine. Eventually, I sent a couple of emails to the Sedona organizers, as well as TEDx headquarters on the East Coast, trying to find out if my talk had sound issues like a few others did, or if something else was keeping it from being uploaded. I found out that it was sent to TEDx corporate for review four months after the event.

Five months after the event, I finally found out that TEDx head-quarters had a problem with my talk. They felt it didn't meet the content guidelines. I was confused because a) I'd submitted many videos along the way and had the approval of TEDx Sedona, and b) I knew there were other TEDx talks that covered topics of intuition and abuse. I wracked my brain trying to figure out what was wrong with mine.

The waiting game continued.

On May 8th, 2017, I finally got a call from TEDx Sedona saying that TEDx wanted to continue to edit the video "because of a few words I used in my talk." What words? I didn't know what that meant specifically. They instructed me to submit my written script to them so they could tell me what was wrong with my talk. Not wanting to be the one who was holding it up any further, I immediately sent my script back.

I let a week or two go by before I reached out to TEDx Sedona to see if they had any updates. Nope, nothing. But they promised they'd poke the bear.

More silence.

I finally decided to write to TEDx headquarters using their general mailbox email again, since that seemed to spur some action. I wanted to know if they had time over the past three weeks to take a look at the script. I received a perplexing reply from TEDx headquarters that asked if I was writing about an upcoming talk. Then came another email from Sedona requesting that I stay out of it because I was making it worse and possibly hurting their relationship with TED.

There it was. Seven months. No real answers. No end in sight with a "butt out" message, to boot.

I had a decision to make. Should I continue to play the game and accept the silent treatment and shaming for trying to get answers from the same folks who forgot to tell me I was a chosen speaker, or do I go rogue and just post my own amateur video? The latter would help me take my power back. I was done being pushed around.

I grabbed the video Noah recorded on the day of the event and taught myself how to use iMovie to prepare it for publication. It's by no means perfect, but it's real. After hours and hours of editing, I posted my video on June 2nd, feeling a quiet knowing that I needed to get it done that day. I shared it with Yvette, who revealed that June 2nd is Jason's birthday. *I've got your back, Kiers* came to my mind again. I was dumbfounded.

I had literally felt pushed all day long—like someone was pushing on my back—to get the video done right then. And now I knew why. *What are the odds that the day I gave my TEDx talk (that he said I would give) was his angelversary, and the day I took my power back by uploading my own video was his birthday?* It was beyond coincidence.

At the end of July, while having breakfast with my in-laws, I hopped on the TEDx Sedona website to see if any of the other talks with tech difficulties had been published. It'd been a long time since I did that.

"Oh my God, guys, it's up," I said to Larry, Judy, and Scott who were all sitting around the dining room table. "It published five days ago, apparently."

Scott jumped up from the table. "Kiers, this is huge! Let's watch it on the big TV!"

"This is gonna be interesting. I still can't believe it published and no one told me. Oh wait...maybe I can believe that."

We watched the TEDx talk for eleven minutes—it was four minutes shorter than my original talk. Their version eliminated all talk of intuition. They even cut out the word *intuition* at the end of the talk where I said, "I hope you're inspired to trust your own intuition."

I felt so relieved that I had published my uncensored video on my website. It's a much better talk that makes sense. It's the talk I know I was meant to give.

Still, even in the censored version of my talk on the TEDx site, the message about wounded attachment is a really important one—one that I wished I'd known when I was coming to grips with the abuse I endured as a child. There are way too many of us repeating cycles of abuse, all the while having no clue as to why. If I've learned anything from being vocal about my journey, it's that we are truly dealing with a silent epidemic of abuse. One that affects millions of people around the globe.

* * *

Between business trips and life with the kids, I continued to find healing in writing about my experiences and solace in simply being with the ones I love most. I still battle the long-lasting physical effects of three years of narcissistic abuse. I'm doing everything I can to reverse the adrenal fatigue and endocrine system issues that stem from high cortisol levels flooding my body for so long.

On occasion, I still get unexpected emails from people related to Tony, but for the most part, that portion of my life is in the rearview mirror. In June of 2020, I heard from a design industry friend— apparently Tony reached out to him for the sole purpose of shaming him for publicly supporting me. It had been three years since I'd left Tony, yet he was still stalking my social media, hell-bent on making sure those who split from him in support of me are made to feel they made the wrong choice. In response, my friend told Tony that if he contacted him again, he'd take legal action.

Prior to that, in early 2019, I received a comment in response to a post I'd written where I combatted lies Tony was spewing about me by posting all of the legal documents documenting the abuse, including the restraining order. The post comment I received read: *Dodged this bullet, only after reading your blog/posts.* This brave woman later confirmed that she was talking to Tony but something felt off. She did a little research online and found my website.

Reading her message filled me with so much gratitude. One of the reasons I decided to be vocal about what I endured was because I didn't want others to fall into the same trap—whether it be with him or someone like him. In circles of folks recovering from narcissistic abuse, it's widely encouraged to not combat the smear campaign that most abusers launch—but in my case, I knew intuitively I need not follow that advice.

It appears this is a recurring theme throughout my forty-eight years on earth: to stand up for what I know is right for me no matter how scary, intimidating, or crazy it might seem. I have been guided my whole life to trust my own intuition no matter how difficult the task.

I've come to realize that the Universe or God or whatever you want to call interconnectedness has a plan, and it's up to us to learn and grow from our experiences. As I've continued to heal, I've experienced a lot of full-circle moments that remind me that there is a purpose in what we endure and what we learn.

For instance, I've had the honor of mentoring an eighteen-year-old named Corey. He's very strong in his Christian faith, as well as highly intuitive. He came to me via his mother, who knew about my story and journey with sudden onset mediumship. This very thing was happening to him, and he was terrified.

I know the only reason he was even open to talking with me was that he didn't perceive me as "Sedona woo woo," as he said. I shared how all of the spirit stuff happened to me and I talked about how I had to learn to set boundaries. And in the circular way these things go when it comes to spirit, he taught me a few things, too.

When Corey and I first sat down together in my office, he was looking for answers about how to protect himself against the energy that was holding him down nightly in his bed. With tears in his eyes, he told me that if he doesn't ask for protection from God and Jesus, he's pinned to his bed, rendering him powerless to move. In addition, he could see an evil-looking figure standing in the corner of his room.

"Oh Corey, I'm so sorry...I know how terrifying it is to experience things like that and have no common sense explanation. I want to help you figure out how to make this stop."

"Thank you, Kiersten. I just don't know what to do anymore and I'm not sleeping."

"I don't have all the answers, but I have experienced dark energy like what you're talking about. I learned through trial and error that I have power over it...if I believe I do. Here's what I want you to do: make a list of rules for yourself, but you have to believe with all of your heart that they are set in stone."

I told him that if he makes rules like *nothing is allowed in my room that isn't for my highest good,* he will control what is coming in and feeding off of his fear. He wanted to believe me, but I could tell he wasn't completely sold. His mom asked if he could do this—if he could truly believe in his soul that he was protected. His answer brought tears to my eyes.

With tears streaming down his face, he said, "I think I can, but what if I'm not good enough in God's eyes? What if I am not doing all I can and risk going to hell?" In that moment, I heard in my mind to say, "You are heaven." I leaned over and put my hand on his knee. "Corey, you are heaven. Right here, right now. You're an amazing human being with a huge heart. You are heaven."

I never could have predicted what happened next. He started shaking violently in his chair. His eyes rolled back in his head as tears continued to fall. His mother and I looked at each other with mouths agape. I turned to Corey "Are you okay?"

"I'm okay, I just can't control this," he said in a very calm voice.

Three minutes went by, and the shaking came to a slow stop. He returned to normal, aside from beads of sweat pouring down his face.

"Kiersten, I feel so much lighter," he said. "I feel different."

"Really? That's fantastic! I have to be honest...I've never seen anything like that in my life, but I keep hearing intuitively that the energy that attached itself to you is no longer with you. By believing that you have control, and that you are heaven right here, right now, you demanded that energy leave you."

I held out hope that when he climbed into bed that night, he would have his first restful sleep in more than six months. Thank God, he did.

Since our meeting, he's been learning to set boundaries and honing his intuitive skills. I mentor him when he reaches out for help. His gifts have escalated significantly, and he's even helped spirit cross into the light. He had to learn to believe that what he was experiencing was real and true, and then he had to own it without fear or shame. Believing that he had power over the dark was key.

It dawned on me recently that what I started with the Little Light Project—helping kids and parents—had come full circle too, because I was finally in a place where I could help kids and parents again. Not only were the kids in spirit back, but so were the intuitive kids who needed help making sense of what was happening to them. I didn't consciously make any of it happen; I was simply living my life away from abuse and darkness. Finally.

Children in spirit still come in when they need my assistance. I help them however I can, whether that means passing information to parents and trusted law enforcement contacts, or simply holding onto their messages for a later time if instructed. I no longer doubt that what I am seeing and hearing is real. I've been through too much to question anything now. I truly believe that nothing is a coincidence...even the toughest lessons of our lives.

CHAPTER 22

Turning the Page

Remembering what Sophia had said all those years ago, I knew it was time to pen my not-so-normal journey. From late 2017 to fall of 2019, I spent early mornings, business trips travel, and weekends feverishly pecking away at my laptop.

At times, the writing process was beyond gut-wrenching. To make sure my memory matched reality, I read through thousands of email and text messages saved from when Tony and I were together. Despite the pain, I pushed myself to keep going, knowing that spirit was guiding me. Jason was guiding me. He even told me in the beginning of the process that it would take me a few years. As usual, he was right.

By the time October of 2019 rolled around, I was finally done with my rough draft. Similar to when I researched how to build furniture and cross spirit into the light, I turned to Google to learn how to pitch literary agents. The kids in spirit said that I'd land a female agent—and that felt right to me—but I also tried to keep an open mind.

First, I researched which agents sold spiritual memoirs. As you can imagine, there aren't many. I even used my pendulum to confirm that I had the right folks on my initial pitch list before sending query letters to fifteen agents. I soon became the queen of kind rejections, or I heard nothing at all. That is until an agent/award-winning fiction writer by the name of Tina Wainscott took a chance on me. She replied to my query asking when we could chat on the phone. When we finally connected in December, Tina told me that her intuition urged her to connect with me despite knowing that a) memoir is not easy to sell unless you're a celebrity, and b) spiritual memoir is even harder to sell.

Chills raced up and down my body when she told me what drew her to my story. I can guarantee it wasn't my writing, nor was it my comma placement. She took a chance on me and helped me prepare a professional book proposal as well as edit my manuscript draft because she saw something unique about my story. And her own intuitive guidance told her twice to add me to her client list.

In March of 2020, a month before Tina started shopping my book proposal with publishing houses, the Coronavirus pandemic hit. While I knew this would throw a wrench in things, I didn't fully understand just what it would take to get a traditional book deal for a book that was anything but traditional. Tina pitched *Little Voices* to the massive publishing houses first. Let's just say I got very used to seeing the word *pass*, even though many editors seemed intrigued by my story.

Thankfully, I did receive some intuitive guidance on the trajectory of the book. Spirit said that the publishing house I'd call home would have a tree in its logo. I knew to trust it because two of my favorite mediums, Cynthia Spiece and Katie Beecher, both told me separately and without knowledge of what the other said, that they were channeling a vision of a tree for the logo.

Naturally, I researched every publishing house with a tree or leaves in its mark, and I made sure Tina knew what was being channeled about my upcoming book deal. So far, all of the publishers with tree logos had already turned me down. Either my platform wasn't big enough or they weren't sure how to sell *Little Voices* because it tackled so many subjects across multiple categories.

One day in September of 2020, I was chatting with Yvette when Jason came through saying that I needed to put the book down for a year. Specifically, he said I would be adding more to it. My first reaction was disbelief. *Why was I supposed to wait? And what would I be adding?* The book was already long enough.

I decided not to tell Tina, because she was about to pitch a few more publishers and why hold her back? I was still hopeful that I'd land a deal before the end of 2020. Three months passed, and I rang in the new year without a publishing contract. *Timing*, I reminded myself. Still, I couldn't help but think back to what Jason had said in September about adding more to my story.

* * *

While I not-so-patiently waited for a book deal and continued to do everything I could to keep all of us safe and Corona-free, the Universe filled my world with *woo woo*. Thankfully, I'm pretty fond of all things spiritual now. And I'm fond of the extraordinary young mom named Alexis who reached out to me for guidance about intuition in early 2021. She isn't a stranger—we've talked once before, and I know her mom and dad from my hometown in Ohio.

While I don't accept every request for guidance I receive (or I'd become completely overwhelmed just answering questions), I knew I needed to help Alexis. I've admired her work as a writer and an activist. And I knew she and her family needed help understanding the strange world of intuition.

After we connected by text, I happily shared what I've learned over the years, and I talked to her about what I was intuitively picking up regarding her house and her family. I heard from spirit that her eldest son was just like her—incredibly intuitive and empathic.

Naturally, after we spoke and I relayed a few resources and tips, I thought that might be the end of our back and forth.

Until *he* showed up in my mind's eye.

When Alexis asked me via text if I could describe any of the spirits I saw hanging out in her house, I shared that one stood out more than the others. He had dark hair, wore a black leather jacket, and looked to be in his twenties.

Alexis sent back a short message: "I'm in tears."

Naturally, I wondered and worried about what triggered her emotional response until she forwarded a photo of a photo that hangs on their wall. She indeed knew the young man well—he was her husband's best friend who passed away when he was nineteen. I was relieved to know that she connected with the person I was seeing in my mind, but I didn't realize there was more to come.

The next day, the young man showed me a vision of John Candy and asked me to share that message with Alexis. I chuckled thinking about the randomness of the message. After all, I've never channeled anything about the late actor/comedian, nor did I even remember his name. I had to ask Scott what Candy's first name was after seeing his face on a movie screen in my mind's eye and hearing the word *candy*. When I passed on the message, and Alexis looked up John Candy on Google, she said the minute she saw his photo, she had chills from head to toe.

Sure enough, the message that I shared with Alexis made complete sense to her husband. When he was in his teens, they used to watch the movie *Spaceballs* together in the basement. It was one of their things.

The beauty of such a simple "evidential" message, as the woo woo world calls it, is that in an instant, Alexis' husband learned that his beloved friend is still with them in spirit. And Alexis understands that her intuitive awakening isn't to be feared, nor is it something she made up in her mind. She even mustered the courage to reach out to the young man's mother to tell her what had transpired, and what she'd picked up using her own sixth sense. By trusting her inner voice and intuitive gifts, she reassured his mom that roughly ten years out from his death, he is still very much alive in spirit, and continues to help guide those he loves from the other side.

Thanks to this young man, Alexis knows without a doubt that her intuition is real, and that it's meaningful beyond anything she can see right now. After all, she's not supposed to see how it all fits together, or know all of the details about what's coming down the pike for her. None of us are. That's the beauty and mystery of life.

CHAPTER 23

Then, Now, and Forever

In early 2021—in addition to continuing to mentor Corey—I began working with several other highly intuitive kids and young adults. Just like before, these families were guided to me through friends and family. I love helping kids make sense of their gifts, and consider it one of my favorite parts of my *woo woo* life. Plus, at that point, volunteering my time in this way helped keep my mind off wondering what Jason meant when he said I'd be adding more to the book.

During the same time, Tina started pitching the smaller publishers. She even hinted to me that we were unfortunately inching closer to the end of the road. After all, there aren't that many houses out there that publish spiritual memoirs. It was time for me to revisit that list of hers—there were roughly five publishers left to pitch. I sat down at my desk, opened my web browser, and got to work. Before I knew it, I'd researched all of them but one.

The words *Post Hill Press* anchored the bottom of the list. The minute I pulled up their website, I started laughing uncontrollably. Their logo was a giant tree! *How had I missed that?*

I knew instantly I'd found my publisher, so I excitedly scanned their website for anything that looked remotely like *Little Voices*. It seemed they mostly catered to politically conservative and/or traditionally Christian authors. I personally don't fit into either one of those categories nor did my book.

I started to lose hope just about the time I spotted Dr. Ramani Durvasula's bestselling book about surviving narcissistic abuse called *Should I Stay or Should I Go? Oh my god, I know her,* I thought. *What are the odds?* Like me, she spoke at the 2018 TEDx Sedona event. I really loved her TEDx talk and all of the work she does to help survivors of abuse. During the Sedona event, I remembered thinking how ironic it was that we were both giving a talk about narcissistic abuse; however, mine was personal and hers was based on her work as a celebrated psychologist. After meeting her at the event, I'd even started sharing with friends and family the videos of her *Red Table Talk* TV segments with Jada Pinkett Smith.

Instinctively, I knew I had to do what I hated most: ask for help. I mustered the courage to write to her that very day. I had no idea if she'd even remember me or my TEDx talk, or if she'd even have time to write me back. Within a few days, she replied telling me how much she loved my talk and that she remembered my beautiful family, too. When I asked if she'd be willing to read and endorse my book, she quickly said she'd be honored.

I was floored that she said yes. I even gave her every out to say no, knowing that some of the subject matter—aka, the *woo woo* stuff—might not be something a well-respected psychologist would want to be associated with. She didn't take the outs I gave her, thank goodness.

We set a tentative date for her to get back to me by March of 2021. As we all know now—having lived through a worldwide pandemic—unexpected things happen that mess up our best-laid plans. It took a few more months for Dr. Ramani to read *Little Voices* and share her endorsement with me. End of August, to be exact. When I received it, I cried tears of relief and gratitude. She personally told me that she loved the book and could even see it as a movie. Her written endorsement blew my mind, too. *Maybe all that stuff I went through with TEDx was really about meeting Dr. Ramani?* I thought as I dialed the phone to call Tina.

Tina and I knew back in January, when Dr. Ramani agreed to read *Little Voices*, that we needed to wait to send a pitch email to the head of Post Hill Press until we had her endorsement. And now we had it. Tina was as excited as I was when I told her what Dr. Ramani had said about my memoir. Within a day of receiving the endorsement, Tina included it in her pitch and sent her email off to Post Hill Press. Now, all we had to do was wait.

* * *

In early November, my phone rang. It wasn't Tina calling about Post Hill Press, but rather Detective Mark Pucci. It had been months since we'd spoken, and it was rare for him to call, so I knew something was up. We normally sent texts back and forth to one another.

"Kiersten, I have an offer for you," he said. "Do you remember when we first met in 2014, and we talked about knowing we'd work together under a bigger umbrella one day?"

"Absolutely I remember that!" I replied excitedly. "It was something I was told by spirit, even. I just didn't know how it would all come together after I closed down the Little Light Project nonprofit."

"Well, now I know how we're going to do this," he replied. "I'm starting a nonprofit that helps crime victims and their families investigate cases at no cost to the families. I want us to help families of missing and murdered Indigenous women and children, missing persons, and homicide victims. And I want to call it the National Institute for Law and Justice…NILJ, for short."

Chills raced up and down my entire body as tears filled my eyes. This was meant to be. This was *it*. I knew it with every cell of my being. It was all coming together. This was what Jason was talking about when he said I'd be writing more in my book.

"Mark, I'd be more than honored to join you…this is absolutely what we're being guided to do…what can I do to help?" I choked out through tears.

That night, I started setting up the website, designed a few logo concepts, and called on a small circle of amazing people I knew would be guided to jump on board, too.

Of course, a few souls already knew what was happening, and they made themselves known that night. In addition to Carrie, Jason, and Nate, a handful of children in spirit I'd never met before came by to say hello. They told me a line was already forming behind them.

They told me it was time.

* * *

A week after Mark and I spoke on the phone about NILJ, I received another call. This time it was from Tina.

"Kiersten!" she practically screamed. "You're not going to believe this! You've been telling me for a year that you knew it would be Post Hill Press! Well, their editor just wrote to say that they want *Little Voices*!"

Everything in my body went numb. I could barely speak. I didn't even know what to say. I just kept saying, "Oh my God" over and over again. Finally, I pulled myself together and thanked Tina for believing in me through forty-four rejections and almost two years of pitching.

"We did it…oh my God, Tina, we did it!" I said, with a smile as wide as Texas spread across my face. "Wow! Okay, so…what happens next?"

Tina and I talked about the next steps while my family looked on knowing that something majorly good had just happened.

We all teared up when I shared the details of my call after hanging up with Tina. I think we even danced around the kitchen, but it's truly all just a blur in my memory at this point. I do remember Scott and me hugging for a very long time, and we just kept saying we couldn't believe that Post Hill Press had a tree for a logo.

Just like spirit said.

* * *

I will never not be amazed by how the Universe works. But if I had to pinpoint one of the most basic lessons my path has taught me, it's to live in the moment like I never had before. I believe in timing and synchronicity more than I ever thought possible, and I truly believe each soul has its own journey. I see it in my own kids every day.

Three years ago, Noah shared with us that he finally realized he'd been dealing with gender dysphoria for ten years. Noah, who has now chosen the name *Natalie* as well as *she/her* pronouns, is currently undergoing hormone replacement therapy to help her become the gender with whom she identifies. Her realization at the age of twenty is part of her path, and we're incredibly proud of Nat's bravery and commitment to honor what she knows is true for her. We're excited for her bright future in the art/illustration world and the ease that will come as she finally feels comfortable in her own skin. This particular journey is not for the weak, but it is for the most compassionate, incredible human beings who are born to help lead us into a future filled with less judgment and more love for self and others.

Grace, who is now nineteen, is fulfilling a soul purpose to touch the lives of others with her music. To watch her write, compose, and sing original songs that are wise beyond her years is such an honor and joy. She's been doing it since she was little but only now understands that not everyone can write, or channel, songs that heal the heart the way she does. And not everyone can teach themselves to play musical instruments. If ever there was a person destined for a music career, it's Grace. She opened for Andy Grammer at just sixteen and was scouted by casting agents for the tv show *The Voice*.

We're incredibly proud of her courage and determination to carve out the life she wants at such a young age.

I see soul purpose in my relationship with Scott, too. Our faith in one another—when we met, during the first eighteen years of our marriage, during our separation, and now—is profoundly soul-based. Turns out, it was *our* love that was, and will forever be, TNF.

I can only speak from my experiences, but I believe we all have purposes and gifts. And yes, it takes guts to follow the invisible roadmap laid out for us. There were many times I wanted to quit Mod Mom or give up on the book, but my intuition urged me to keep going.

In 2019, the Frank Lloyd Wright Foundation approached me about designing and producing the first-ever line of kids' furniture inspired by Wright. Never did I imagine that I'd partner with the most celebrated American architect of all time. The reason it was even an option was that I kept listening to my intuition, never giving up on Mod Mom no matter how hard it got. Turns out, all of those mistakes, hurdles, and failed deals along the way were just redirections to something better. If we could all see those detours and "failures" that way, we'd endure a lot less pain.

I see soul purpose around the abuse I endured, too. I could have stayed angry with my uncle and Tony for the rest of my life, but what if there's a bigger picture I just can't see? Now, I'm not saying I did anything to deserve what my uncle did—I was a young child who was preyed on by a predator. But what if, as Jason said, some of the things in my life—like meeting Tony—were planned before I took my first breath? What if my soul chose specific experiences to endure, learn from, heal, and then ultimately help others through? What if all of the people in our lives are playing roles for a greater purpose?

I don't know anything for certain, but if the answer to all of these questions is yes, then I choose to be grateful for the healing journey. And grateful for the cast of players who helped me and continue to help me live out my soul purpose.

It doesn't mean I condone abusive behavior by any means. I also know that the men who abused me didn't deserve to be treated the way they were when they were young. They, too, were forced into the cycle of abuse and, thus far, have not been able to break free in all areas of their lives. That's their choice and journey.

I recognize that I don't fit the mold of the *abused woman with self-esteem issues* that is widely believed and spread throughout our society. As a woman with a great deal of confidence, I'm quite the opposite, actually, and I know I'm not alone. Every woman I've met who has escaped an emotionally abusive relationship is strong, successful, smart, determined, courageous, driven, empathic, and empathetic. After all, narcissistic abusers frequently seek out those who have what they don't in hopes of absorbing it all and then moving on.

The narcissist's perfect target is someone who is wounded, regardless of whether the target is conscious of the trauma or not. Many women I've met who found themselves in abusive relationships as adults are childhood abuse survivors. Many of those same women are incredibly intuitive. Based solely on discussions I've had with survivors, there seems to be a link between intuition and trauma.

As someone who had no idea I was abused as a child until I was forty years old, I finally understand that I didn't need to know the abuse happened to recreate similar trauma as an adult. It's widely known in scientific circles that our subconscious drives roughly 80 percent or more of our behavior. Even if you don't remember you endured some sort of trauma as a child, you're still being driven by it. But as a grown-up, I had the opportunity to say *no* to more abuse, create boundaries, eradicate all codependent behaviors, heal subconscious patterns, and finally end the cycle I had unknowingly, unconsciously been locked in since childhood.

I don't have all the answers but I've finally learned three things I didn't understand when I was younger:

1. Intuition is real and has always been a part of me.
2. Intuition is what I ignored when I was being abused as an adult.
3. Intuition is what ultimately saved me, and helped me climb out of the darkness and begin to heal.

I think back to my time with Sophia—almost fourteen years ago—and marvel at all I've learned since she took my hand that day in her psychic shop and started an avalanche of change inside of me. Without that change, I wouldn't be where I am today.

One thing is for sure: I may never have had the strength to get out of the abusive relationship and open myself to understanding the power of subconscious programming had I not believed in the power within me. I had a choice to make—to believe in the unknown and dive headfirst or run from it. I'm grateful that I chose to embrace intuition. And I'm beyond grateful for the children in spirit who quite literally saved my life. Many of them perished at the hands of sexual predators and they made damn sure I wasn't going to suffer the same fate.

I'm finally able to see what Sophia saw a decade ago. She said I had a lot of healing to do but that in the end, it would be beautiful. And boy, was she right. Today, love and light are all around me—love from my husband, my kids, my family, my friends, Mark and everyone at NILJ, and the beautiful eternal lights like Carrie, Jason, and Nate who helped me stand up to abuse. And it truly doesn't get any better than that. Then, now, and forever.

In Carrie's case, I continued digging for answers beneath that tree. When I found what I was unknowingly looking for, I wept. For her. For countless others whose voices haven't been heard yet. And for Little Kiersten who, for almost forty years, silently waited to make herself known. Solving most cases is a long road—as is healing—but what I learned is this: they both always start with the courage to unbury the deep secrets and bring truth to light.

CHAPTER 24

Final Thoughts

Tips for Developing Your Intuition and Healing Old Wounds

Like the day I spent digging beneath the tree, I knew there was more to uncover. I still feel that way today. I will forever be digging for answers to many questions about life, the afterlife, and healing.

With that said, over the past ten years, having lived through narcissistic abuse, experienced so much of the unseen world, and founded a nonprofit that helps highly intuitive kids and grieving parents, I do have a few tips and practices to share with you about how you can better develop your intuition as well as heal subconscious wounds.

We all have the gift of intuition; we just don't always know how to recognize or trust it. My hope is that you'll be able to apply some of these tips and techniques to your own life. And if you're an abuse survivor who has not yet climbed out, or is thinking of ways to escape, I hope you find this chapter helpful as you rise up, out, and fully heal.

Developing Your Intuition

Here are a few ways to develop and hone your innate intuitive abilities, in addition to a few things I've learned along my journey about the act of developing your intuition:

1. **Tapping into your intuitive side doesn't require that you sit cross-legged meditating for hours on end.** Think back to some of your best ideas. Did they happen while you were driving? Or in the shower? Many of mine did. I've found that actively doing something with your physical body helps you to get into a state of mind that is conducive to receiving intuitive guidance. You're concentrating on performing an activity that is familiar to you (like driving or taking a shower); therefore, it gives your intuitive self a chance to take center stage. Simply knowing this will help you recognize intuitive guidance while you're just moving about your life.

2. **Ask your loved ones in spirit to help you become more intuitively open.** Our guardian angels (also called guides/loved ones in spirit) are around us always, but because we have free will, they can't necessarily step in on both subconscious and conscious levels unless you ask them for help. You can fix this by requesting (in your mind or aloud) that they show you signs. Many grieving parents I've worked with over the years have talked of signs such as nickels or other common items showing up out of nowhere. Another sign I've seen quite a bit is lights turning on and off on their own.

   Also, ask that your guides/angels come into your dreams with messages. Your sleep state is a closer vibration to their state of being in spirit form; therefore, it's easier to connect with them in dreamland. For that reason, keep a journal or piece of paper and pen by your bed. For example, early in my intuitive awakening, I remember waking up from a very vivid dream in the middle of the night in order to write down a word I was told to remember. The next morning, I told Scott what had happened and asked if he knew the meaning of the word. Lucky for me, he did. After he explained what it meant, I realized it was tied to a case I was working on, and it helped me make sense of something I never would have come to on my own.

3. **Take a walk while listening to instrumental music.** Music touches the creative, intuitive, subconscious part of our being. Use it as a catalyst to become more intuitively receptive while walking about.

4. **Listen to a guided meditation on YouTube.** If you're like me, and your mind jumps around a lot, try listening to a guided mediation on YouTube. They're free and easy to use. I personally have had much success with several meditations called Violet Flame.

5. **Commit to memory this easy mediation.** If you're also like me and suffer from memory loss, trying to remember a lengthy meditation without guidance is difficult. Here's one that is relatively easy to commit to memory: Close your eyes and take three deep breaths. Now, in your mind's eye, see a big movie screen. It's in front of you and completely white. Take three more deep breaths and ask to be shown on the screen a symbol, photo, or mini-movie pertaining to something your loved ones in spirit/guardians want you to know. Continue to ask more questions, or simply take three more breaths and thank your loved ones for their assistance before opening your eyes. Record on paper what you received, and continue to record what you get intuitively.

6. **Pay attention to your body's intuitive signals.** When I was awakening to my intuitive skills, I felt more sensations and emotions than I saw or heard. Chills were, and still are, a very strong intuitive signal for me. They signal different things, but

mainly they alert me to the truth. And they point out that I need to pay attention to what is happening in that moment. Nausea is another intuitive sign, especially when it's fleeting and without a foreseeable cause. As you read in my book, I experienced a lot of physical signs while I was enduring Tony's abuse. The buzzing sensation on my right hip and the panic attacks I endured let me know that I needed to take care of myself and stand up for my inner child, who did not want to live a life of abuse.

7. **Explore intuitive tools like tarot cards and pendulums.** Many tools like these have gotten a bad rap over the years. Again, the intention is key when using tools that foster intuition. Prior to testing them out, simply say a short protection intention, either in your head or aloud. Then, ask that your loved ones in spirit to surround you with light and protect you and your intuitive session from all lower vibrational energies that are not good for you. If you're uncomfortable with tarot cards, there are many other types of decks, including angels, oracles, and nature.

Setting Boundaries

Over the past ten years, I've noticed a pattern in my own life with regard to who is guided to me for help. In most all cases, learning to set boundaries is needed, which is something I gleaned in a big way when I was figuring out how to manage my intuition, and then again when I was finally out of the abusive relationship.

I learned that I needed to make rules in my home and space, just like I taught Corey to do when he was struggling. First, write down on a piece of paper what you will allow in your home and space, and what is not allowed. If you are being woken in the middle of the night by unseen energy that you'd rather not deal with, write that down. List it all. Write that you will only allow energies that are for your highest good to connect with you. After you're done penning your list, hang it up in your home or your room, and watch what happens. When you set boundaries, you get results. It's all about intention. I've seen it work 99 percent of the time with dozens of adults and children I've shared this technique with over the years.

In addition, many families have reached out asking about how to help their highly sensitive little ones feel more comfortable in the world. If they are old enough to understand capes, I encourage them to put on an invisible cape before they walk out the door. The cape surrounds the child and creates a barrier to others' energies. Not only does it give kids a sense of control, but it sets the intention that they will not take on another person's energy. They are protected and safe from feeling everyone else's emotions and energy. Additionally, I frequently surround myself with white light (in my mind) before I go into crowded places like grocery stores and malls. This creates the same boundary as the cape exercise.

Clearing Your Space and Energy

Helping friends and family clear the energy of their homes is something I'm called to do quite a bit. I've seen everything from dark energies wreaking havoc in a house to minor energy disturbances due to negative emotional energy. I've found the key to clearing a home is believing you have the power to rid the space of what is not for your highest good. Also, I've found that intending that the energy is cleared in all space and time works well. As humans, we forget that time is actually a human construct, not a Universal one. Some folks recite clearing rituals to clear their space. Those can easily be found online. You can also try lighting a bundle of sage or palo santo wood and intend that your house be cleared as you waft the sage smoke throughout all rooms. This particular clearing is common within many cultures. Additionally, Reiki energy can be used to clear a home as well.

Similarly, you can clear your personal energy. Many intuitive people are highly empathic, which means they not only feel what others are feeling but they take on their energy like we talked about with children. Some say they feel tired and heavy, a sign that they may be taking on additional energy. To ensure that you're only working with your energy, try one or both of these techniques:

- **Ask if what you are feeling is yours or others'. Listen for the answer in your mind.** Then ask that all energy that is not yours leave your body. It's as simple as that. Remember, the intention is everything. You can also use a pendulum to get the answer, but remember to ask only yes/no or either/or questions.

- **Try this visualization.** Sit down in a chair and place your feet flat on the floor. Close your eyes. Visualize cords of light (your choice of light color) coming out of the bottom of your shoes/feet into the ground, traveling all the way down to the core of the earth. Now, see the light coming back up the cords into the bottom of your feet, up through your ankles, shins, knees, upper leg, groin, stomach, heart, out through your arms, then back up your neck and out the top of your head into the sky. Now, envision the light coming back down starting at the top of your head and going down your body, only this time, you see all energy that isn't yours or isn't good for you falling off of your body as the light passes through. See the energy that isn't good for you as black sand falling to the ground and down into the earth. Open your eyes after you perform the visualization. You should feel a bit lighter.

Healing Old Wounds

There are millions of grown childhood abuse survivors in the world who are struggling with daily life and relationships. In addition to my own experience as a survivor, I've worked with many abuse survivors who are unknowingly, subconsciously recreating similar abuse in their teen and adult lives. I talked quite a bit about this in my TEDx talk and the concept of wounded attachment, which is the unconscious way of being attracted to or attached to someone or something that reinforces the childhood wound/trauma. In addition to talk therapy, here are a few intuitive therapies that I used to help me heal from the abuse I endured:

- **Hypnotherapy.** During a few hypnotherapy sessions with my hypnotherapy doctor, I was able to access my subconscious, see my abuser in my mind's eye, and reduce his presence in my life. As you read, it was instrumental in helping me clear the energy of grief that was lodged in my lungs and impeding my ability to breathe.

- **EFT (Emotional Freedom Therapy).** My psychologist, Dr. Botello, introduced EFT to me while I was recovering from the narcissistic abuse I endured with Tony. EFT, or Tapping, is a form of psychological acupressure, based on the same energy meridians used in traditional acupuncture to treat physical and emotional ailments for over 5,000 years, but without the invasiveness of needles. Instead, simple tapping with the fingertips is used to input kinetic energy onto specific meridians on the head and chest while you think about your specific problem—whether it is a traumatic event, an addiction, pain, and so on—and voice positive affirmations. This combination of tapping the energy meridians and voicing positive affirmation works to clear the "short-circuit"—the emotional block—from your body's bioenergy system, thus restoring your mind and body's balance, which is essential for optimal health and the healing of physical disease. https://www.tappingsolutionfoundation.org/

- **Reiki Healing and Energy Healing.** As a medium and someone who helps others, I've found it critical to also take care of my own energy on a regular basis. I seek out practitioners who resonate with me to help me stay balanced energetically.

Einstein is widely quoted with saying, "The intuitive mind is a sacred gift and the rational mind is a faithful servant. We have created a society that honors the servant and has forgotten the gift."

It took me forty-three years to learn this truth, but in the end, it saved my life. I hope that as you move through your life, you develop strong faith in your own intuition and a better understanding of just how much our subconscious rules our conscious world. And I hope you use my story—and the tips included in this last chapter—as a guide to help you get there.

APPENDIX

Resources

Narcissistic Abuse Survival and Healing Resources

When I was trying to understand what was happening to me while I was with Tony, and then again after I left the relationship, I scoured the internet looking for anything that resembled the relationship in which I was living. I found a few online resources and books that helped me. I highly recommend these resources to others who are dealing with or healing from narcissistic/sociopathic abuse:

- *Why Does He Do That?* by Lundy Bancroft
- *Should I Stay or Should I Go?: Surviving a Relationship with a Narcissist* by Ramani Durvasula, PhD
- *Power: Surviving and Thriving after Narcissistic Abuse* by Shahida Arabi
- *Healing from Hidden Abuse A Journey Through the Stages of Recovery from Psychological Abuse* by Shannon Thomas, LCSW

- *Psychopath Free: Recovering from Emotionally Abusive Relationships with Narcissists, Sociopaths, and Other Toxic People* by Jackson MacKenzie
- *Letters From a Better Me* by Rachael Wolff
- Lisa E Scott's book series on narcissism

Intuition and Healing Using Intuition Resources

I could write for days about the topic of intuition and healing from abuse, but I hope I've provided a few techniques and resources that will help you feel empowered to take control of your intuition and your healing. In addition to what I shared about healing old wounds, consider these books for further exploration on the subject of intuition. They have helped me navigate my intuitive awakening and healing.

- *Heal from Within: A Guidebook to Intuitive Wellness* by Katie Beecher
- *The Afterlife of Billy Fingers* by Annie Kagan
- *Ghosts Among Us* by James Van Praagh
- *Between Two Worlds* by Tyler Henry
- *The Highly Intuitive Child* by Catherine Crawford
- *Dr. Judith Orloff's Guide to Intuitive Healing* by Dr. Judith Orloff
- *How to Heal Yourself When No One Else Can* by Amy B. Scher
- *Brave New Medicine* by Dr. Cynthia Li, MD

Acknowledgments

With Love and Gratitude...

To my husband, Scott, and daughters, Natalie and Grace: There aren't enough words to describe how deeply I love you and how profoundly thankful I am for you. I am still here in this world because you believed in me during the best of times, and remarkably, during the darkest of times. You've always seen me and loved me, even when your hearts were breaking. Even when I didn't know who I was anymore. When I started writing this book, you patiently and supportively listened to me peck away on the keyboard during road trips, during your favorite TV shows, and sometimes even during dinner. We're talking hundreds of hours of keyboard tapping. You gave me the space, strength, and confidence to write *Little Voices*. You even bought me a bracelet that reads *Keep Fucking Going*. And I did. And you did. Simply put, you are my everything, always and forever. I'm so incredibly grateful that you feel the same way about me. Let's keep fucking going together...forever.

To my family: Mom and Dad, Traci, Judy, Larry, Annis, and Laura. Thank you for believing in me and supporting me, even when it made no logical sense to do so. I love you all with my whole heart.

To Egan, my soul sister: No matter space nor time—no matter the hardships and triumphs we endure in this life—we are always connected. You are forever my soul sister. Thank you for your unwavering protection, your courage to stand up for me, and your support and love, in both light and dark times.

To Lorraine: I wouldn't have survived all of these years without you. Thank you for lending an ear (and a shoulder) without judgment, and for encouraging me to write my story. It's hard to believe that our communication class at Ohio University started this soul-sister connection almost thirty years ago. This, of course, means that you are truly stuck with me until the end of time.

To Andy: Thank you, my warrior cousin. You stood up to the dark when few would. You even made TikToks with me. I'm forever grateful that your love knows no bounds.

To Cynthia: Thank God we met that cold, sunny day in Sedona. I'm eternally grateful for your intuitive guidance and friendship over the past seven years. There is no one I'd rather paint kitchen cabinets for than you. You are forever part of our family.

To my literary agent, Tina Wainscott, at Seymour Literary Agency: You took a chance on me and I'll never forget that. I thank God that you not only took me on as a client but that you continued to shop the book for almost two years despite an extraordinary number of doors being slammed in your face. Thanks to you, we found the open door that was meant to be. And even better than that, I found a lifelong friend. Thank you for all of your edits, support, love, and mentorship.

To Rachael: Thank you for helping keep me sane during our early morning Zoom calls. You're not only an incredible author, brainstormer, and mother, you're one hell of an amazing soul sister. Your support and friendship mean the world to me.

To Post Hill Press: Special thanks to my editor, Debra Englander, for believing in *Little Voices*. I'm also immensely grateful to Heather King, Rachel Hoge, Allison Henson, Devon Brown, and everyone else at Post Hill for helping make this book the best it can possibly be.

To the incredible doctors, therapists, intuitive mediums, healers, and detectives who've been with me on my intuitive journey: Dr.

Botello, Deanna, Dr. Proiette, Necole, Katie, Vicki, AJ, Macie, Jeneda, Craig, Mark, and Cynthia—I wouldn't be here without all of you. Thank you for your support and friendship.

To Mark Pucci: Your faith in me changed my life. Thank you for believing in this furniture company CEO turned intuitive medium even when she didn't quite believe in herself. And thank you for penning such a beautiful, touching foreword for *Little Voices*. I can't wait to do what we know we're meant to do at the National Institute for Law and Justice. I'm forever honored to work alongside you helping families find loved ones, closure, and justice.

To Amy B. Scher: Who knew waiting together could be so much fun? But seriously, thank you for your support, mentorship, and friendship. And for being a champion for my story and for domestic abuse survivors everywhere. On a literary note, if, one day, I possess even a quarter of your beautiful writing talent, I'll be one happy woman. Here's to many more celebratory happy hours in our future!

To Erica Vhay: Thank you for allowing me to feature your stunning artwork on the cover of Little Voices. You are and will always be my favorite painter.

To my Cherry Hill family: Karen, Nicole, Theresa, Amanda, Darryl, David, and Dave, thanks for supporting me along this stranger-than-fiction book (and life) journey. I love and adore you all. You are my people.

To my friends-like-family: Stacey B., Ben, Janine, Krista, Cindy, Tracie, and Melissa, thank you for your support, love, friendship, and adventures. Love you all.

To all of my readers, endorsers, and editors, I truly appreciate your time, advice, and help. You encouraged me to keep going and made me a better writer.

And finally, to the little (and not-so-little) voices in spirit, Jason, Nate, Amalia, Carrie, and the many kids and adults in spirit who've come before and will come after, thank you for trusting me with your messages. And thank you for saving me in every possible way there is to save a person. There would be no me without you. I'm thankful for your beautiful families, too. To Yvette, John, Denise, Jack, and Camilla, getting to know all of you has been one of the greatest blessings of my life. I'm eternally grateful.

About the Author

KIERSTEN PARSONS HATHCOCK is an award-winning self-taught carpenter/furniture designer, and founder of Mod Mom Furniture, a kids' furniture company featured on ABC's Shark Tank. She's also a TEDx speaker and intuitive medium who works for the National Institute for Law and Justice helping detectives and families uncover truth in missing persons and homicide cases. In her previous work life, Kiersten was a staff writer for Northern Arizona University and TV marketing executive for A&E and the History Channel. An Ohio native, she now resides in Phoenix, Arizona with her husband, Scott, daughters, Natalie and Grace, and pup, Scout.

About the Contributors

Erica Vhay is known for capturing the emotion and movement of a moment in time. Her fascination with patterns and negative shapes can be seen in both her figurative and abstract work—with her focus on the negative shapes as much as the positive.

From a family of artists, her mother was a painter and her great grandfather was the 20th-century American sculptor Gutzon Borglum—most notably known for his sculpting of Mt. Rushmore. Other influences in her work can be seen in Egon Sheile, John Singer Sargent, and the more recent Malcolm Leipke and Michael Carson.

Mark Pucci (Founder and President of The National Institute for Law and Justice) is a highly decorated, retired NYPD Detective. Mark's investigative experience while working for the New York City Police Department encompassed all facets of law enforcement from Vice, Narcotics, Illegal Firearms, Gangs, and other violent crime related investigations, to Special Operations Division, city-wide major-crime pattern identification, and the apprehension of many of the city's most wanted criminals.

Mark's extensive undercover, observational surveillance, and covert / special operations' training and experience during his tenure as a Detective with the NYPD are considered by many to be unparalleled in the private sector. Since Mark's retirement from the NYPD and re-entry into private sector investigations, Mark has worked with several large scale National & International Investigative Firms in the capacity of Executive Vice President, Chief Investigator, Chief Compliance Officer, and National/International Investigative Consultant.

Throughout his career in the private sector, Mark has successfully investigated and supervised the completion of thousands of cases in a wide array of investigative practices, (many of which have garnered "national and international" media coverage and attention), encompassing, civil/criminal law, accidental/wrongful deaths, homicides, missing persons, child abductions, cold cases, white collar, corporate, and cyber-crimes, insurance defense, matrimonial practice, and a passionate personal specialty in "Adoption-Adoptee Location" (birth-parents/children/siblings); and the "identification, location and reunification," of those who desire to be reunited.